Managing Teleworkers and Telecommuting Strategies

Managing Teleworkers and Telecommuting Strategies

Gina Vega

Foreword by Joanne H. Pratt

Westport, Connecticut
London

Library of Congress Cataloging-in-Publication Data

Vega, Gina.
　　Managing teleworkers and telecommuting strategies / Gina Vega ; foreword
　　by Joanne H. Pratt.
　　　p. cm.
　　Includes bibliographical references and index.
　　ISBN 1-56720-552-6 (alk. paper)
　　　1. Telecommuting.　I. Title.
　　HD2336.3.V44 2003
　　658.3′12—dc21　　　　2003045789

British Library Cataloguing in Publication Data is available.

Library of Congress Catalog Card Number: 2003045789
ISBN: 1-56720-552-6

First published in 2003

Praeger Publishers, 88 Post Road West, Westport, CT 06881
An imprint of Greenwood Publishing Group, Inc.
www.praeger.com

Printed in the United States of America

The paper used in this book complies with the
Pemanent Paper Standard issued by the National
Information Standards Organization (Z39.48-1984).

10 9 8 7 6 5 4 3 2 1

Copyright Acknowledgment

Extracts from Alvin Toffler, *The Third Wave.* New York: William Morrow, 1980,
page 235. Reprinted with permission of the author.

To Robert

Contents

List of Illustrations

TABLES

FIGURES

Foreword

One day the word will disappear, signaling that telework has become institutionalized as "just the way we do business." But now we are still in transition from old, tightly structured patterns for organizing work to new, more flexible patterns enabled by evolving technologies.

Telework crept into the organization as a strategy to reduce trips. Originally called telecommuting, it has been not of great moment to organizations that understandably care more about employees at work than they do about how they get to work. Yet after 20 years, although lacking dramatic growth, it has claimed notice by even the most traditional companies. Why? Because telework proved to be the opening wedge for organizational change—inevitable change due to the nature of the new digital tools, telecommunications, and the Internet. As it now demands attention from a management perspective rather than a solely transportation viewpoint, more serious consideration needs to be focused on the two-way interaction between employer and employee—particularly the unintended consequences of working remotely from one another.

As Gina Vega so aptly points out, "Telework is not an endeavor per se; rather it is the embodiment of a philosophical and humanistic movement." In that spirit Vega probes the literature to contemplate issues that managers and workers must address if both are to succeed in the developing eWork, information age.

In lively, engaging prose, Vega raises the questions every organization should consider. She interweaves issues of telework, wisely focusing on communication as key to the "mutual understanding" and
"trusting relationships" that managers and workers must achieve when
they no longer see one another throughout the workday. Particularly
instructive is her setting the historical context for working at home or
distant locations. Starting as far back as smoke signals, she traces the
course of telecommunications and technology as they force both organizational and personal change.

The challenges she cites from academic research and practical practice will inform any reader who is interested in the impact of technology
and communications on work and private life. She speaks to my own
concern that we can anticipate a backlash when we tire of our high-tech
toys and become fully aware that, for better or worse, our cell phones
and the Internet are tying us to 24/7 weeks. The consequence is a
blurring of the old boundaries that separated our work and personal
lives.

One refrain that bubbles through the literature is the seemingly
universal urge to decide definitively whether telework is a good thing
or a bad thing. In trying to arrive at a quantifiable, logical, proven
judgment of telework, we are frustrated as we try to "ascribe direct
linear advantage to the implementation of telework." But do we need
to arrive at an absolute value judgment of telework?

We may be craving the wrong thing—the 1940s' and 1950s' idealized
movie life in black and white: mom in the kitchen, dad "at work," and
the kids at play. Maybe this imagined utopia is not what we should be
seeking. Maybe the message of telework is that each of us is different,
and not only that, each of us has different priorities, motivations and
responsibilities that change constantly throughout our lives. Similarly,
the organization is not the cookie-cutter model of efficient production
that we remember as comfortable and reassuring just because it was so
unchanging.

The more fruitful approach may be to break out of the old models and
develop new models congruent with the old. Or more boldly, to cut all
ties and explore what is logical and desirable in new organizational
models for the new age.

As we attempt to quantify the changes that telework brings, perhaps
the most enlightening insights can be gleaned from the detailed case
study that concludes Vega's inquiry. She accomplished something unusual and valuable—a four-year longitudinal study of an organization,
Putnam Investments.

You will enjoy this book. Vega leads us toward developing new
theory that relates the impact of remote work to a reshaping of the
organization. She gives us grounds from which to derive new guide-

lines and rules for the virtual organization. What those will be is not yet obvious. But she also gives us the proper questions to ask. This remarkable book will help find the best answers.

Joanne H. Pratt
Founder and President, Joanne H. Pratt Associates

Preface

In 1997, Scott Adams published one of his Dilbert cartoon episodes, in which Dilbert himself undertook to work from home. We watched Dilbert as he worked in bunny slippers and pajamas, while his peers in the office thought he was out playing despite his apparent productivity, and as his evil boss instituted all sorts of nefarious monitoring processes. Articles began appearing on a regular basis in the popular press about the benefits and drawbacks of telecommuting, and, in the academic press, concerns about this emergent work structure began to surface, ever so gently. Technological advances leapt from the drawing board to the marketplace. Stock markets were booming worldwide, and business was becoming more and more global each day. The air crackled with excitement, Web-citement, and investment in this new and glorious age of electronic information sharing. Work and workplaces were changing quickly.

It was that environment that prompted this book about the phenomenon of telework and the management of teleworkers. My research has taken me in several directions. It began with my concern about potential worker alienation and loneliness that could result from working in isolated environments, far from the normal interactions of coworkers. This focus on "the human disconnect" led to further concerns about workers: Would working at home put even more pressure on workers to produce? Would teleworking encourage the ominous drift of workplace concerns into the home? Were workers destined to work ever more hours, shifting their personal focus away from their families and on to their jobs, all under the code name "Family-Friendly Workplace"? What sort of values were being reinforced by telework? These questions are addressed in Chapters 6, 9, and 12.

I was surprised to discover that the most common concerns regarding teleworking in the United States revolved around managerial issues, specifically those that were based on the control traditionally wielded by managers in their oversight capacities. How could managers confirm that people were working, not playing, when they could not actually see them? Stopping by cubicles in the course of "managing by walking around" could not work with teleworkers. Most business cultures did not support the trusting relationships known as Theory Y management (McGregor, 1960). Managers were both frightened by their loss of control and frustrated by their inability to keep tabs on distant workflow. Chapters 4, 5, 7, and 8 deal with these issues.

The nature of work had also changed. The impetus provided by electronic technology and its promise of freedom from onerous commutes matched by the desire of a new breed of worker to seek freedom from time clocks and the formality of office environments created a living laboratory of willing test subjects for telework. Since the early 1990s, workers have accepted the reality of a changed social contract, one in which they are responsible for their own careers rather than depending on their employers to look after them. They reason thusly: If we are responsible for our own futures, we can also make our own rules.

Rule #1: Dress casually.

Rule #2: Report to yourself.

Rule #3: Do work rather than do time.

Rule #4: Be at home for your children.

What do these rules mean for society and community? Some of the answers are in Chapters 3 and 10.

The new rules applied to those individuals fortunate enough to work for enlightened companies, or companies that, during a period of extraordinarily high employment, were willing to take a chance on trying new ways to recruit and retain the employees they desperately needed to run their businesses. The U.S. federal government was one of those employers, and I looked into the way in which the government was implementing telework in its own offices. I found a lot more talk about telework than action in implementing it. When I pursued the topic, I located some creative and novel telework programs within several government agencies, but I also discovered that the government was trying to imitate programs initiated in the private sector, while companies were looking at government programs for effective ideas. Numerous researchers were seeking out information about telework programs and teleworkers, but none of the data sources was comparable to any other data source. As a result, no one knew even approximately how many people were teleworking in America. In fact, there was no agreement on a common definition of telework. Confusion reigned, both in the United States and abroad. I looked at the implementation of telework programs in several countries and was once again surprised by what I learned. It is indeed a small world, but national implementation problems vary wildly from country to country, as demonstrated in Chapters 1, 13, and 14.

Were it not for technological advances that led to the growth of entire new industries, the nature of communication would likely have remained unchanged. However, the digitized world demanded a new form of communication, with different relationship models, and evolving social networks. New ways to get in touch, keep in touch, and stay in touch without actually being in touch are discussed in Chapters 2 and 4.

For four years, from 1998 through 2002, I studied the evolution of a successful telework program at Putnam Investments and learned that, with proper management, effective hiring, on-target training programs, and continuous reevaluation of the model and its goals, telework can work very well. I tell Putnam's story in the final chapter of the book, with the methodology used to conduct this research described in a closing appendix.

Sources come from many academic disciplines: management, economics, communications, ergonomics, philosophy, technology management, psychology, and history. But most importantly, this research is reality based. I have listened to workers, to managers, to executives, and to government employees. The story that you read in the following pages is sure to engage your interest in the growing phenomenon of telework.

Acknowledgments

As all who write books know, the process is all-consuming. It pushes in front of other projects that have been patiently waiting. It wakes you in the night. Ideas appear when you are eating breakfast, dancing, driving to work, chatting with friends. The book is a topic of conversation that never fails to fascinate you, even when it bores everyone around you. If you are fortunate, your family tolerates this nonsense until you have completed the task. I am among the very fortunate, having a husband who not only tolerates my work and its demands, but supports it, endorses it, and proofreads it as well. I cannot acknowledge him enough for his contribution.

Others have also made important contributions to this book. Support for my interim research came from PricewaterhouseCoopers Endowment for the Business of Government and the U.S. GSA Office of Governmentwide Policy, Office of Real Property. Putnam Investments has been generous for four years in opening their Work@Home program to me and my student researchers, whose names appear in the Appendix. They did wonderful work, and I commend them for it. Three different collaborators have researched several of the chapter topics with me: Louis Brennan, Martin Hanlon, and Gregory Simpson. I appreciate their insights and wisdom, which have made this book better. Several colleagues at Merrimack College have gone out of their way to read, comment, edit, correct, adapt, and make altogether valuable suggestions for the improvement of this work. These include Robert Bruen, Robert Chwaliszewski, Mary McHugh, and Gary McCloskey, OSA.

And, without the generous support and resources of Merrimack College and the Francis E. Girard School of Business and International Commerce, I would not have been able to complete this volume in a timely way.

For your support, both actual and virtual, I thank you all.

The Story of Telework

Since the 1960s, the world has been rocked by rapid, discontinuous change. It does not take the apocryphal rocket scientist to recognize that the history of the world is the history of change, but in the case of telework, it did take a rocket scientist to ignite our interest in the potential for a dramatic shift in workplace and work process based on evolving telecommunications technology.

A BRIEF HISTORY OF WORK

Work has always been with us. Derived from old English, the word "work" is related to *ergon* (Greek), meaning "deed" or "action." The earliest recorded "work" included activities performed by slaves captured in battle, in exchange for their lives (Donkin, 2001). These deeds or actions set the stage for our current transactional focus on work (something we do in exchange for some payback). That payback continues to be our lives, or our livelihood, as we refer today to the income that allows us to live.

Leaping over some 3,000 years of history, our "New Work" at the turn of the twenty-first century differs significantly from the work of the past, even from the recent past of the late twentieth century. However, our language, our thinking, and our behavior have not yet caught up with these changes (please see Chapter 5 for a full discussion about the New Work), so we often still think in traditional terms. The picture that may spring to mind when we think about work, or employment, is a picture of production—work with a tangible outcome. This work may be conducted in a factory, a farm, an office, a restaurant, a retail store, a school, or a hospital. The workers in these venues have specialized names—cutters, finishers, polishers, farmers, office workers, wait staff, sales associates, teachers, doctors, and nurses. The outcomes of their work are products or services—cars, textiles, food, insurance policies, finished goods, education, medical care. These workers are not perceived as slaves in the traditional image of slavery despite the designation "wage slave" bestowed upon them, but they do work for a living—for wages—and they serve the priorities of their employers.

As we see in subsequent chapters, the New Worker is different from the specialized workers with whom we are familiar. The New Workplace differs from the workplaces with which we grew up. But the products and services produced in the New Economy are substantially the same as those we have always used. We continue to drive cars, wear clothing, eat food, get educated, and survive with the help of medical care. However, the very successes we experienced in the twentieth century through the processes of industrialization have created a set of challenges that we must address in this new century.

SUCCESS CREATES PROBLEMS

The great engine of progress that made life comfortable for so many in the twentieth century had unanticipated economic, cultural, and political consequences, among which we can count the following:

- Pollution and other threats to environmental integrity
- Excessive energy consumption and overuse of fossil fuels
- Traffic and related transportation and commutation problems
- Weakening family structure as the nuclear family reduced further in size
- Increasingly overworked citizens in an aging workforce
- Trust in technology as the ultimate solution for all the preceding problems

There are other challenges facing America as well, including the economic and social impact of globalization, a changing demography based on world migratory movements, and a weak educational system that threatens to reduce opportunities for the next generation.

Pollution, Energy Consumption, and Traffic

We can look at these three problems as one unhappy and codependent triangle that originated in our love affair with the automobile. When, in 1913, a new Model T could be purchased for under $500, all the rules changed. The automobile changed the way we humans did our work, the way we got from one place to another, the amount of freedom we had, the way we met, dated, and married, the way we spent our leisure time, the way we spent our wages. According to Richard Donkin (2001), "For the worker, the change was incalculable. At work he was rooted to the spot, but outside work he and his family could move around at forty miles per hour in their new Model T. They could live outside town if they felt like it, free from the necessity to live in rows of worker housing close by the factory" (149).

The development of paved roads and easy cross-country access took a long time to accomplish. As early as 1919, Lt. Colonel Dwight D. Eisenhower, later to be the president under whose leadership the interstate highway system was developed, participated in the U.S. Army's first transcontinental motor convoy where he experienced "all the woes known to motorists and then some—an endless series of mechanical difficulties; vehicles stuck in mud or sand; trucks and other equipment crashing through wooden bridges; roads as slippery as ice or dusty or the consistency of 'gumbo'" (Weingroff, 1996, 5). In later years, President Franklin D. Roosevelt indicated "interest in construction of a network of toll superhighways as a way of providing more jobs for people out of work," but his plan was accused of "jitterbug economics" and it failed. Roosevelt was looking further ahead, to the end of the war that America had not yet entered, and "he feared resumption of the Depression if American soldiers returned from the war and were unable to find jobs. A major highway program could be part of the answer" (Weingroff, 1996, 1-2). The highways were to be located "so as to promote a desirable urban development . . . [and] to connect by routes, as direct as practicable, the principal metropolitan areas, cities, and industrial centers, to serve the national defense, and to connect suitable border points with routes of continental importance in the Dominion of Canada and the Republic of Mexico" (Federal Highway Act of 1944).

Political arguments kept the development of the interstate system on a back burner until the mid-1950s, when Eisenhower eloquently proclaimed, in a series of speeches over several years,

Our unity as a nation is sustained by free communication of thought and by easy transportation of people and goods. The ceaseless flow of information throughout the republic is matched by individual and commercial movement over a vast system of interconnected highways crisscrossing the country and joining at our national borders with friendly neighbors to the north and south. Together, the united forces of our communication and transportation systems are dynamic elements in the very name we wear—United States. . . . More than any single action by the government since the end of the war, this one would change the face of America. . . . Its impact on the American economy—the jobs it would produce in manufacturing and construction, the rural areas it would open—was beyond calculation. (Weingroff, 1996, 10–15)

Plans to build the interstate with the traffic of 20 years in the future in mind backfired, because 20 years after the construction was completed, the roads were already overcrowded and excessive numbers of automobiles with their noxious exhausts were polluting the environment. By 1970, four years after the fiftieth anniversary of the Federal Aid Road Act of 1916 that launched the federal-aid highway program, the Clean Air Act directed the Administrator of the EPA (United States Environmental Protection Agency) to reduce auto emissions of carbon monoxide and hydrocarbons by 90 percent from 1970 model levels in the 1975 model levels. By 2000, cars were a major source of air pollution, including smog, emissions, and global warming. The growing use of America's interstate system had spawned its own series of unintended consequences.

From 1969 to 1990, annual person-miles of travel increased by 65 percent, from 1,404 billion to 2,315 billion. Twenty-two percent of these trips were made as part of earning a living. Person-miles of travel made by private vehicle increased by 144 percent, from 41.4 million to 99.6 million miles per year. Concurrently, carpooling decreased by 19 percent, and the use of public transportation decreased by 22 percent. People were traveling alone. The majority (62 percent) of vehicle trips made in the morning peak hours between 6:00 and 9:00 A.M. were home-based work trips (Ball, 1994).

All these trips were made without regard to the rising price of oil controlled by OPEC, temporary rationing of gasoline during the 1970s, the proliferation of fuel-inefficient vehicles, and constant road delays resulting in parts of the interstate system being nicknamed "The World's Longest Parking Lot."

People in Families, People at Work

Family structure changed dramatically in the third quarter of the twentieth century. Just as we became comfortable with the shift from the extended family that was "normal" in pre-industrial society to the nuclear family consisting of two parents, 2.5 children, and a dog that was so familiar to Baby Boomers in their youth, the family unit was pulled out from underneath us once again. Gone were the two parents, replaced by single head of household families. In 1970, 70.6 percent of families were married couple households, and 10.6 percent of families were "other family households" (single parent households). By 2000, the percentage of married couple families had dropped to 62.5 percent and "other family households" had increased to 16 percent (Fields & Casper, 2001, 3). And gone were the 2.5 children as well, as families of five or more members decreased as a percentage of the household population from 20.9 percent in 1970 to only 10.4 percent in 2000 (Fields & Casper, 2001, 4).

One result of this trend coupled with the population explosion of 1946 to 1961 was that the population of the United States as a whole became older. The median age of the population in 1970 had fallen to just over 28, but by 2000 the trend reversed and the median age had risen to 35.4 (U.S. Census). As this demographic bulge works its way through the national pipeline, it continues to have an inordinately large impact on society. It earns more, it consumes more, its expectations and desires become the will of the majority, and its needs become the burden of the subsequent generations.

When this group becomes tired, everyone yawns, and this is the group of workers who have been working hardest, longest, and more hours than any other in modern history. In 1999, the average American worked almost 2,000 hours for pay. This is 350 hours a year more than the average European, who worked only 1, 656 hours in the same time frame (Reich, 2000, 112). When we add to this figure travel time of 40 minutes per day to the workplace (Nilles, 1998, 7), it's no surprise that Americans are exhausted.

Technology

Telecommunications technology is the automobile of the twenty-first century. The development of the Internet and World Wide Web seems to parallel quite closely the development of the interstate highway system. Initially established for use by the military, then opened to academic institutions, the Internet provided a unique, elite means of communication for the privileged few. However, when opened to the general public in the late 1980s and commercialized and popularized in the 1990s (Kahn, 1995), electronic communication took on a transformative role in world society. Daily trumpeting about the need for expanded bandwidth and broader access to the information highway are reminiscent of the clamor that encouraged legislation (passed in 1966) requiring all parts of the interstate highway system to be at least four lanes regardless of traffic volume. The goals of the development of the transportation system are the same as those encouraging the development of the Internet: defense, jobs, connection of locations, opening of rural areas, and improved flow of information.

PIE-IN-THE-SKY SOLUTIONS

Along came Jack Nilles working for NASA in 1970, the rocket scientist mentioned in the beginning of the chapter. Now celebrated as the "father of telecommuting," Nilles was seeking potential civilian applications for satellite communication technology, and directed his efforts toward some of the problems created by the successes of industrialization. Transportation alternatives became his key focus, gaining him support from the National Science Foundation and the state government of California. Clearly, anyone who could resolve the transportation and commutation woes of California would have a bright future. His work in reducing pollution and dependence on fossil fuels, and alleviating the personal energy- and life-sapping process of simply getting to work and back home again made Jack Nilles the go-to guy in the development of telework.

Nilles designed a series of telecommunications-transportation trade-off projects for the federal government in the 1970s, then turned his attention to the State of California in the 1980s. The results of these projects were impressive, particularly the demonstration of teleworking conducted following the Loma Prieta earthquake of 1989 (Nilles, 1998; Pratt, 1991). Telecommuting, and later teleworking, words coined by Nilles, became the unpublicized competitive advantage for a group of Fortune 100 companies willing to try something new.

Location or Technology?

This is a good place for a definition of telework and how it differs from telecommuting. In general, telework suggests computer-based distant access to company business systems (Vega & Brennan, 2000b). According to Nilles (1998, 1), telework is "any form of substitution of information technologies [such as telecommunications and computers] for work-related travel; moving the work to the workers instead of moving the workers to work," while telecommuting reflects "periodic work out of the principal office, one or more days per week either at home, a client's site, or in a telework center . . . [via] the partial or total substitution of telecommunications technologies . . . for the commute to work." In other words, telecommuting is a form of telework, which is the more generic term.

But there is no generally accepted definition of telework or telecommuting (Avery & Zabel, 2001; Pratt, 1997a) and the actual number of definitions goes far beyond the ability to present a universal collection of them. According to Amy Helling (2000: 54), telework can "be defined primarily by the location at which work takes place, and secondarily by frequency and effects on commutation, rather than by the use of telecommunication devices." Daniel Pink (2001) agrees, suggesting that telecommuters "work for an organization, but do so from a remote site, usually their home" (2001, 42). The U.S. government also focuses on the location of the work rather than the technology required to perform the work: "Telework means performing work on a regular basis in a location other than the principal office, such as the employee's home or a nearby telecenter" (GSA, 2000, 16). The 1999 ITAC (International Telework Association & Council) Telework America survey states, "Teleworkers, also called telecommuters, are defined overall as employees or independent contractors who work at least one day per month at home during normal business hours" (Pratt, 1999, 1). But the following year, the organization's definition had changed: "With the help of modern technologies many types of work can now be done at home using telephones, faxes and computers. This is called teleworking or telecommuting" (Nilles, 2000, 7). Gil Gordon (2000), a consultant in this area, begs the question, claiming, "It doesn't make much difference . . . what you call it—as long as you do it."

I agree that the definition is less meaningful than the concept; therefore, I use "telework" more often than "telecommuting" as the broader, more inclusive term.

Specifically, telework refers to "normal" work performed away from the office on a regular basis using telecommunications technology.

ALL ABOARD . . .

No matter which definition we choose, proponents of telework would have us believe that workers are swarming to the alternate workplace. If we use Helling's definition of telework, as it relates to location and commutation, with no emphasis on telecommunication technology, teleworkers made up 16.7 percent of the American workforce in 1995, according to the Nationwide Personal Transportation Survey (2000). If we use ITAC's definition, 12.2 percent of American workers are teleworking (Nilles, 2000). If we use the U.S. government definition, this figure drops to 3.2 percent (Kulish, 2001). Even 3.2 percent of the population means that more than four million Americans were working at home in 2000, a significant number. Regardless of the definition we select, it is clear that the American workforce has become, at some level, touched by telework.

Despite or possibly because of these numbers, some researchers suggest that telework has failed to attain its original promise. Early estimates of the potential of telework to engage the imagination of the American worker, solve the unanticipated consequences of industrialization, and enhance the weakened family structure that developed after the 1960s have fallen short of the mark. One popular newspaper article on this topic generated an explosive response from telework supporters when it stated, "Mounting studies and new research suggest that telecommuting isn't living up to expectations" (Armour, 2001). Citing corporate reports from AT&T, a leading supporter of telework, along with many smaller and recognizable firms, and such research leaders as the American Management Association and Boston College's Center for Work and Family, the article suggested that the climate of teamwork, the damage to family relationships, and the need to work face-to-face have been drags on the growth of telework. This claim was substantiated by the U.S. 2000 Community Census; "The fraction of Americans breaking free from offices and cubicles stayed about the same, with 3.2% working at home compared with 3% in 1990."

A look at who is teleworking and where telework takes place may help to shed some light on this phenomenon. There are several work location configurations that fall under the general rubric of alternate work sites for telework, including the home, business or telecenters, temporary "hot-desks" in the familiar office building or satellite office across town or across the country, and a variety of plug-in locations in hotels, restaurants, coffee-houses, and public facilities such as libraries or schools. The vast majority of teleworkers work at home (89 percent), with business or telecenters housing the second largest group, at 7 percent (Nilles, 2000).

A business center or telecenter is a workplace designed for use by the employees of one or more businesses. It is generally located away from the congested inner city, and is accessible to commuters who would ordinarily clog the access roads to the main workplace. "Across the country, some 4,000 business centers offer flexible space—from cubicles to private offices—at costs ranging from $500 to $2,500 per month (Zbar, 7/20/01). These telecenters provide all the conveniences of an office, such as photocopy machines, fax, phone, computers, network connections, and ready access to the necessary information. They provide privacy so that workers can use confidential documents without removing them to a home (and thereby, unsecured) location. They also permit workers to learn teleworking skills in a supportive environment, so that the worker is truly prepared to work at home at a later date (Zbar, 7/27/01). What they do not provide is a manager on site. They act as a sort of halfway house instead, keeping workers out of the office, but not in their homes. Workers can share the company of other workers, yet still put their jobs behind them at the end of the day.

Interest in the third category of alternate work sites is growing. The proliferation of coffee houses–cum–meeting space makes it easy to meet with people out of the office. These limited-menu restaurants provide convenience, comfort, and a place to plug in. "In short, they provided a four-hour office rental for the price of a three-dollar latte" (Pink, 2001, 161). In fact, Pink claims the real estate market is about to be turned on its head as a result of the movement to free agency and away from traditional work in traditional offices.

> Today, the typical non-retail commercial space consists of 80 percent offices and cubes and 20 percent meeting rooms. That arrangement forces people to travel in order to perform heads-down work they could easily do somewhere else—and it leaves insufficient room for doing the collaborative work that is the chief reason for people to share the same space . . . the workplace of the future will likely consist of 20 percent private offices, 20 percent 'touch-down' spaces (where people can plug in their laptop, check their e-mail, or make a quick phone call), and 60 percent meeting rooms and other venues for group interaction. With this configuration, some employees of companies would still come into the office every day, but most would have to do so only for a specific purpose. And for free agents working with that company, they'd have ample room to hold a meeting or connect their laptop instead of hastily grabbing the office of someone who happens not to be at her desk. (267–268)

Certainly, serious work of a confidential nature is not going to take place in a public coffee shop, but there are a great many work tasks that do not require the formality of an office in order to be completed effectively. Teleworkers may be crunching numbers, performing writing tasks, analyzing data, designing marketing programs or other projects, updating spreadsheets, or doing any other sort of focused work that is best handled without the interruptions of coworkers, telephone calls, and the demands of office collegiality or home availability. Venues like these are also suitable places for teleworkers whose responsibilities include client meetings or short, face-to-face interactions with business associates as they can be more professional away from the home environment.

Profile of a Teleworker

The description of the prototypical teleworker has changed since the early days of telework. The early teleworker was narrowly described as someone whose work did not require contact with a work team or contact with customers (other than as mobile sales personnel), and who could work alone and did not have to manage others. This description was based on what the worker did not do, instead of the work the teleworker actually performed. But all that has changed. Part of this change is the result of improvements in electronic work devices and our subsequent dependence on technology. For a full discussion of technology, please see Chapter 2.

In the late 1980s, as telecommuting was capturing the imagination of workers and employers, about one third of those teleworkers were able to perform their tasks at home one day a week without computer involvement. But that number has gradually diminished as more and more workers use computer technology in their daily work (Nilles, 1998). Workers without electronic access today are unlikely to be able to perform their normal responsibilities or fulfill their employers' expectations. However, the teleworker at the beginning of the twenty-first century not only has computer access but also carries a cell phone. These teleworkers have ready access to copy shops with fax machines and sophisticated printing technology so that their written reports are indistinguishable from those produced in the corporate office.

Teleworkers are no longer limited by distance—teleworkers can (and do) perform nearly every task from a remote location that they could while actually in the office. Teleworkers at the turn of the twenty-first century are managers, customer service representatives, members of virtual teams, administrative assistants, engineers—nearly every traditional office job can be performed by a teleworker at least part of the time. According to ITAC's 2000 survey, teleworkers are working at home or in telecenters about 20 hours each week, and more than half of them have been doing so for at least three years (Nilles, 2000). Most of the home-based teleworkers are employees (53.9 percent) or contract workers (12.6 percent), but an increasing percentage are operating home businesses (9.4 percent) or are self-employed (23.8 percent).

Oddly, since the concept of telework was designed to lessen commutation stresses, nearly 58 percent of teleworkers live in cities, whereas only 52 percent of the entire workforce consists of city dwellers. In fact, the effectiveness of telework to address commutation issues is somewhat suspect, as only 13 percent of teleworkers live in rural areas, whereas nearly 19 percent of the workforce includes those who live in rural areas. The greatest density of teleworkers is found in New England, the Mountain region from Idaho through New Mexico, and the Pacific coastal states (Nilles, 2000).

Median annual income is higher for teleworkers than for non-teleworkers, the former in the $50,000 range and the latter in the $30,000 range. Not surprisingly, teleworkers have attained a higher level of education than non-teleworkers, with 80 percent having completed at least some college compared to approximately 60 percent in the non-teleworker group. And this teleworker is probably a White male in his early 40s (Nilles, 2000).

THE TEMPESTUOUS ADOLESCENCE OF TELEWORK

Telework is still a young trend, and it is suffering the natural strains of adolescence. The numbers of teleworkers rise and fall with the economy. The development of e-commerce and Internet-related projects with their rocketing and plummeting fortunes have made telework into the solution-du-jour for every work-related problem

Aging workforce tired of commuting? Try telework. Young workforce unwilling to spend hours on the road? Try telework. Unable to recruit and retain qualified and desirable employees? Try telework. Pollution from automobile emissions? Try telework. Decreasing natural resources? Excessive strain on the infrastructure? Globalization? Absenteeism? Telework may be the answer.

Stand clear—the tectonic plates of change are shifting once again.

2

All Circuits Are Currently Busy

The signal fire suddenly flashes out. Oh welcome, you blaze in the
night, a light as if of day, you harbinger of many a choral dance in
Argos in thanksgiving for this glad event!
                    —Aeschylus

Or, in today's parlance, "You have mail!"

DEMYSTIFYING TELECOMMUNICATIONS TECHNOLOGY

In the last century, only technicians needed to understand the way
their equipment worked. Today, no one has the luxury of taking the
technology that business uses for granted. Throughout the ranks of
the corporation, all the way to the CEO's office, each day each
individual must come in contact with some form of telecommunications technology.

As frequently occurs with technological developments, a gatekeep-
ing mystique has arisen about telecommunications that limits its use-
fulness by shrouding both complex and simple concepts with complex
explanations. An entire lexicon has been developed to explain, or perhaps confound, this technology. Newly coined words, such as *connectivity*, with no intrinsic meaning, keep all but the most diligent language
sleuths in the dark about their implications. The time lines and descrip-
tions that follow take much of the mystery out of telecom while allow-

ing us to continue to take pleasure in the remarkable engineering that has brought us these communication tools.

Telecommunications Time Lines

"Before" the Internet. Moving beyond the smoke signals that introduce this chapter, communication methods advanced rapidly from the French Revolution through two world wars and their aftermath, the Cold War. Table 2.1 presents the flow of patents and developments in communication technology during the 180-year era from 1790 to 1970. Some of the entries in the table will surprise you—you may not have connected the developments in telegraph, telephone, television, radio, radar, computers, and the Internet as part of the same movement, as you will see that they are. You may also be surprised at how long ago some of our current innovations were conceptualized and designed. Who would have thought that the first mobile phone was used in the Boer War in South Africa in 1889? Table 2.1 is, of necessity, limited in length. Particularly in the world of computers, I have left out many interim developments in order to avoid repetition. But even without all of the inventions listed in sequence, several trends become apparent.

You will note that although engineers and inventors from all over the world have sought improvements in information sharing and have labored in multiple related technological arenas to develop the pieces of the telecommunications puzzle, the United States has dominated this field since the beginning of the twentieth century. Why is this so?

One reason for America's early dominance in telecommunications has to do with the motivations behind developing these technologies. Most of the inventions occurred either in wartime or by the military, with commercialization coming later. Throughout history, military success has been based on competitive advantage, and that advantage often is surprise. If a new weapon is invented, it is most effective when the enemy does not know about it. During the French Revolution, with France under siege from five other countries and internal revolt adding to the confusion, Chappe's optical telegraph (1790) gave the French government a significant military advantage in terms of deploying troops. The telegraph system consisted of tall poles with movable arms, mounted on hills, and visible one to the other. The arms of the machine were moved into configurations that represented different letters and were relayed from one tower to the next. The enemies were beaten handily because of the ease of communication between Paris and Lille, 23 kilometers distant. But the system was slow and could not operate in the dark or in bad weather, leading to the search for a more reliable, less expensive, and more readily available method of long-distance communication. After Benjamin Franklin discovered electricity in 1780,

TABLE 2.1 Before the Internet (1790–1970)[1]

Year	Development	Country
1790	Claude Chappe's Optical Telegraph System (range: 230 kilometers)	France
1796	"Telephone"—word invented by G. Huth for trumpets connecting towers by sound	Germany
1832	Charles Babbage introduced the "analytical engine"—first computer (steam powered)	England
1839	Charles Wheatstone's Electric Telegraph (range: 13 miles)	England
1845	Samuel Finley Breeze Morse's Electric Telegraph (Washington to Baltimore)	U.S.A.
1858	First submarine cable telegraph message from North America to Europe (Newfoundland to Ireland)	Canada/ Ireland
1876	Elisha Gray and Alexander Graham Bell applied for patents on the telephone	U.S.A.
1884	Paul Nipkow patented selenium cell television	Germany
1888	Heinrich Rudolf Hertz discovered microwaves	Germany
1889	Almon B. Strowger invented the Automatic Exchange for telephone Central Offices (subscribers could dial their own calls)	U.S.A.
1889	Herman Hollerith invented the punch card reader (used in the 1890 U.S. Census)	U.S.A.
1889	Lars Magnus Ericsson developed the first mobile phone (using transportable connections)	Sweden
1894	Alexander Stepanovich Popoff completed first "radio" transmission	Russia
1896	Guglielmo Marconi received the first patent granted for the radio	Italy
1904	J. A. Fleming developed the "valve," or vacuum tube	England
1907	Lee de Forest developed the control grid to amplify power levels	U.S.A.
1924	H. Nyquist developed "telephotography" for AT&T (later developed into facsimile process—"fax")	U.S.A.
1926	J. L. Baird and C. F. Jenkins developed a mechanical television system using photoelectric cells	England and U.S.A.
1928	V. K. Zworykin patented the electronic scanning television system	U.S.A.
1929	BBC begins broadcasting television	England
1935	Sir Robert Alexander Watson-Watt patented radar (Radio Direction and Ranging)	England
1939	David Sarnoff (RCA) introduced electronic television at the World's Fair in New York City	U.S.A.
1940	John V. Atanasoff and Clifford Berry developed the first all electronic computer (the binary-based Atanasoff-Berry Computer)	U.S.A.
1940s	Broadcasting in newly discovered VHF (very high frequencies) by relay	U.S.A.
1945	John Presper Eckert and John W. Mauchly developed ENIAC	U.S.A.
1948	John Bardeen, Walter Brattain, and William Schockley patent the first transistor	U.S.A.
1940s/ 1950s	Development of cable television (CATV or community access television) in Pennsylvania and Oregon	U.S.A.
1951	Remington Rand built UNIVAC I	U.S.A.
1951	CBS began first regularly scheduled color television broadcasts	U.S.A.
1953	50% of homes in the United States had television sets	U.S.A.

[1]Data for all charts in this chapter are compiled from Augarten (1984); Brown (1970); Federal Communication Commission, myhome.hananet.net; U.S. Census, www.earlytelevision.com; www.novia.net, www.pbs.org, www.privateline.com, www.javaworld.com, www.digitalcentury.com, www.technicalpress.com, www.islandnet.com, www.inventors.about.com, www.sci.sdsu.edu.

TABLE 2.1   continued

Year	Development	Country
1956	Transatlantic cable laid between New York, London, and Montreal	U.S.A./ U.K
1956	Picturephone first tested	U.S.A.
1956	TX-O—first transistorized computer completed	U.S.A.
1958	Jack Kilby developed the integrated circuit—semiconductor origin	U.S.A.
1960	78.5% of homes in the United States had access to a telephone	U.S.A.
1960	ECHO I launched by NASA—first communication satellite	U.S.A.
1960	Digital Equipment introduced the first minicomputer, PDP-1	U.S.A.
1960s	IBM 1401, the "Model T" of the computer industry, is a solid-state design (transistors rather than vacuum tubes). COBOL and FORTRAN were introduced.	U.S.A.
1963	Douglas Engelbart patented the mouse	U.S.A.
1964	John Kemeny and Thomas Kurtz developed BASIC	U.S.A.
1965	"Hypertext" is coined by Ted Nelson (text that is not linear)	U.S.A.
1965	Donald Davies invented "packet switching"	U.S.A.
1965	INTELSAT launched—first commercial communication satellite	U.S.A.
1967	IBM built the first floppy disk drive	U.S.A.
1968	First networking hardware and software developed	U.S.A.
1969	ARPANET—origin of the Internet—connected 4 universities	U.S.A.

electricity became a reliable source of power. Later versions of the telegraph powered by electricity were used both for military purposes and limited commercial ones.

Overall, a surprising number of inventions were first developed for military or government ends. For example, Marconi's radio was originally designed to provide communications for naval operations. This radio technology was used by the British in developing the radar that would protect the United Kingdom from attack by air. It was a short but significant leap from radar to television. Television was an invention that was commercially based from the outset. Developed concurrently in several countries—most prominently the United Kingdom and the United States—television owes its origins to the mechanical selenium cell scanning technology developed by Paul Nipkow in 1884. The 1920s were calling for entertainment after the rigors of World War I and before the traumas of international financial depression, and television was an instant hit. The BBC began broadcasting a mechanical version of video over low bandwidth audio frequencies in 1929. Television technology continued to improve, and David Sarnoff introduced electronic television at the 1939 World's Fair. Despite the intervention of World War II that suspended licensing of stations in the United States, television continued to grow in popularity. By 1953, half the homes in the United States had television sets. Cable television was introduced at the same time, to provide service to areas that either were less economically appealing to the commercial interests that backed this technology or were in geographically challenging parts of the country.

The development of the telephone was nearly an afterthought, as Alexander Graham Bell and Elisha Gray were trying separately to invent a "multiplexer," a method of transmitting several messages simultaneously over the telegraph lines. In the process, Bell became interested in transmitting sound via electricity and was encouraged by Joseph Henry, the Secretary of the Smithsonian Institution, to pursue that course of action and drop the telegraphy. Although there was little early interest in the telephone, there is no need to document either the importance or the popularity of this critical technology. Over 10,000 telephones were in service in the Bell Operating System by 1878, only two years after its patent was received; twelve years later 240,000 telephones were under Bell's control (Farley, 2001).

But the telephone was not a stand-alone invention; it became possible because of its closeness to earlier technologies, and without the later invention of the vacuum tube and the transistor, the telephone would not work the way it does today. The integration of the technologies loosely referred to as telecommunications technologies is what creates the complexity of our existing systems and what makes them difficult to understand. Many different parts of the system shared the foundational technologies but subsequently developed in different directions.

Between the wars. With the entry of the United States into World War II, the considerable strength of the U.S. military pocketbook supported telecommunications technology. The results included the computers that created ballistic charts for the U.S. Navy, and later ENIAC, a general purpose computer that led to the commercial applications of UNIVAC. Most of the computers developed during the 1940s and 1950s were sponsored and purchased by the military, both in the United States and in England, where similar advances were being made. When commercial applications and military applications matched, the technology entered the marketplace, but that happened rarely until the 1960s (Augarten, 1984). Early computers were designed to tackle one specific task, but second generation computers became more flexible and considerably smaller than the original block-long mechanical models. The development of the transistor allowed for size reduction, and the development of programming languages such COBOL and FORTRAN encouraged corporate interest. Kilby's development of the integrated circuit further reduced the size of computers and in 1960 the first minicomputer was produced. Shortly thereafter, BASIC (the first high level-language of microcomputers) was developed and the mouse was invented. Networking hardware and software was designed, and the Department of Defense's Advanced Research Project Agency (ARPA) designed a small network of supercomputers that allowed researchers in the United States to share data. ARPANET, the forerunner of the Internet, connected Stanford Research Institute, UCLA, UC Santa Barbara, and the University of Utah in 1969, and within a few years many major colleges and universities nationwide.

By 1960, it had become apparent that a new technology was required to carry voice and data over long distances and across oceans. One new technology would be satellite based. Development of satellite communication systems was spurred by the Cold War and its proliferation of intercontinental missiles, which demanded a method of communication and control that had a greater range than previously possible. The original radio technology, now enhanced by microwave transmission and transistors, led to the commercial use of satellites by 1965. Television and telephone transmissions became global, and an international agreement to share in the development and organization of satellite communication was signed by most of the noncommunist countries in the world (Brown, 1970).

The technologies had merged.

The Internet and WWW. The developments over the next thirty years, from 1970 to 2000, were no less dramatic. (See Table 2.2.) The computer continued to shrink in size and price and grow in power, memory, and capacity, as did related technologies. In the heyday of the minicomputer (1965–1975), the typical machine with 8–16 bit word length, 32–64 KB of RAM, a teletype (CRT terminals were not yet available), and a magnetic or paper tape reader cost between $20,000 and $150,000. The typical mainframe with 16–32-bit word length, 256 KB of RAM, and hard disks cost between $100,000 and $1,000,000. Supercomputers with 32 bit, 1 MB memory, and with various peripherals cost, from $1 million to $10 million.

By 1980, microcomputers designed for home use had been introduced, and were 8- or 16-bit machines with up to 128 KB RAM, floppy disk drives, and 10 MB hard drives. They cost between $3,000 and $15,000. Three years later, the Apple IIe with 64 KB RAM and 1 MHz processor cost only $1,400. As of 1997, microcomputers were 32-bit machines and, equipped with 32 MB RAM, a 3½-inch floppy drive, a 6 GB hard drive, and a 24X CD-ROM player, sold for around $2,000 (www.sci.sdsu.edu) or less, if you caught a good sale.

In 1982, the first videoconferencing system cost $250,000 with $1,000 per hour line charges. Less than ten years later, a videoconferencing system cost $75,000 with $30 per hour line charges. And, in 1992, the home videophone was introduced for $1,500. Ericsson's early mobile phone was replaced by a series of sophisticated cellular models that allowed remote locations to be connected seamlessly with the rest of the

TABLE 2.2 The Internet and the World Wide Web (1970–2000)

Year	Development	Country
1971	Ericsson made the first transatlantic video telephone call	Sweden
1971	The Intel 4004 chip was developed for microprocessing	U.S.A.
1973	Motorola filed a patent for cellular telephone	U.S.A.
1973	ARPANET connected with England and Norway	U.S.A.
1974	Telenet opened—first commercial version of ARPANET	U.S.A.
1974	Bill Gates and Paul Allen founded Microsoft	U.S.A.
1976	Stephen Wozniak and Steve Jobs introduced the Apple	U.S.A.
1977	Digital Research developed CP/M (Central Program for Microprocessors) operating system	U.S.A.
1977	FCC granted a license to operate a cellular system	U.S.A.
1978	Bahrain Telephone System operated the first mobile cellular radio	Bahrain
1978	Advanced Mobile Phone Service (AMPS) in North America improved car phones	U.S.A.
1978	Stromberg-Carlson introduced the digital X-Y switch (a simple switch that competed with earlier Strowger technology)	U.S.A.
1979	Cellular system introduced in Tokyo	Japan
1979	Compuserve was founded	U.S.A.
1979	USENET newsgroups were started	U.S.A.
1980	Commodore VIC-20—first computer with a color monitor	U.S.A.
1980	Hewlett Packard bought its chips from Japan	Japan
1981	Adam Osborne introduced the Osborne—first portable computer and first computer to be sold with software	U.S.A.
1981	Hayes Micromodem introduced the Modulator/Demodulator (MODEM) to market for PCs	U.S.A.
1981	Cellular system introduced in Mexico City	Mexico
1981	Cellular service introduced in Europe	Denmark, Sweden, Finland, Norway
1981	IBM introduced the first PC	U.S.A.
1982	5.5 million PCs were in use	
1982	Compression Labs introduced the first video conferencing system	U.S.A.
1982	TCP/IP was created and the "Internet" was born	U.S.A.
1983	First Windows product was developed	U.S.A.
1983	Texas Instruments introduced the single chip digital signal processor	U.S.A.
1983	Canadian cellular service began	Canada
1984	Commercial mobile telephony on aircraft	U.S.A.
1984	Apple's Macintosh introduced	U.S.A.
1986	WYSIWYG display facilitated desktop publishing	U.S.A.
1987	Panasonic took over an Ericsson plant	Japan
1987	The number of Internet hosts exceeded 10,000	
1985	Cable television began replacing earlier coaxial cable with fiber optics	U.S.A.
1990	ARPANET decommissioned, leaving only the Internet (more than 300,000 hosts)	
1990	In flight radio telephone became digital	U.S.A.
1990	95% of U.S. homes had telephones	U.S.A.
1991	PictureTel and IBM demonstrated the videophone on PC	U.S.A.
1991	The World Wide Web was established as a commercial network	U.S.A.
1991	"Gopher" was introduced (the first point-and-click Internet navigation tool)	U.S.A.

TABLE 2.2   continued

Year	Development	Country
1991	Tim Berners-Lee posted the computer code of the WWW on the alt.hypertext newsgroup	Switzerland
1992	Videophone became available for the home market	U.S.A.
1992	65 million PCs in use	
1992	MBONE introduced audio and video broadcasts; the Internet had more than 1,000,000 hosts	
1993	Apple introduced the Newton Personal Digital Assistant—first PDA	U.S.A.
1993	Nippon Telephone and Telegraph introduced digital cellular	Japan
1993	Mosaic became available and traffic exploded; the Internet expanded at an annual rate of 341,634%	
1995	NSFNET left the entire Internet in commercial hands	U.S.A.
1995	Cablevision introduced Access Plaza—users could surf the Internet, get interactive news, and do home banking through the normal cable drop	U.S.A.
1996	Nearly 10 million hosts on the Internet	
1996	Microsoft introduced NetMeeting software	U.S.A.
1997	36.6% of U.S. households have computers and 49.8% of employed Americans are using computers at work	U.S.A.

world. Successive waves of miniaturization encouraged the entry of Japan into this electronic playground. By 1980, Japanese technology and work systems were considered the most reliable in the world and had become the supplier of choice of Hewlett Packard.

The Internet exploded, with annual growth estimated at 341,634 percent in 1993. Access expanded exponentially; by 1996, there were nearly 10 million hosts on the Internet. In 1997, the U.S. Census Bureau captured a picture of an electronic America, with nearly 50 percent of employed civilians using a computer in their daily work and 36.6 percent of American households with home computers. Of those adults with home computers, 44.5 percent of them were using it for email, among other activities. The demand for Internet access had gone off the charts. Additional technologies were required to handle this demand.

The world beyond. As I write this chapter, it is out of date. Changes are occurring daily—we are making history and, curiously, can feel ourselves doing so.

In the summer of 2001, *Fortune* magazine's special technology issue claimed, "new products and technologies grab headlines, but simple utility and value often win the day. That's why standards such as the Palm V and Iomega's 100MB Zip Drive still place among our 100 most popular products, though both have been available for nearly two years" (Halpin, 2001, 40). Two years—two years is a lifetime in twenty-first century technology. Wireless LANs were tempting IT professionals as a cost-effective way to keep their teleworkers connected despite the uncertain standards in effect in 2002 (Taschek, 2002). More than 1,500 telecommunications companies were competing for customers and markets. Battle lines were drawn between providers of DSL, ISDN, cable-modem, T-1 or T-3 lines, and fiber optic data links. As demand soared, innovators were challenged to find new solutions, and business-as-usual companies were being left behind.

But new problems are created as older ones are solved. The demand for storage capacity overwhelmed the ability of most businesses to handle the situation. The assumption of instantaneous availability of records has forced the development of data caching for instant access to files. The need for rapid transfer of funds has created the electronic bill presentment and payment (EBPP) technology. Home networking and home phone LANs, faster PCs, lighter weight laptops, sophisticated peripherals (such as laser printers, scanners, flat screen monitors, CD burners, handhelds, and wireless phones that rival the most powerful business systems available, and software that blurs the line between computer and telephone, radio and computer, television and computer, cable and computer, and home or car and business) are all responses to problems created by the solution of older problems. Old problems have resurfaced, now dressed in electronic clothes, forcing the development of email content managers (for censoring email), powerful firewall breach protectors, and similar items. AT&T Labs has put together an "Imagine Kit," which can be viewed on their Web site: www.att.com. Some of the prototypes shown seem less strange than one would expect: A wireless phone/watch would allow the wearer to communicate directly through the wrist piece (Dick Tracy, come in please); the Internet Gamer wireless would allow people to compete in their favorite games over the Internet from any location and at any time; and The Kids Communicator would allow parents and children to see each other through a digital videophone mounted inside a transparent ball and talk to each other through wireless Internet links.

Two Tin Cans and a String

How are all these computers connecting to the Internet? How are all the telephones connecting to one another? What impact is wireless technology having on this process? The answers are no more complex than the telephone systems you made as a child out of two cans and a string. They just cost more. The two components of telecommunications technology are infrastructure and equipment, with bandwidth defining the major constraint of the combinations of the first two. These items are addressed in turn next.

Infrastructure. Infrastructure identifies the power resources and technical assets necessary for the transmission of messages through telecommunication media. In this case, the power media may be wire (electron based), radio (electromagnet based), or fiber optic (photon based), or they may be a combination of the three.

People are most familiar with the wired infrastructure, which requires wires connecting to an electrical source. Whenever an appliance must be plugged into the wall or run via battery, it is using electrons for power. That includes telephones, computers, radios, and toasters. The electrons may be on call permanently, full-time, as in direct wired telephones (open line intercoms, for example, or a wired system from your kitchen to the garage), or they may be available on a temporary basis, through dial-up equipment (traditional line telephone service in which you "dial" a number to connect with your sister in the next town or across the country). This is a simple and familiar process.

Radio technology is a bit more complex. It uses electricity for energy, but converts the electricity into an electromagnetic form that has the ability to leap or be pushed off the wires on which it started and be recognized by other wires many feet (or many miles) away. These radio signals project output at varying frequencies that are described on a continuum from ultralow to ultrahigh frequencies. The earliest radio technology functioned at the lowest frequencies, those most reachable by primitive equipment. As our ability to gain access to different frequencies increased, so has the possibility of sending bits of data and voice on microwaves, via satellite, and ultimately to date, by cell phones. Satellite communication, which began in the 1960s, allowed the transfer of data (radio, computer, or video) over great distances, even globally, but has been superseded domestically, for the most part, by land-based microwave transmission that carries voice and data for whole systems.

All of these changes have been incremental, but the earth-shattering technological change was the development of fiber optics and the possibility of transmitting evergreater amounts of voice and data over the same facilities. Fiber optics uses units of light—photons—instead of electrons, and its widespread use allowed the transformation of the world's communication infrastructure that was necessary to develop the Internet as a functional communication method. When the shift from analog signals to digital signals that took place in the 1960s was coupled with the fiber optics developed in the 1970s, the results were dramatic. Analog signals are continuous transmissions, controlled by the flow of the original input. Digital signals are units of light, electricity, or electromagnetism that run in an on/off process (commonly represented by 1 and 0). The functional result of this shift from analog to digital is an enormous expansion in terms of the volume of bits of information going from place to place. The on/off process allows smaller or lower-priority items to be sent along with the larger or higher-priority items (data bits between voice bits, for example), both speeding up transmission and expanding capacity.

Equipment. Equipment is the broad term for the hardware and software designed to operate within one or more of the structural constraints just described. Equipment is what we refer to most often when we talk about advances in technology, and these advances are, for the most part, incremental. The flow of these inventions was dependent on the supporting technologies of electricity, radio, and fiber optics, but the user equipment itself has been limited only by the imagination of engineers and inventors. Engineers' and inventors' minds are so fertile that we, as end users, have had increasingly shorter periods of time in which to become accustomed to a technology before it is overtaken by another. This was particularly evident from the mid-1980s to the mid-1990s, when each generation of PC quickly became obsolete because of enhanced chips, microprocessors, fancier peripherals, and new versions of our favorite software.

What seemed like a miracle on Monday became an entitlement by Thursday. Companies made massive investments in systems that nearly became out of date while they were being installed, creating among corporations what we may term "cutting edge anxiety," a late twentieth century phenomenon reminiscent of the gold rush of 100 years earlier. Part of the attempt to encourage acceptance of computers was the movement to make them "user-friendly." User-friendliness was meant to help office workers unfamiliar with the technology overcome their fear of computers and of the blank computer screen, populated only by DOS system C:\, the dreaded C prompt or "command line interface." The result was the integrated GUI (Graphical User Interface) and the WYSIWYG (what you see is what you get) display, encouraged by the development of the mouse and the Windows operating system. The familiar color and graphic displays of the video game systems (such as Atari) that had become popular with American children of that era were used to try to make the technology fun.

Advances in personal computing technology sped alongside advances in telephone technology, supported by the movement to wireless communication. It is interesting to note that wireless communication devices developed more rapidly and became popularized earlier outside the United States, where the wired infrastructure was not as well developed or pervasive as the existing U.S. wired infrastructure. Countries where telephone wire access was limited, such as remote areas of Scandinavia and many other parts of Europe, areas where war frequently interrupted civilian service such as the Middle East, areas where the infrastructure had never been fully developed with the earlier technology, such as the Far East, and countries whose land area and population were a fraction of the United States welcomed wireless technology with gusto. While Americans were enjoying car phones in 1978, the Bahrain Telephone System had instituted mobile cellular radio. Shortly thereafter, cellular service was introduced in Tokyo, then Mexico, then the Scandinavian countries (Denmark, Sweden, Finland, Norway). By 1993, Nippon Telephone and Telegraph had introduced a digital cellular system to Japan, and a walk down the street in the major European cities was accompanied by the trilling of "mobile" phone calls and the sight of people talking into their fists. In America, PDAs (personal digital assistants) were leading in appeal, followed by the introduction of cable access through which users could then surf the Internet, get news, and do banking at home, as well as watch special television shows, sports events and movies. Half of American workers used computers at work, and more than a third of American households had computers at home. There were nearly 10 million hosts on the Internet by 1996, when Microsoft introduced NetMeeting software, making it possible for users to create video, audio, and graphical connections over the Internet among multiple participants. Something had to give.

Bandwidth—from soda straw to garden hose to fire hose. Bandwidth is the term used to describe the overall capacity of the telecommunication environment. Bandwidth also describes the major limitation of communication-facilitating technologies. Bandwidth is the conduit through which items of information travel. When the bandwidth is narrow (straw sized), demand for connections can easily overwhelm existing capacity for transmission. The result? Busy sites on the Internet, painfully slow access, crashing connections, "circuit busies," and even inability to get a dial tone. It is as if the sky were filled with smoke signals coming from many hills, mixing in the atmosphere and filling space with the unreadable details of lost messages.

One way bandwidth can be increased is by boosting the speed of the transmission through enhanced technology such as expanding the size of the conduit, allowing the larger downloads demanded by graphics and video as well as speedier connections and broader access. Instead of sending voice and data on the same frequency, DSL technology permits a wide variety of frequencies to be accessed by the same lines, making it possible to separate the voice (larger) from the data (smaller) and send them each on different frequencies. DSL (digital subscriber lines) are subdivided into the equivalent of multiple tracks along which information can be sent, and then reassembled at the appropriate destination. As standard wiring is converted to fiber optics, more and more information can pass through the conduit. Nonetheless, each message is self-contained and travels as if in a private railroad car on its own circuit.

Another way to move messages and data faster is packet switching, a just-in-time technology developed in 1965. Packet switching allows sending messages without requiring them to remain in strict order along a track. They take the shortest available route (OSPF—Open Shortest Path First) to their final destination and are then re-ordered by a packet assembler. This causes no problems with data, but when voice packets are delayed, reassembling can be distracting and unsatisfactory. That is why video conferencing can seem awkward and less smooth than we may expect (*www.privateline.com*), but dedicated telephone lines and other technical solutions to these reassembly problems relieve most discontinuities.

THE COLLISION OF PEOPLE AND TECHNOLOGY

Related Costs and the Technological Downside

Technology, inventions, innovation, and creativity are fun and stimulating. They encourage us to think in terms of possibilities instead of sinking back into our intellectual comfort zone. In the short term, novelty creates a sense of newfound freedom that can overshadow its drawbacks and second order consequences. Telecommunications advances have permitted us to make connections with counterparts around the globe; with coworkers in offices regardless of location; with customers, suppliers, and all those who ordinarily participate in our business lives. But these connections do not come without costs, and the costs are not all directly financial.

Choice. How do you select from among the multiple options available for computers, telephones, cellular phones, Internet access services, broadband or dial-up connections at home, or tomorrow's latest and greatest invention? This is far from a frivolous concern, as the financial impact as well as ease of use, ergonomic issues, speed, and reliability can turn the teleworker's environment into a technological disaster area. To complicate matters, new choices are often appearing; since 1996, "hybrid technologies such as fixed wireless, a technology that provides homes and businesses with local-phone and data-transmission service over an antenna instead of wires" [have emerged] (Cauley, 2001, R6). Merely keeping up to date on emerging technologies and technological change and determining the lowest-cost/widest-access telephone calling plans every few months can become a full-time job.

Knowing where to start can help. When selecting telecommunications devices and access routes, the wisest course begins with the basics—your business goals. What is it that you are trying to accomplish? Do you need new technology to get there? How? If your organization employs workers at home to respond to customer service calls, your selections will differ significantly from those of a business that employs teleworkers to edit manuscripts, prepare graphics for advertising campaigns, do market research, or sell cemetery plots. There is simply no getting away from good business-planning practices and clearly thought-out strategies. Without these, technology cannot help you attain success.

One of the considerable difficulties in making choices is the allure of focusing on only one small component of your system. This is dangerous because the resulting suboptimization can have negative impacts across a whole system. Though you are happy that you have reduced your long-distance charges by a penny per minute, the requirement for dedicated interfaces can create unexpected administrative, technical, and operational headaches far exceeding your savings.

Access. Is there room for you on the Internet? This is not an idle question, as space is *not* unlimited. The Internet was built under a communications system "designed for no more than 4.3 billion computers and devices" (Jesdanun, 2001, C2). In the 1980s, that was deemed sufficient. However, as more and more users log on and more countries connect, some suggest that the remaining connection points will be used by 2006. The next version of the Internet (v6) was in development in 2001, with some major manufacturers of routers and software providing v6 compatibility for software developers in the spring of 2001.

What about the reliability of your access? When workers at home need speedy connections like those available in the office, they must use broadband services such as cable to gain Internet access. But broadband services can go out of business, leaving customers unable to work or dependent on commercial ISPs with dial-up connections, resulting in slow downloads, intermittent disconnects, weak security, and an unprofessional presentation. One survey showed that cable modems were being used by 25 percent of teleworkers, DSL by 18 percent, and ISDN by 13 percent. Overall, however, more than 40 percent of those working at home used dial-up access, with all of the drawbacks mentioned (Osterman, 3/28/01).

The same survey showed the impact of connection speed on the productivity of teleworkers. Each worker surveyed sent and received approximately 70 messages daily when working on the office system; the same workers working at home on dial-up systems sent and received 30 percent fewer messages a day than those on high-speed access connections (50 messages as compared to 65 messages). Email down-time, whether caused by access failure or network messaging system failure, is particularly disruptive, often requiring multiple telephone calls and tests before resolution. The impact on productivity can be a 25 percent decrease.

Evolving Technology and the Teleworker

Why do we need to know so much about the technology? As managers, our job is not necessarily technological. We have an IT department for that. After all, we do not need to understand how the ABS brakes work on our automobile in order to drive it. However, we do need to understand that ABS brakes will affect the way our car functions in certain environments and that in order to drive it both wisely and well, we must be aware of how this technology changes the rules of safe driving.

In the same way, not understanding the basics of telecommunications technology keeps us from understanding how to maximize its uses and thereby to optimize our own professional capabilities. By allowing ourselves to be limited by someone else's vision of technological advances, we automatically limit our success and that of our organization. Specifically, managing workers in remote locations creates a set of demands that must be satisfied either through technological innovations or by the creative application of existing devices.

Although many configurations are possible, a typical telework setup will include, in the remote location, a computer (laptop or desktop model), a telephone, a fax machine or fax access through the computer, a printer and other peripherals, and Internet access. If the teleworker also works in the office, the entire environment may be duplicated. The specifics of these allocations will differ from company to company according to needs and pocketbooks, but the basics are consistent: a way to communicate by voice, a way to communicate in writing, and connections between the parties to the conversation.

The technological revolution of the past 100 years has changed the means of communication dramatically, but the evolution of the parties to the process (people) is both exponentially and immeasurably slower. Whether face-to-face or technologically assisted, people continue to make connections through the old-fashioned expedients of language and social interaction, always demanding more information.

The more diverse the civilization—the more differentiated its technology, energy forms, and people—the more information must flow between its constituent parts if the entirety is to hold together, particularly under the stress of high change. . . . As the people around us grow more individualized or de-massified we need more information—signals and cues—to predict, even roughly, how they are going to behave toward us. And unless we can make such forecasts we cannot work or even live together. As a result, people and organizations continually crave more information and the entire system begins to pulse with higher and flows of data. (Toffler, 1980, 183)

A full discussion of the way we communicate in our digitized society appears in Chapter 4.

3

The Rewards of Telework: *Cui Bono?*

STAKEHOLDER THEORY

Any discussion of the rewards or benefits of telework must begin with a consideration of the interests at stake. Stakeholder theory takes into account the needs and interests of all institutional stakeholders, typically including stockholders, employees, customers, suppliers, the local business community, and political interests. The primary stakeholders may vary according to the focus one wishes to place on each major player and on whose interests are paramount at the time (Mitchell, Agle, & Wood, 1997).

In the case of a movement such as "telework" (as opposed to the behavior of an individual or corporation), stakeholder theory can serve as a starting point for the determination of motivations for supporting or rejecting the large concept. As Max Clarkson (1995) eloquently argues,

The moment that corporations and their managers define and accept responsibilities and obligations to primary stakeholders, and recognize their claims and legitimacy, they have entered the domain of moral principles and ethical performance, whether they know it or not. So long as managers could maintain that shareholders and their profits were supreme, the claims of other stakeholders could be subordinated or ignored. There was no need for the manager to be concerned with fairness, justice, or even truth. The single-minded pursuit of profit justified any necessary means, so long as they were not illegal. But as managers make decisions and act in terms of stakeholder management in resolving inevitable conflicts of interest between stakeholder groups, they can no longer rely on "the invisible hand" to solve problems. (111)

The four central theses of stakeholder theory (Donaldson & Preston, 1995, 65–91) are:

- Stakeholder theory is descriptive: "It describes the corporation as a constellation of cooperative and competitive interests possessing intrinsic value."
- Stakeholder theory is instrumental: "It establishes a framework for examining the connections, if any, between the practice of stakeholder management and the achievement of various corporate performance goals."
- Stakeholder theory is normative: Stakeholders maintain legitimate interests in various aspects of corporate activity, and these interests have intrinsic value (not to be measured solely in terms of the potential impact on the interests of another stakeholder, such as stockholders).
- Stakeholder theory is managerial: "Stakeholder management requires, as its key attribute, simultaneous attention to the legitimate interests of all appropriate stakeholders, both in the establishment of organizational structures and general policies and in case-by-case decision making."

The Constituents

Exactly who are these constituents or stakeholders, and what is their interest in telework? The six primary stakeholders that appear in Figure 3.1—workers, employers, equipment suppliers, telephone companies, public agencies, and consultants—have distinct and specific interests in the pursuit of telework. The unnamed stakeholder can be referred to as the amorphous "social interest" that, although difficult to measure, plays a major role in the acceptance or rejection of telework and other alternate, virtual life style changes. An examination of the concerns of each of these stakeholders helps to identify the net benefit provided by the incorporation of telework into a business's operations.

Workers. The subtext of this book is a consistent interest in the experiences and needs of people, of individual workers and the impact of new technology on their lives. Although in the year 2002 less than 5 percent of the American workforce was directly and personally involved in telework, telework had a secondary impact on a far larger portion of the working population than represented by this figure. The movement toward a "family-friendly workplace" counts telework as a significant element in attaining the goal of having most work-

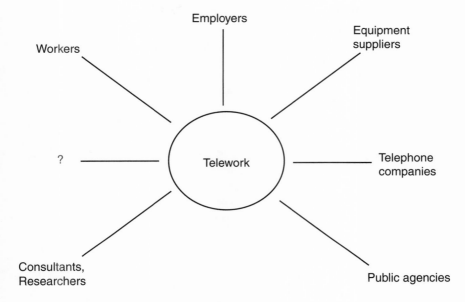

Figure 3.1 Teleworking Stakeholders

places consider the needs of employees as primary. (Please see Chapter 9 for a full discussion of the family-friendly workplace). Family-friendliness is a euphemism for employer attempts to meet the following challenges:

- Recruiting a skilled workforce in a competitive environment
- Retaining valuable employees in the face of a booming economy that provides multiple options for workers
- Providing a way for overworked Americans to care for young children, the elderly, and the other demands of running a household
- Improving the overall quality of work life (QWL) as a means of maintaining productivity during periods of high employment

When unions protected most workers, a national movement toward family-friendly workplaces was unnecessary. During the period from 1850 to 1950, the typical workweek decreased from 72 hours to the 40 hours with which we are more familiar today. Leisure time increased commensurately, and projections from that period suggested that the trend would continue, with the workweek decreasing to 36.5 hours by 1960 (Kaplan, 1960). This never occurred—as of 2001, the average workweek for nonagricultural full-time workers in America was 42.8 hours, reversing the anticipated trend (www.stats.bls.gov).

The increased workweek, coupled with dramatically increased labor force participation by women, has very nearly eliminated earlier concerns about what to do with the greater leisure afforded by shorter workweeks. The studies that were conducted during the heyday of the decreasing workweek indicated that the preference of American workers was for "leisure bunching," or providing more days off rather than shorter workdays. An eight-hour workday provided sufficient time for twentieth century workers to handle their normal household responsibilities on a daily basis; gaining another hour of personal time per day did not provide a significant benefit to them.

But Americans at the end of the twentieth century and the beginning of the twenty-first century have experienced different needs. As the average workday for technical, professional, and other non-service sector workers has increased to meet the demands of a 24/7 society, people are eager to protect time for home life, for family, and for community away from their employment and to preserve some vestige of the leisure time that seemed to be a challenge 50 years ago. The time away from work is once more desperately needed on a daily basis, rather than bunched into days off.

One way for workers to reclaim some personal time is to eliminate commuting, one of the great time-wasters of modern society. Although the average teleworker saves one hour per day while working at home (Pratt, 1999), commuting eats as much as three hours a day that can be returned to workers through telework (see "Public agencies" later in this section). The vast majority of those commuting hours are spent in cars rather than on public transit. Elimination of the high stress, heavy traffic commute during the morning and evening hours allows a gentler entry into the workday and can even provide time for exercise or other personal activities at the end of the day. These salvaged hours can also be used by workers to fulfill their "second shift" responsibilities; the many hours absorbed by child care, elder care, and household maintenance.

Time is the scarcest resource, and the one that is most difficult to obtain. Telework can help people "get more time" for the activities they want to perform, whether these are the required second shift or the opportunity to get to know their families and friends better. The value system of Generation X, the generation of those born between approximately 1964 and 1975 and who enjoy growing clout in the workforce, focuses less heavily on getting ahead within a company and more on maintaining a measure of personal control over their lives. They are more unwilling to place work ahead of family needs and personal development, and for them, telework is a blessing. A study of American workers conducted in 1999 indicated that 95 percent of the respondents felt enormous time pressure, most significantly related to spending insufficient time with their families (Heldrich, 1999). A subsequent study by Catalyst confirmed these findings, making it clear that flextime, telework, and access to technology are the key motivators for Gen X. Of the respondents, 61 percent of the women and 54 percent of the men in the study (1,263 professionals) wanted to be able to telework, whereas only 17 percent have the opportunity to do so (Kistner, 1/1/02). The latitude to work less-scheduled hours, to be almost entrepreneurial in their approach (but without the entrepreneur's responsibility for corporate success), and to feel more freedom in their jobs—all this satisfies many of their needs and motivates them when traditional means do not.

Another benefit of telework to workers includes decreased expenses related to employment. Teleworkers pay less for travel, for clothing (despite the nation's movement toward casual dress, if you are in an office you still need to wear clean, neat, and professional attire), for makeup and other personal care items, and for food (eating at home always costs less than eating in restaurants). By 1997, the trend toward eating in restaurants and bringing home takeout had picked up speed and accounted for more spending than did shopping for the groceries necessary to prepare meals at home. According to the "16th Annual Report on Eating Patterns in America," although 83 percent of meals were eaten at home, pizza and hamburgers were top preferences whether at home or in restaurants (Wetzel, 2002). Although costly and unhealthy, this approach to food preparation serves as a time-saving alternative of last resort for time-poor workers. With their increased participation in teleworking noted over the five years from 1997 to 2002, and encouraged by renewed interest in cuisine and increased time to cook, this generation may reverse the trend.

Employers. The benefits and rewards of telework that accrue to employers is a long list indeed. These include increased productivity and effectiveness, decreased absenteeism, increased retention, ease of recruiting, and lowered cost of doing business.

From the employer's perspective, productivity is key to organizational success. Telework has been shown to be effective in decreasing absenteeism and thereby increasing productivity. According to a 1999 survey of teleworkers who were heads of households, the time spent on planned and unplanned absences from work (doctor and dentist appointments, family care emergencies, personal illness, waiting for service personnel to arrive) cost three times as much for nonteleworkers as it did for those who work at home. Individual illness decreased, and shorter times were required for many personal appointments due to the closer proximity of services to home rather than to work. Companies that supported telework saved over $2,000 per employee per year (Pratt, 1999). Other research reports confirm these findings: a 1998 study showed that teleworkers take two days less sick leave per year than office workers (Nilles, 1998).

In addition, teleworkers consistently report increased personal productivity when they work at home over when they work in the office. The teleworking population interviewed by Pratt claimed a 22 percent increase in personal productivity. This increase, based on the estimated average daily wages of her study group ($169.00), netted a total productivity increase of $37 per day teleworked. Annualized for 50 days of telework, this amounts to $1,850; for 150 days of telework, the net productivity gain is $5,550 per worker. Again, these data are corroborated by other studies indicating annual productivity gains between $4,800 and $8,300 per teleworker (Nilles, 1998). AT&T reported in 2002 that their teleworkers gained an hour a day of productivity, retrieved from time ordinarily spent commuting. These generous teleworkers added an estimated $65 million in business benefit to the company in 2001 (Kistner, 1/1/02).

It is important to remember that these productivity data are all self-reported and must be viewed with a measure of skepticism due to the inherent self-interest involved in this kind of data collection. Issues of self-reporting aside, however, part of the problem in generating accurate productivity data lies in the difficulty of measuring the knowledge work that is the greater part of most teleworkers' normal responsibilities. Very few companies have found a reliable measure of productivity for knowledge workers; each individual's work tends to be quite specific in nature and difficult to slot into broad categories. Until reliable measures have been developed and adopted by a broad cross section of organizations, it will continue to be a challenge to measure productivity objectively.

Lowering the cost of doing business creates an additional impetus to employers to expand their telework programs. One of the major costs of doing business is the expense of real estate. In 2000, the U.S. GSA (General Services Administration) Office of Governmentwide Policy issued a document that provided a method for calculating the per person cost of office real estate, benchmarked by 10 government agencies with data contribution by nearly 20 additional public and private organizations. The resulting Cost Per Person Model spreadsheet can be retrieved at www.gsa.gov. Any company can use it plugging in its own data. The GSA cautions against the temptation of making a linear connection between telework and real estate savings. Nonetheless, it is indisputable that desks will be freed up by telework and that space can be reconfigured to result in real property savings through creative redesign. AT&T, one of the largest teleworking employers in the nation, has claimed to have reduced office space costs by 50 percent and freed up $500 million in cash flow from 1991 to 1998. They also estimate an annual real estate savings of $2000 per teleworker (Lovelace, 2000; Nilles, 1998). Nortel claimed a one-time real estate savings of $60 million, and Siemens foresees a savings of $1 million in real estate costs over five years (Lovelace, 2000).

Retention and recruiting are two sides of the same issue, and both are addressed by telework. If no one provides workers with the opportunity to telework, then there is no benefit attached to it. But once one company in an industry provides this opportunity to workers, it becomes a competitive advantage to do so and a strategic disadvantage to those who fail to offer this benefit. The critical nature of telework programs in worker retention cannot be overstated. Organizations have found it difficult to recruit workers who are in high demand if they do not have a telework program in effect (Pratt, 1999; Vega & Brennan, 2000b), especially in a strong economy. Companies estimate that recruiting a new worker and training that person to full productivity can cost up to half a year's salary, making serious inroads on corporate profitability. In addition, during periods of high employment, those new workers can be hard to find. Telework capability provides access to an expanded labor force, unlimited by distance or convenience of public transit. If a company has teleworking capacity, it becomes easier to locate potential employees regardless of where they live, as well as to retain those valuable workers already on the payroll.

Equipment suppliers. Telework is big business. Manufacturers of dozens of identifiable pieces of equipment and software as well as myriad less identifiable hardware items participate in the generation of revenue and profit from this lucrative industry built around sending people home or to alternate locations to do their normal work. Suppliers of routers, switches, central office equipment, fiber optics, computers, specialized software, modems, cable modems and other connectivity equipment, and telephones with sophisticated options all participate in the financial rewards associated with telework and have a significant interest in its success.

Although it is not possible to distill revenues generated solely by teleworking from those generated by the networking and IT industries overall, a look at this economic sector reveals an arena of massive production and spending. In 2001, the federal government anticipated spending nearly $42 billion on information technology, and state and local governments nearly $39 billion. This accounts for only one tenth of the annual network industry sales for 2001—$890 billion, and that $890 billion represented a 4 percent decrease in sales from the previous year (Croci, 4/29/02). The top 10 manufacturers in the networking industry (IBM, Hewlett-Packard, Compaq, Dell, Motorola, Intel, Microsoft, Cisco, Lucent, and Sun) recorded $342.9 billion in sales in 2001, a figure that may be misleading because many of these companies were selling to each other, generating additional revenue within the industry. This issue aside, it is clear that there is a great deal of money to be made from telework support, implementation, training, and service, even when the technology sector overall suffers decline. A small piece of an enormous pie can satisfy a great many hungry companies.

Telephone companies. What I have identified as "telephone companies" includes long-distance providers, ISPs (Internet service providers), local telephone service providers, and service integrators. Some of these companies provide lines, some satellites, some cellular services. The top ten local, long distance, and Internet service providers had revenues in 2001 of $344.1 billion, surpassing the equipment providers by over $1 billion. These top 10—Verizon, AT&T, SBC Communications, AOL Time Warner, WorldCom, Sprint, BellSouth, Electronic Data Systems, Qwest Communications, and AT&T Wireless—represent moving targets. They combine with one another, recombine, separate, and meet up again in an orgy of electronic mating dances, all with the same purpose in mind—to gain market share. They have controlled the industry for years, with only minor variations in their rank order.

This stakeholder group would be incomplete without a discussion of IP VPN (Internet Protocol Virtual Private Networks). IP VPN appears at the nexus of the previous stakeholder category of equipment provider and the stakeholder category of telephone company. VPN technology assures privacy for corporate networks while providing access over the Internet, bridging two sectors of stakeholder interest (see Chapter 2). IP VPN usage has been growing steadily, with more than 83 percent of U.S. companies using it as of 2001, permitting teleworkers to secure access into the corporate LAN over the Internet via inherently secure connectivity (Harris, 2002). Since most medium and large U.S. companies provide Internet access to employees—some 99 percent of companies do this—the Internet provides the WAN (Wide Area Network) connectivity, eliminating the need for some of the older types of private-network connections and may be more cost-effective as a result. Bottom line interest for this stakeholder? Economic gain.

Public agencies. It is the responsibility of public agencies to implement the social, political, and legal agendas subscribed to by both government and business interests. Sometimes these are in conflict and must be carefully managed in order to satisfy disparate interest groups. The public agencies most concerned with environmental impact, energy consumption, and expansion of opportunity for all members of society are federal, state, and local transportation boards, environmental agencies, and departments of labor and employment.

Beginning with the unholy triangle of pollution, energy consumption, and traffic, telework seems likely to provide a way to some relief. From the late 1960s to 1990, the number of trips made in private vehicles increased dramatically from 145 billion to nearly 250 billion, an increase of 72 percent. Almost one quarter of these trips were made as part of earning a living, either commuting or in other job-related activities. In just the 10 years from 1980 to 1990, the number of workers driving to work alone in their cars increased by 35 percent, from 62.2 million to 84.2 million (Ball, 1994). By 1999, 87 percent of teleworkers reported that when working in the office rather than at home, they commuted alone in their vehicles (Pratt, 1999, 4). The Metropolitan Washington [DC] Council of Governments forecast a 44 percent increase in vehicle miles traveled by 2020, whereas highway capacity increases were only 11 percent (West, 2000). Anyone who has experienced rush hour in the areas surrounding New York City, Boston, San Francisco, Los Angeles, Washington, or other major U.S. cities knows what these figures mean in terms of time, frustration, strain on the infrastructure, and delays. As the number of these trips continues to mount, our air quality plummets due to the carbon monoxide, nitrous oxide, hydrocarbon, and particulate matter emissions we are generating; we are killing ourselves in the rush to work.

The ideal commuting alternative has been the Holy Grail sought by public agencies since the 1960s. Proposed solutions have included increased public transportation, carpooling, technological solutions such as emission control devices, and working at home. These solutions have been effective to varying degrees, but the greatest impact has resulted from working at home. One California proposal indicated the potential annual reduction in pollution for 16,000 teleworkers working at home only 1.4 days per week as over 6 million pounds of carbon monoxide, 380,000 pounds of nitrogen oxides, over 1.1 million pounds of unburned hydrocarbons, and 26,000 pounds of particulate matter from brakes (Nilles, 1998). The same study indicated "an average annual energy saving of 4,200 kilowatt-hours per teleworker . . . [potentially resulting in a savings] of 60 million kilowatt-hours, about 1,600,000 gallons of gasoline" (147). An AT&T Telecommuting Calculator computes that a full-time teleworker will save 3,200 pounds of carbon dioxide from polluting the atmosphere each year; even telecommuting just one day per week will save 640 pounds of carbon dioxide (www.att.com).

California has been a leader in this research, as the environmental impact has been particularly severe in California cities, but studies in

Texas, Oregon, Colorado, Michigan, Georgia, and the Washington, DC area have confirmed these findings. The result has been a plethora of federal and state laws meant to address the issues of air quality, pollution, and the conservation of natural resources via control of traffic and commuting. Telework stands as a key component of these programs.

Consultants. A small industry that deals with issues surrounding telework has developed since the 1970s. It includes consultants, academics, researchers, trainers, associations, and government agencies, and others who support telework projects. Conferences are held, international meetings are conducted, books and monographs are published, and grants are offered and written on this topic. Each individual thus engaged has a significant stake in the future of telework and must be considered a prime constituent. Therefore their interests must be considered. Most of these interests are financial—consulting and conference organizing are lucrative businesses and engage many other substakeholders in the process of doing business. Publishing is less lucrative, but far more influential in terms of public opinion and political influence, and it also engages a wide variety of substakeholders in its operations. Researchers, academics, and trainers have professional interest in telework, as well as career building and influence on public opinion.

Social interest. This "stakeholder" includes the focus on environmental impacts, air quality and traffic congestion mentioned previously, but that is not its only focus. At least two more important social issues are addressed by telework: disaster planning and the expansion of employment opportunities for all people.

Disaster planning is an oxymoronic concept of the highest order. Although it is possible to plan for regularly occurring weather-related disasters such as tornados, hurricanes, floods, and blizzards, it is not possible to plan for a specific disaster in advance of its occurrence. However, proponents have provided ample evidence of telework's effectiveness in dealing with the unexpected.

When a fatal car crash shut down the GA 400 (one major access route to Atlanta) during one morning rush hour, the Metro Atlanta Telecommuting Advisory Council (MATAC) was able to put an emergency telework program into action. The media were alerted to inform workers who had not yet left home for home to work from home until the traffic problems were cleared. The workers were able to check email, hold telephone meetings and conference calls, and perform other activities rather than sit in traffic or add to the road congestion (Zbar, 5/27/02). Immediately following the terrorist attacks on the World Trade Center and the Pentagon on September 11, 2001, many firms whose workers had been displaced and offices destroyed implemented telework programs on an emergency basis. Six months later, some of the companies continued to see telework as a good stopgap measure but were eager to get back to "business as usual." Other companies had such a positive experience with telework during the crisis that they advanced their existing plans to incorporate telework on a broader basis immediately (Zbar, 3/18/02). This replicates the experiences of other disaster plan implementers. Telework has proven to be a valuable tool during hurricanes, earthquakes, and traffic emergencies, as well as being helpful during periods when large crowds (such as for the Olympics or for national political conventions) are likely to disrupt regular commuting schedules but the work of the nation must go on.

Another major social concern relates to increasing employment opportunities for all people. Telework has the potential to advance entry into the workforce of previously unemployed or underemployed populations, such as people with disabilities, people who have caregiver responsibilities, people with limited access to transportation, or those who live in remote areas. America has made a commitment to provide opportunities to all citizens. In particular, the Americans with Disabilities Act of 1990 (ADA) was designed to protect the interests of the vast majority of the American workforce (Cascio, 1998) by requiring that reasonable accommodation be made for the special needs of people with limiting disabilities. Working at home can make these company-supplied accommodations unnecessary and can open the doors to employment for the twothirds of working-age people with disabilities who are currently unemployed (Burkhauser, Daly, & Houtenville, 2000). The labor force could be expanded by 8 percent if the 11 million working-age people with severe disabilities were employed (Kruse, 2000).

Telework can also help to bridge the digital divide—the gap between the technological haves and have-nots—which had become apparent in America in the mid-1990s. In 1984, only 8 percent of U.S. households owned computers. By 1994, only 24.1 percent of U.S. households owned a computer, with ownership slightly higher in cities (24.8 percent) than in rural areas (22.1 percent). In 1997, computer ownership began to increase—37 percent of U.S. households owned a computer Then, growth in computer ownership and Internet usage exploded in the three-year period from 1998 to 2001. A report issued by the Census Bureau in September 2001 indicated that 51 percent of U.S. households (54 million) owned one or more computers in 2000 (*Falling Through the Net*, 2001).

Shortly thereafter, a measurement of Internet usage by the National Telecommunications and Information Administration, the Economics and Statistics Administration, and the U.S. Census Bureau showed that by September 2001, more than half the nation was online—54 percent of the population, or 143 million individual Americans (*A Nation Online*, 2002). The same report showed a 5.5 percent increase in home computer ownership from 2000 to 2001. In 2001, 56.5 percent of U.S. households owned a computer, and this number was closely linked to computer usage at work. Home ownership of a computer was found twice as often among those people who use computers at work than among those who do not (77.9 percent versus 35.9 percent). Telework can encourage both home and office computer usage, increasing mainstream participation in the U.S. economy and social engagement for the groups with lower current participation (including Blacks, Hispanics, people with disabilities, and those with family incomes below $24,999).

The Four Central Theses

Stakeholder theory is descriptive. Each of the aforementioned constituents has valid and legitimate interests in the expansion of telework. The individual's desire to improve the quality of work life and lead a more balanced life overall while recovering some of the personal time that has been lost to the American work ethic seems to combine well with employers' desire for increased productivity and improved effectiveness that plays out through recruiting and retention figures. Even sectors of the economy that do not directly use telework benefit from it through sales of consumable and nonconsumable products, services, and their related taxes. Social interests and concerns are favorably affected by the trend toward increased computer and Internet usage, and a greater sense of national equity can be achieved as telework increases.

Stakeholder theory is instrumental. Telework functions as a high-level abstraction that operationalizes many of our national propensities and explicit and implicit goals in one convenient package. Convenience is one key to American popular philosophy, and anything that enhances our convenience tends to be accepted as good or worthwhile. Telework is convenient for workers, for employers, and for the rest of the constituent stakeholder community as well. What could be easier than commuting from one's bedroom to one's basement workroom? What could be more cost-effective than to supply workers with equipment at home while compressing the office workspace in a shared or hoteled manner to reduce real estate costs? What could be better than developing an entirely new market for existing products by extending WANs and LANs to the home environment and providing home Internet access at the same levels that, until recently, had only been provided to companies? What could be more convenient for researchers and consultants than to perform their own activities online, in a virtual environment, from the convenience of their own locations or attending and participating in conferences via teleconnections from their laptop computers? And what could possibly be better than performing all these activities and protecting the environment, reducing pollution, and conserving resources all the while?

Stakeholder theory is normative. According to the stakeholder analysis in Table 3.1, telework provides intrinsic value not only individually to all constituents but in some categories to several stakeholders simultaneously. Seven themes (recruiting, retention, reduction of commutation, QWL, cost/expense reduction, improved profitability, and environmental protection) emerge that indicate telework's value to at least two other identified stakeholders in addition to the stakeholder whose interest may be considered primary. Considering Table 3.1, it is easy to spot the overlapping areas of individual interest.

Stakeholder theory is managerial. According to this stakeholder analysis, telework provides intrinsic value to all constituents collectively, thereby offering an opportunity that is attractive because it is both negotiable and manageable. The development of appropriate policies, guidelines, and case-by-case decision making appears to be a straightforward process, easily managed by the matching of reciprocal interests on the part of the constituents.

TABLE 3.1 Stakeholder Analysis: Patterns of Benefits

	Workers	Employers	Equipment Suppliers	Telephone Companies	Public Agencies	Consultants	Social Interest
Recruiting	X	X					X
Retention	X	X					X
Second Shift	X						X
QWL	X				X		X
Commute reduction	X				X		X
"Free" time	X						X
Cost reduction	X	X					
Productivity		X					
Effectiveness		X					
Profitability		X	X	X		X	
Environmental protection	X				X		X
Equity					X		X

Who Is Being Served? Who Is Paying?

It's hard to imagine, with all the foregoing benefits and rewards in mind, that anyone could be opposed to the expansion of telework and its attendant positive impacts. As we proceed with our look at telework in subsequent chapters, we do, however, uncover some valid concerns, and a few disturbing consequences, and we look closely at the hidden costs of telework.

Communication in a Digitized Society

Humans communicate through language and social interaction. In 1969, more than thirty years ago, Peter Drucker (1970, 4–5) shared the four fundamentals of communication with the Fellows of the International Academy of Management in Tokyo:

1. Communication is perception.
2. Communication is expectations.
3. Communication is involvement.
4. Communication and information are totally different. But information presupposes functioning communication.

These four simple claims define our continuing belief in the relational nature of communication. We know that communication is perception, because we are all too aware of the human phenomenon of hearing what we want to hear, and disregarding the rest of the message. Words without context have less meaning to us than the same words embedded within a recognizable context—a simple statement like "That was an interesting speech you made" can have a wide variety of meanings depending on who the speaker and the listener are and what their relationship is. The same example explains why communication is expectations. We hear (read, understand, intuit) what we expect to hear (read, understand, intuit) and, as a result, we can hear the congratulatory nature of the comment on our speech or we may hear a snide undertone that undermines our confidence in the presentation we made. The words alone carry less meaning than the expectation of the words carries.

An additional impact is made by the relative personal importance to us of the communication. We naturally prefer to hear pleasant comments on our activities rather than scornful ones; we will normally suppress unpleasant connotations and emphasize those that give us enjoyment or satisfaction. We are also likely to misinterpret communication for information, as these two are closely intertwined. Information suggests a logical transfer of data (there is some way in which your speech was "interesting" on an objective, impersonal level), whereas communication suggests that your speech addressed some specific interest of the listener as an individual (a relational and personal level). The encoding of information requires mutual understanding on the part of both sender and receiver (speaker and listener), and this mutual understanding is what we understand to be communication.

The complexity of the communication process is exacerbated by the electronic interface that keeps us at arm's length while connecting us over great distances. When we use computers to communicate, what we send and receive is primarily information. Decontextualizing such information removes it from the realm of communication and may limit our ability to understand the messages in the context the sender desired (Bluedorn, 1998). The impact of such decontextualization on our social networks is worth considering.

SOCIAL NETWORKS

Social networks have long been the subject of research and investigation. What makes people want to interact with one another? How do they develop compatible worldviews and cohesive relationships? What role do these networks, or loose connections, play in organizational communication and, by extension, effectiveness? A landmark study about how people get jobs provides some answers.

Focusing on the professional, technical, and managerial workers (PTM) that we are concerned with, Granovetter (1974) determined that more than 50 percent of successful job searches were the result of personal contacts rather than the more formal means of answering ads, direct application to companies, or the use of a paid intermediary. These personal contacts fell into two categories: social (family, friends) and occupational (colleagues, teachers), and both were instrumental in assisting job seekers at various stages of their business careers.

This "Rolodex" concept of relationships and connectedness has implications for organizational behavior that go beyond the obvious (and well-researched) claims that people who like one another are likely to spend time together (Homans, 1950); that spending time together influences people because of the frequency, intensity, and proximity of their interactions (Burt, 1987); that people are likely to conform when in close and cohesive groups (Levine & Moreland, 1990); that people who get along well with each will have a positive impact on one another's work while those who do not get along well will have a negative impact on group productivity (Brass & LaBianca, 1999); and that people depend upon the others in their social network to reduce uncertainty and develop a sense of security and stability (Shah, 1998). What it suggests is that, despite any efforts we may make to the contrary, all our relationships no matter how strong or how weak are transactional and are fair targets in the game of business.

One key to the instrumental value of these relationships is our own placement within the social network, known as embeddedness. The more connected we are within our own circles of influence, the more likely we are to develop trusting relationships with the others in our social network. These trusting relationships can lead to effective business operations and to the development of standards of business behavior that are shared by the specific community overall. Furthermore, these trusting relationships extend to the "widely variegated social network of interaction that spans firms" (Granovetter, 1985, 498). Issues related to cost accounting, pricing, and hiring are often more dependent upon the influence of the social network than upon the objective or rational decision-making process.

It should be no surprise that centrality (being in the middle of things) provides power, influence, and other personal advantages to those situated either in the center of their own network (Sparrowe, Liden, Wayne, & Kraimer, 2001) or at the nexus of two or more networks. Nor should it be surprising to learn that cohesive relationships (friendships) and structurally equivalent relationships (people who hold the same position in their network as you hold in yours) will result in a mutual chain of influence as well as a sense of rivalry among peers (Shah, 1998). What is surprising is the extent to which this influence and rivalry have an impact on the effectiveness of organizational communication processes, and the way in which technology mediates them.

Strong Ties/Weak Ties

The language describing the level of our connectedness with others refers to strong ties—very close personal relationships—and weak ties—relationships that are less personal, somewhat more distant. Ties and their strength can be defined as follows: "The strength of a tie is a (probably linear) combination of the amount of time, the emotional intensity, the intimacy (mutual confiding), and the reciprocal services which characterize the tie" (Granovetter, 1973, 1361). A curious finding about these relationships is that weak ties often are more instrumental in assisting us in accomplishing our work goals than are strong ties and, as we become more experienced, weak ties become increasingly valuable to our professional success (Granovetter, 1974). This somewhat contrarian finding has been replicated many times; however, correctly understood, this does not suggest that personal relationships (strong ties) are dinosaurs with no place in the world of work. Instead, it suggests that those relationships that we may have considered less important because of their weaker personal impact do play a significant role in the life of an organization. It is the weak ties, or bridges between social networks, which allow for the successful crossing of boundaries and diffusion of information that otherwise would likely have remained within small groups with strong social ties (Granovetter, 1973).

The foundation of this curiosity is the nature of the relationships themselves. When ties are strong, connections are emotional and close; they are unlikely to be open to new members. In contrast, when ties are weak, connections are more instrumental; that is, we feel less uncomfortable about bringing new people into the relationship and using their influence because we have not developed significant emotional attachments to them. The weaker ties actually encourage broader communication and wider, more inclusive networks.

Nurturing these weak ties is a significant managerial responsibility, with the terminal goal of facilitating the transfer of information while freeing up time to improve human communication. As Drucker (1970) so eloquently wrote, "The test of an information system will increasingly be the degree to which it frees human beings from concern with information and allows them to work on communications. The test, in particular, of the computer will be how much time it gives executives and professionals on all levels for direct, personal, face-to-face relationships with other people" (18). Today, many of those relationships are conducted within a team structure and more and more of those teams have become "virtual."

Virtual Teams

One of the challenges of virtual teaming has been the development of homophilic relationships (relationships among people with similar interests)—how can people find common personal ground when they cannot see each other? The classic *New Yorker* cartoon with the punchline "On the Internet, no one knows you're a dog" refers to both the benefits and drawbacks of remote communication. Most often, people look to others similar to themselves for friendship and social identity (Burkhardt, 1994; Mehra, Kilduff, & Brass, 1998). When social context is absent, distinctive characteristics disappear, thus allowing tradition-ally marginalized populations to become central and requiring tradi-tionally central groups to provide evidence to sustain that central position. While this process fosters a society of striving meritocrats (sometimes seen as a benefit), it also creates a sense of personal discon-nectedness, even anomie (often considered a social deficit). According to Robert Putnam (2000), "The poverty of social cues in computer-me-diated communication inhibits interpersonal collaboration and trust, especially when the interaction is anonymous and not nested in a wider social context" (176).

In other words, a focus on the development of weak ties within teams to the exclusion of strong internal ties, although increasing the likeli-hood of information transmission, will have a formidable negative effect on the development of social capital. This can be seen readily in the reports of some disgruntled teleworkers who feel isolated from coworkers, managers, and direct reports due to the lack of contextual-ized communication (Zbar, 6/28/01; 3/7/02). Information transfer is a poor substitute for relationship building and the development of trust that leads to effective organizational operations (Pratt, 1997b). Yet, we continue to support and sponsor information transfer over relation-ship-based communication.

THE ELECTRONIC TETHER

How many times a day do you check your email? your voicemail? Do you carry your cell phone at all times? turned on? Do you answer your phone when someone else is in your office? while you are at dinner? while reading a book? Do you use your Instant Messaging system? Do you check these systems while on vacation?

Technological Impacts of Communication Devices

Every technological advance in communication devices creates a new environment for personal relationships. Some of the resulting techno-logical ecologies are more welcoming to human interaction than others, and as they evolve, they may add or remove a layer of context from our communication processes. The telegraph speeded up the accurate trans-fer of information, but it eliminated the visual and auditory contexts, supplanting the elegance of the written word with the economy of the coded word. The telephone restored the auditory, with the life, weighty silences, and rapid-fire exchanges of everyday conversation. Emotion returned to communication, although context was still limited by the omission of the visual connection. Television returned to us the visual along with the auditory, but it made interactive communication impossible, as the medium was unidirectional. The communication chain (send–receive–acknowledge) could not be completed. Interim technologies such as the videophone replaced the missing visual component while maintaining voice and timely interaction but have not been widely adopted. The computer has, for the most part, relieved us of the real time visual and auditory connection, while enhancing our ability to "communicate" speedily and economically, and to transfer information efficiently. It is impossible to determine whether the meaning of the information sent electronically is received accurately due both to the lag time between send and receive and the lack of contextual clues, during which many misunderstandings can occur. Video conferencing and Net meetings address some of these weaknesses, but they have not progressed to general acceptance.

As we saw in Chapter 2, the development of communication technologies has been an evolutionary, rather than revolutionary, process. Technologies have their own life cycles, during which they move through several stages until arriving at the optimal version, the one that endures until its own ultimate displacement. Ray Kurzweil (1999, 19–20) has identified seven stages through which technologies pass during their "lives." These stages are the *precursor*, the stage in which dreamers are imagining the possibilities of a particular technology; the *invention* of the actual device; the *development* and additional related creation; *maturity* and independence; the rising of *pretenders*, or upstart technologies that fail to supplant the existing technology; *obsolescence* or gradual decline; culminating in *antiquity*, like the manual typewriter.

When applied to digital communication and telework processes, the stages look like this:

- The word "telephone" is coined and serves as the herald or *precursor* of what is to come (1796).
- Charles Babbage *invents* the analytical engine (1832) leading to the computer and Alexander Graham Bell patents the telephone (1876).
- The *development* phase occurs in the late 1960s and early 1970s, when voice and data transmission technologies begin to merge through ARPANET.
- We have entered into the *maturity* stage of both telecommunications and computing. Although we are aware that changes are in the offing, we believe that work designs based on digital communication (as we know it) will endure at traditional locations.
- Some interim models *pretend* to take over (telecenters, hotelling, work-at-home) and are proposed as alternatives to office-based telework.

- *Obsolescence* threatens to supersede the new technologies with which we are becoming familiar and on which we have based our work designs. What is on the horizon to supplant cell phones? How far can we shrink a laptop computer and still maintain functionality? Where are all those Palm Pilots people received as gifts in 2000?
- *Antiquity*, still in the future for our existing human-technology interface, promises to reorient us once again and challenge our ability to adapt.

Living in the maturity stage of technological development has encouraged the technological advances that pretend to replace our limited, earlier technologies. Some claim that bandwidth is the solution to all electronic communication challenges. According to Werner Schaer, president and CEO of the Software Productivity Consortium, "With 20M to 30M bit/sec connections, you can have people communicating over video connections, helping bosses interpret physical cues" (Kistner, 11/11/01). He claims that telework will both drive the expansion of bandwidth and provide the "killer application" for its development.

Perhaps. Or perhaps the killer app will be the ability to "Collaborate on demand with remote colleagues naturally, the way you do in person. A company called Axiom8 has built a system that allows just that and puts an end to telephone tag once and for all" (Kistner, 1/2/02). Telephone tag has been the enemy of timely communication ever since the operators who answered the phone for American businesses (and even took messages) were replaced by automated telephone systems. This new device promises to track down the intended recipient of your uncompleted telephone call by text, voice, or video using either a telephone or Web-based PC, and collaborate via file transfer, document sharing, whiteboarding, presentations, and desktop sharing. Its future versions promise text-to-speech, speech-to-text, and language translation abilities, along with recording, storing, searching, and communication editing processes. Oh, brave new world. . . .

Collaboration software makes another promise to users—it claims to "free up workers to think more creatively," provide new opportunities to connect resellers and markets, synchronize design processes, and match trucking companies with schedules and loads (Keenan & Ante, 2/18/02). Remarkable returns have been reported using collaboration software, despite its inherent limitations. These limitations include the difficulty of changing human behavior and attitudes, the challenge of training professionals to change their accepted work patterns, the need to make technology accessible to people who are unfamiliar with the intricacies of computers, and ironing out those irrepressible computer bugs that seem to arise from nowhere to plague the very processes that computers are being employed to address. The solutions to these problems include communicating face-to-face, in person. Keenan and Ante report that "One of the key early lessons is that for collaboration to work well, it has to be between people, not just machines. Management experts say digital workplaces can't completely replace more traditional interactions, especially in the creative process. In-person communication is important for training, building relationships, and riding herd on a difficult project" (16).

THE ELASTICITY OF TIME

But face-to-face real-time communication poses some logistical challenges to virtual teams. Some of these challenges reflect national cultural differences (see Chapter 14), but others arise even within the same country, the same coast, the same region, the same organization. One such challenge is the way we view time. Time, like communication, is contextual. "A long time" means one thing to someone waiting for a bus in the rain and another to someone waiting for their loved one to return from war. "A few minutes" is a "short" time when waiting for a cake to come out of the oven and a "long" time when waiting to be seated in a popular restaurant. "All our representatives are busy right now helping other customers. Your call is important to us and will be taken in the order in which it was received" means that you are going to wait "a long time" before the representative gets to your call.

In the past, when we received a telephone call at home before 8:00 A.M. or after 11:00 P.M., we knew that something untoward had happened. Those hours were sacrosanct, protected private time, and interruptions could only mean bad news. But "times" have changed—and a 9:00 a.m. call from the worker in New York to the colleague in San Francisco is no cause for alarm. In fact, it is no longer considered unusual, and companies with bicoastal workers are expected to make accommodations for the time differences. This reflects a shift from the traditionally monochronic approach of American business to the polychronic approach taken by much of the rest of the world.

Monochronicity is a linear approach to time, one in which people tend to engage in one activity at a time. Polychronicity is a nonlinear approach in which people conduct multiple activities concurrently. The United States has shifted over time from being a primarily monochronic culture, which developed from its origins in other monochronic cultures (England, Germany, Scandinavia) to a more polychronic one today, based on immigration patterns and demographic shifts that include the influences of high-context societies, such as those in Latin America and the Mediterranean. This movement has created tension between the "natural" tendencies of low- and high-context cultures, and low and high comfort levels with technology. According to Edward Hall, the early identifier of this trend, the pulls of monochronicity (as evidenced by low context and high technology) are competing at present with polychronicity (as evidenced by high context and personal influence and less emphasis on technology) (Bluedorn, 1998).

These opposing tendencies make communication, collaboration, and relationship building ever more difficult to accomplish, especially as technology removes more context from our interactions, leaving us information or data but no way to make sense of it. Communication without exposure to cultural cues is destined to be incomplete, as we can only guess at intentions, meanings, and patterns (Hall, 1959). Participants in electronic communication miss more than visual and auditory cues; they miss the "foreshadowing part of a communication from the barely perceptible signs of annoyance to open hostility. In the animal world, if the adumbrative [foreshadowing] process is short circuited or bypassed, vicious fighting is apt to occur. In humans in the international-intercultural sphere of life many difficulties can be traced to failure to read adumbrations correctly. In such instances, by the time people discover what is going on, they are so deeply involved that they can't back out" (Hall, 1982, 5). Hence, the prevalence of "flaming," or multiple angry responses to a possibly innocent online comment. According to Hall, "preoccupation with the content of communications often blinds us to the adumbrative or foreshadowing functions of communication" (183), and we find ourselves negatively engaged in what could have been a simple, direct, and open communication process. This downward spiral can be blamed, in part, on our need for speed and instantaneous satisfaction.

Instant Gratification

We live in a world of instant gratification. We are no longer used to putting off our purchases—credit cards are held nearly universally, making buying, if not paying, easier and faster. Satisfying our needs and wants has become second nature as well as first priority. Fewer meals are cooked at home than ever before, replaced by take-out fast food, picked up on the way home from work. Instant ordering online makes trips to the supermarket and mall superfluous. We can pay our bills online, eliminating the trip to the post office to purchase stamps and physically drop our envelopes into the mail slot. We carry our telephones with us, unwilling to wait as long as it might take to pick up a message at home or to find a coin-operated telephone on the street. Even this speed of interaction is too slow for many—we use instant messaging to speed things along.

One of the more promising speed-satisfiers will be the introduction of voice-to-text unified messaging, a system that would allow voicemail to "be accurately converted to text in near real-time and sent to an email client as traditional text-based email" (Osterman, 1/15/02). Used at present for people with impaired hearing, this costly alternative will make information transfer quicker, if not more accurate, because we can only speak at about 60 words per minute, but we can read at about 200 words per minute. Efficiency is driving our communication forward at breakneck speed, at the cost of replacing the auditory with the visual.

The velocity of our business interactions spurred the title of one article about videoconference, "No Time for Face Time" (Rosen, 2/11/02). In an eerie implementation of a virtual hallway, members of a team in Ohio can see the secretaries walking across the corridor in California. Said the IS manager, "The accounting person in Ohio can see us and wave." Casual meetings in the virtual hallway can spur brainstorming sessions, chat, and fast answers to complicated questions. However, after all is said and done, the managers involved with this sophisticated system claim that periodic face-to-face meetings are critical, because videoconferencing, no matter how fast and how fancy, cannot develop the relationships for you.

That process must be initiated in person, in real time, intentionally, and then can be continued online, in peer-to-peer environments. There is technology available that can facilitate small group collaboration among people who interact frequently, who trust one another, and who have no business secrets from each other (Kobielus, 6/25/01). This software allows the invited users to share one another's desktops, files, and systems to an even greater extent than they might be willing to do in person. The result can be extraordinary productivity, high-quality communication, and efficient information sharing. Or, it can be chaos, depending on the type of organizational structure and group goals to be met.

Networked Organizations and Attaining Group Goals

The emphasis placed by business on teamwork focuses our attention on ways to get work done by groups rather than by individuals. As a result, motivational methods must be adapted to satisfy group needs, with less consideration paid to hierarchical structures and individual achievement and more to collaborative structures and joint accomplishments. Creating a corporate culture that supports group effort and rewards it evenhandedly is one way to flatten the hierarchy and elevate the team.

Eastman Chemical Company, a Malcolm Baldrige National Quality Award winner in 1993 and a traditional manufacturing company, has succeeded in shifting its culture to incorporate virtual teams as well as traditional teams (Lipnack & Stamps, 2000). They wrestled with issues of trust, benefits and equity, and employee development that would generate value for the organization as well for the individual. One of the most important learnings that arose from the change process was to keep the focus on the big picture of organizational goals. If that can be done, then the small picture of the mechanics of implementation takes care of itself.

In Eastman's case, the organizational big picture—the way their corporate hierarchy was being redrawn—indicated a major change in the way communication took place. This change had nothing to do with location. Instead, it had to do with permeable communication boundaries within the organization and less permeable ones surrounding it. Sometimes this process is referred to as "managing in the white space" on the organization chart. What this presupposes is that the organizational elements, each group (temporary or permanent), each small team, each dyad (relationship pair) has a sense of goal interdependency, and that they are all aware that they are working toward the same end. The organization is suffused with consistency: attitudes, actions, and intentions are identical throughout because there is universal commitment to the goal. Reciprocated interest increases cooperation, and each individual's acceptance of responsibility and accountability nurtures the further replication of that commitment. This sense of commitment is not dependent on time or location.

The Impact of Time and Place

Time and place do have an impact on the successful operations of an organization, but one that is readily managed if all members are mindful of the variations in these two components of organizational life. There are two kinds of time and two kinds of place in which the organization can function. Clock Time (or real time) is time as measured by devices and calendars. It is stable and immutable, and it cannot be stretched except through perception (as in visiting the dentist or listening to a children's elementary piano recital). Task Time (or virtual time) is measured by process duration and can easily be stretched by extending deadlines for completion. In terms of the location of workers (Place), they can be collocated, that is, in the same location, which permits visual cues and speed of action. Or, workers can be distributed, that is, in different locations, which provides privacy and the opportunity to think out actions before taking them.

As can be seen in Figure 4.1, when a matrix of time and place options is developed, the benefits and drawbacks of each element become clear. Clock Time privileges speed of action; Task Time privileges reflection on action. Both are important in the normal activities of every organization. Collocation provides multiple cues for participants—visual, verbal, written, semiotic. Distribution provides fewer cues but allows for personal privacy that is not available in a collocated environment. Specific activities and communication patterns are suitable to each quadrant, as indicated below. Cycling through the four quadrants in sequence, we can see the gradual decrease in speed of action and consequent increase in quality of reflection—an increase in creativity concurrent with a decrease in the ability to take concrete action.

Quadrant 1, the Convergent nexus, is the natural home of the department meeting. Its focus on speed and the availability of multiple communication cues support activities such as agenda building, task allocation, and scheduling. The main obstacle to success in this sector is the arrival of latecomers, both literal and figurative, who want to provide input after most of the discussion has been completed. This violates the concrete, touch-it-once-and-move-on attitude of the Convergent organization.

Quadrant 2, the Impersonal organization, fully supports remote work and virtuality. Teleconferences, online live chat, and net meetings make this an ideal organization in which to share information, perform orientations, and listen to the words of the CEO as broadcast to all. Workers in the Impersonal organization have the least voice time of any of the four groups, because the communication focus is on efficiency with the fewest possible stimuli.

Quadrant 3 is the Inclusive region. Here, communication takes place on a personal and individual level, and all the time. Threaded email, voice messages, snail and express mail all encourage individual participation, time and space for reflection, and equality in sharing the

TIME

		Clock Time (real time)	Task Time (virtual time)
P	**Collocation**	(1) Convergent	(4) Divergent
L			
A		+ Speed	+Thought
C		+ Cues	+Cues
E	**Distribution**	(2) Impersonal	(3) Inclusive
		+ Speed	+Thought
		+Cues	+Cues

Figure 4.1 Determining Group Parameters for Attaining Group Goals

available voice time through "brainwriting" (an electronic form of brainstorming) and continuous evaluation. The primary barrier to success in the Inclusive organization is the high frequency of interruptions and resultant disorder in process.

Quadrant 4 houses the Divergent organization, with conditions that support creativity. People meet in small groups or teams to work on specific projects. They use various techniques to encourage brainstorming and idea creation. They thrash out their solutions by sharing information, combining data and proposals, negotiating mutually advantageous (or, at least, acceptable) conclusions, and making final decisions that satisfy their articulated needs. All this takes time and, in this quadrant, participants take all the time that the task requires.

None of the four quadrants is ideal; they are interdependent and all are necessary for the long-term success of an organization. Decision-making styles vary within each, authority and power shift from one sector to another, and, within all quarters, goals are attained within the context of membership—commitment to the organization as a whole and to the group in particular. Telework generates benefits in some areas and not in others. Notably, the incorporation of telework and the diversity and weaker social ties that it brings can boost creative contributions.

The nature of work in the twenty-first century that we consider in the next chapter is both the consequence and the architect of the evolution of these new communication models.

5

New Work, New Worker

In January 1999, at the Summit on 21st Century Skills for 21st Century Jobs, before the series of events that shook our world appeared on the national radar, Vice President Al Gore declared optimistically, "America's competitiveness and the prosperity of our people in a changing economy depend increasingly on high-skill high-wage jobs." Some of the changes in the "changing economy" have been downward, and the impact on high-skill high-wage jobs in a time of economic downturn is, naturally, downward. Three short years after Gore's pronouncement, unemployment had soared, the stock market had plummeted, and the high-tech and telecommunications sectors were suffering significant setbacks. Work was changing, and the worker was changing—but not in the direction anticipated five years earlier.

CENTENNIAL SHIFTS

In 1699, Peter the Great decreed that New Year would begin henceforth in Russia on January 1 instead of the traditional September 1. In the American colonies, recently recovered from witch hunt hysteria, the Anglo population was booming, and had reached 250,000 by 1700.

In 1799, the Rosetta Stone—the key to deciphering hieroglyphics—was discovered, and Beethoven wrote Symphony #1 in C major. The following year, Alessandro Volta produced electricity from the first zinc and copper plate battery. Thomas Jefferson was elected President of the United States. Napoleon continued his assault on Europe.

In 1899, the first magnetic recording of sound took place, followed the next year by Max Planck's formulation of the quantum theory. William McKinley was reelected 25th president of the United States in 1900, only to be assassinated the following year and succeeded by Theodore Roosevelt.

New centuries often bring with them a sense of buoyancy, a sanguine attitude toward the future, and enthusiasm for what is to come. Our 2000 centennial transition was no different, except for fears of mysterious, pervasive, and nonmaterializing Y2K computer problems. The turn of our century has been marked, however, by a series of unforeseen events that were no less shattering than Napoleon's march, Volta's and Planck's scientific advances, and Beethoven's genius. Our significant events revolve around the impact of technology on work, on the economy, and on global interactions.

WORK IN THE TWENTY-FIRST CENTURY

According to the U.S. Bureau of Labor Statistics in 1998, the U.S. economy was projected to generate nearly 19 million new jobs in the period from 1996 to 2006. Those jobs were to appear primarily in the service sector, a sector that requires above-average educational attainment and a high comfort level with rapidly changing information technology. Furthermore, computer skills were on their way to becoming baseline requirements for many jobs long before Vice President Gore's proclamation that opened this chapter. Technology has always been the driver of change in the workplace, but the impact of information technology on employment and career development has been both more immediate and more emphatic than any such change since the Industrial Revolution.

Employment and Careers

One impact has been the shift from production work that kept warehouses full to just-in-time delivery of target-specific items, one-of-a-kind businesses, and a focus on agility rather than stability (Reich, 2000). What this has done is to create a contract-worker mentality on the part of companies, which companies readily dispose of unnecessary workers through rounds of layoffs, downsizings, and reorganizations that leave the firms human-resource-poor. These layoffs help keep the economic wolf from the corporate door by eliminating the need to pay for employee benefits, retirement plans, and basic health insurance, but they also successfully eliminate any sense of employee loyalty to the firm. What-have-you-done-for-me-lately came to permeate work relationships and, as a result, working environments and production processes. The organization began to flatten, and the individual independence that results from mistrust of one's employer generated a commitment crisis that threatened the well-being of existing corporations as well as of individuals (Moss Kanter, 2001).

Not surprisingly, this independence plays out naturally in a rise in entrepreneurship, in me-first-ism, and in individual creativity and innovation (Reich, 2000). This confluence of attributes leads to the formation of new companies led by the traditionally fearless young. In this century, the fearless young are technological freethinkers, believers in the redemptive value of all things computer-related. Whereas traditional workers sought long-term employment and strong leadership, the new worker prefers a job to be interesting and challenging, and to provide opportunities for growth. Whereas traditional work values suggested that experience and maturity lead to success, the new work values suggest that emergence, gaining experience on the job through the fast reflexes developed while playing video games, and without any fear of failure are the keys to the economic kingdom. Autonomy and "coolness" are prerequisites in the vocabulary of the New Work.

Autonomy, or at the least the illusion of autonomy, can be provided through telework. Workers who have restrictions on their ability to work outside their homes, workers who have physical restrictions that make it difficult to work in traditional job locations, workers who need or want flextime arrangements to build a more balanced life, workers who cannot find employment locally, military spouses, and workers with specific skills that are needed on a changing schedule can all find semi-autonomous employment via telework arrangements. A headline for this movement could be "Contract Workers Fight Back"—as people have been laid off, furloughed, or downsized, thousands of them have identified themselves as independent contractors and are making a living via remote work as virtual assistants of various kinds, including consulting, IT work, paralegal and comptroller activities (Kistner, 11/27/01; 12/4/01; 8/28/01). The translation of New Work language to traditional work processes in new locations has helped alleviate the pain of unemployment for many American workers, including those for whom opportunity has been harder to locate.

Women and other marginalized groups have found telework and virtual organization an appealing alternative to the traditional work environment. According to a study of 675 women conducted by the Simmons Graduate School of Management, two thirds indicated that their colleagues are more responsive when they do virtual work and that their ideas are more likely to be heard. Eighty-four percent of the women claimed that they are more productive when using online collaboration tools, and 75 percent claimed they can do more work in less time when online (Scully, 2002). It is curious, therefore, to learn that the typical teleworker is male rather than female, but at least it is clear that telework may open some doors to workers, particularly those in search of autonomy.

"Coolness" is harder to come by, especially following the dot.com meltdown that began in late 1999, leaving many Gen X entrepreneurs and workers confused and lost. During the mid-1990s, companies had wooed Gen X workers by picking up the tab for such workplace amenities as concierge service, health club memberships, regular massages, and convenient cappuccino machines in the lounge. These quickly disappeared, along with the sign-on bonuses and even the basics, such as employer-paid health care. Elaborate corporate parties gave way to donuts and coffee, and designer office furniture could be picked up for a song in used furniture stores. Abuse of executive privilege, accounting and financial scandals, and the prevalence of greed in the higher echelons of business made working for large corporations less appealing than ever before. Fear, previously absent from the conversation of the cosseted worker, began to infiltrate daily discourse, and coolness slipped away.

Stock Market Fluctuations and Economic Turmoil

The question posed to economists, stock market gurus, and academics day after day since the business community discovered that it had been supporting dot.coms that were walking about in the Emperor's new clothes was, "When will the market stop falling?" A better question might be, "Why did we think that businesses built on air could possibly turn a profit?" How were our national sages so deluded?

A complex set of causes participated in the collapse of the dot.com bubble. Excitement over new technology, the fickle nature of venture capital availability, Darwinian competition that leads to natural thinning of the herd, flawed implementation of new business models by copycat startups, the optimism of a bull market, and of course greed worked together to create a false belief in an ever rising and indefatigable stock market. The six-month period from March to September 2000 was particularly devastating to the economy. By November 2000, nearly all publicly traded Internet companies had accumulated losses of at least 75 percent of their 52-week high (Kleinbard, 11/9/00). Two years later, in the autumn of 2002, the situation had not improved, with the markets at a four-year low. All sectors of the economy, from IPOs to the blue chips, had been affected, or infected, with the downhill market trajectory. The telecommunications sector was especially hard hit.

One of the myths of telecom and Internet growth has been the promise of greater access bringing hugely increased profits. This myth has successfully been debunked by the empirical evidence of the international telecom debacle. In the fourth quarter of 2002, telecom usage was only 35 percent of capacity in the United States and Europe, with increases in capacity continuing to appear in markets whose demand could not keep up with the supply (Rosenbush, 10/7/02). The excess of capacity will be exacerbated by the 2003 rollout of a new transatlantic cable able to carry 3.2 terabits of data per second, nearly one third more than all previously existing transatlantic capacity combined. Profits from this venture are not anticipated until mid-decade at the earliest, and, at that, are likely to come at the expense of consolidation of some of the telecom giants, and of the development of new services that these companies can provide. Some of those services could include entertainment, consulting, personal services, and telework enhancements.

However, as significantly increased unemployment floats in the wake of the economic downturn, hopeful proclamations about telework's ability to bridge the unemployment gap ring thin. Some economic analysts have put a positive face on the employment shortfall, claiming that "Among the structural changes, the importance of temporary workers and variable pay, both of which allow businesses to match payrolls and labor costs to changes in demand, is already evident in the recovery" (Cooper & Madigan, 4/22/02) and is certainly, in their estimation, a "good" thing. The same analysts remind us that "Businesses will be slow to add on more costly permanent staffers," making it clear that the economy is likely to be rebuilt on the backs of those least able to support it—temporary workers, contract workers, and the independent self-employed. These groups will be challenged to find a technological path to employment security.

As described by Joe Roitz, AT&T's telework director, one such pathway is "The decentralization of the enterprise into a work structure that is more efficient, effective, flexible and resilient. Not to have more employees taking advantage of a perk, but to change the structure of the firm as we know it" (Kistner, 2/18/02). In other words, telework is not different from work; it is work in a different place. As such, it fits quite well into the paradigm of the four organizations as described in Chapter 4.

THE FOUR ORGANIZATIONS

The four organizations illustrate four collaborative approaches for accommodating to the demands of time and place in work processes (refer to Figure 4.1). Time, defined as Clock Time (real time) and Task

Time (virtual time) interacts with Place, defined as collocated or distributed, to emerge as four different types of structures, each with its own internal decision-making system, relationship structure, and optimal work-flow design. Each approach works well, as long as it is appropriately contextualized—matched to the group's goals and to its membership expectations. Today's emphasis on teamed approaches to work comports well with these models.

The Convergent Organization

The convergent organization is the one with which most traditional workers are familiar. It is hierarchical in nature, with a designated leader who performs the carefully articulated classical management and leadership tasks of planning, organizing, leading, and controlling. The designated leader may undertake responsibility for all or most of the informational, interpersonal, and decisional roles that fall to the appropriate managerial level, including monitoring and disseminating information, acting as liaison, allocating resources, and handling disturbances, among others (Mintzberg, 1972). Because there is a formal, "legitimate" leader in this organization, assigned by those in higher positions, the power to make things happen originates from the top (French & Raven, 1960). Decisions are also likely to be made in a top-down style, even when subordinates are consulted (Vroom & Jago, 1988).

This organization has provided the model for all subsequent iterations, be they improvements or less well-designed structures. The convergent organization allows for the least amount of teamwork, although it does encourage working in groups as an accepted form of work process. Because people are working in physical proximity, the distribution of information is generally timely and complete. The manager can readily fulfill the duties assigned to the position, and can easily monitor both workers and work accomplished. In fact, it appears that the work structure has been designed for managerial ease rather than worker effectiveness or excellence of outcome. The convergent work group is likely to look like Figure 5.1. People work together physically, separated by low dividers that provide minimal privacy and maximum availability. When one of the cubicles becomes empty, whether through attrition or downsizing, it is rarely refilled.

The Impersonal Organization

The Impersonal organization functions, like the Convergent organization, on the basis of speed of operations. In order to boost speed further, the Impersonal organization has provided the "always on"

Figure 5.1 The Convergent Organization

option for its team members. It is not necessary for Impersonal team members to work in the same location, as long as they can always be reached by telephone, Internet, or other means when the manager or team leader needs to make contact. This structure is also top down with a formal leader, although the leader's power derives from the ability to provide or withhold rewards and thus to coerce others into action rather than solely due to legitimacy (French & Raven, 1960). Because workers are often physically separated, top-down decision making continues, and communication processes related to decision making tend to be informational rather than participative. As a result, the Impersonal organization allows the least voice from its membership. To combat this loss of potentially valuable input, in the 1960s the Rand Corporation designed a method to increase the participation of distant organizational members through a process known as Delphi technique. This technique involves the sequential iterative combination of expert opinions until a consensus is reached (Dalkey, 1969). Although direct interactive communication does not take place, at the least, multiple opinions are heard despite the distributed nature of participants. The Impersonal work group may look like Figure 5.2. Some people work in the same location; others are accessible by computer or telephone. When a worker in the office is lost due to attrition or layoff, that worker is rarely replaced *in office*. Instead, more workers find themselves at the

Figure 5.2 The Impersonal Organization

electronic, remote end of the communication and work system, having gained privacy but having lost access.

The Inclusive Organization

The inclusive organization shifts its time orientation from real time to task time, the duration required to complete a specific task. Speed is no longer the most valued attribute in this work group, having ceded its position to universal participation of team members. This is the team with which the new worker is most familiar. Team members are equals; leaders are not formally assigned but rather emerge from the group as each individual's skills are called upon for specific elements of task completion. The authority and power reside in the expert, the one who can solve today's problem by the application of needed mental resources. Because the group values and appreciates the input of all, each expert enjoys his moment in the sun, only to be supplanted as the next challenge arises and is solved by a new expert. People are not invested in their offices, their keys to the washroom, or their reserved parking spaces. They are invested in their personal freedom, their privacy, and their ability to be heard. They enjoy the obeisance others pay to their particular knowledge base and expertise, and they are willing to admire others' expertise in order to gain later personal credibility.

Decision making comes easily to this group, as they naturally yield each decision to the appropriate expert. In the process, they learn how to increase their own capabilities in the future and are thus most likely to turn their team into a learning organization (please see Chapter 10

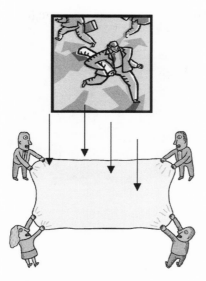

Figure 5.3 The Inclusive Organization

for a full discussion of learning organizations). The inclusive organization may look like Figure 5.3.

This is the teleworking organization. Regardless of location or formal work title, the Inclusive organization respects, supports, and protects its members. Although team members may rarely see one another, any of them may call upon any other for assistance. When a team member is lost due to attrition, the member is likely to be replaced by another with a similar skill set. The depersonalization of individuals to their specific skills is an unintended consequence of the impersonal organization; however, it does not limit the loyalty that the group presents to its members.

The Divergent Organization

As the team shifts from separate and parallel existences for each of its members to collocation, working closely together and building upon one another's creativity and insight, innovation thrives. Brainstorming and consensus decision-making result in novelty and in the optimization of inventive and original solutions to difficult problems, to marketing decisions, to contract negotiations, and to dilemmas that require collaborative solutions. This team willingly assigns power and authority to the most likable, admired, and charismatic member. This is known as referent power and, once bestowed, commits the team membership

Figure 5.4 The Divergent Organization

to that leader and to that leader's ideas. The divergent organization may look like Figure 5.4.

Because of the multiplicity of cues sent and received by the members of the divergent organization, members may know each other on a personal level and may share friendship as well as collegial relations. The divergent organization represents a long-term association and a closed corporation. Therefore, the loss of one of the members due to attrition or downsizing is a painful process and such a loss changes the nature of the team such that it may become ineffective.

These four models have developed as an involuntary response to the flattening of the organization and the human desire for an entity to which they can be loyal. Some suggest that new organizational forms such as the ones I have described represent a last ditch, desperate effort to come to grips with the emerging cyber-landscape that destroys institutional boundaries and relationships (Reich, 2000, 84). According to Andrew Grove, CEO of Intel Corporation, we must "adapt or die" (Townsend, DeMarie, & Hendrickson, 1998, 17). Adaptation is the answer in any complex system, and few systems are more complex than management systems.

EMERGING FROM CHAOS

Since the enormous popularity of the *Jurassic Park* movie series, we have all become familiar with the butterfly effect—the magnification of small changes to create increasingly dramatic repercussions. The origins of the butterfly effect lie in the technology of computer modeling and weather forecasting (Gleick, 1987), where the casual fluttering of a butterfly's wings in one part of the world could be mapped as massive tornadoes in another due to the escalation of effects. These unintended consequences could be tragic or delightful, but either way they would be large, even larger than life. The idea of the butterfly effect was appealing, as it explained a great deal in many areas unrelated to meteorology and technology. Chaos theory promised to explain natural mysteries to us through the beauty of computer-generated models. Chaos theory made us feel better about not being able to trace so many effects back to their multiple causes. Chaos theory was the answer in a world, although inhabited by mostly linear thinkers, that had become nonlinear; and chaos theory was marketable.

Chaos explained a great deal, and explained it with the clout of science, long admired in management circles. It was, therefore, no surprise when management theorists accepted and endorsed chaos as a metaphor to make the ineffable concrete, to make the cloudy clear, and to turn the unexpected into business as usual. The world of management began to use the language of chaos theory—fuzzy boundaries, system complexity, self-organizing systems, and information as more than bits of data that could be encoded into a program or a memo. Information became the "key source of structuration—the process of creating structure" (Wheatley, 1992, 104). The resulting information structures were described in terms of systems and networks.

Systems and Networks

If we consider our organizations as open systems or networks rather than as closed models of functioning, we can take a holistic, or whole system, view of the way they operate (Senge, 1990). When we look at whole systems, we discover that control becomes an issue of lesser importance, while interaction and relationships become more important to organizational success. Information does not have to be controlled; it must be allowed to distribute itself throughout the system. Information can flow within a network and reach all connected members without being formally directed to each one because information itself is nonlinear; it flows in the fluid way that electrons flow rather than in rigid columns (Wheatley, 1992).

Each of the four organizational models in this chapter reflects a systems perspective, and each one handles information flow differently. These four models have been designed with information flow in mind, but with neither a hierarchy of functionality nor a preference for one over the others, except as appropriate for the activities to be conducted within each system and their relationship to the needs of the organization as a whole. The convergent and the impersonal organizational subsystems prioritize information dissemination in terms of speed and accuracy, whereas the inclusive and the divergent subsystems prioritize the creation of "new" information to be shared with others. None of the four can function alone, for without the whole system, each lacks critical components for success. The four subsystems must meet and, through influence rather than control, share their resources in a process known as "coupling" (Eoyang, 1997). This coupling process in complex systems is managed around the flow of information.

Coupling Structures

According to Eoyang, there are three kinds of couples that exist in complex systems: tight couples, loose couples, and uncouples. A tight couple describes a very close and responsive relationship between two unequal parts of a system. In a tight coupling, an action on the part of one of the couple results in an immediate response from the other partner to the couple. This response is unpredictable and may be positive or negative, but it will certainly be escalating in nature. For example, an email written tongue-in-cheek by a member of a work group can touch a nerve unexpectedly in another group member. The second group member responds with a nastygram, other group members weigh in with their own opinions of the exchange, and before you know it, a wholesale flame erupts.

The tight couple can be balanced by a loose couple, where boundaries are less permeable and responses less extreme. The loose couple can be described as a coupling of equals who gently influence one another until they ultimately synchronize their activities. In an extension of the previous example, the email war would likely be averted in a loose coupling. The first joking email would be written in such a way as to be unlikely to be misconstrued by the recipient, and if the recipient should actually misinterpret the intentions of the writer, instead of attacking in return, her response would be more measured, more inquiring in nature. Clarification would be sought and received, and mutual understanding would result. When this type of rational response extends to an extreme, uncoupling can occur.

An uncouple describes two parts of a system as distinct and having no impact on each other. Because they do not influence each other, they cannot generate a response in the other. They do not communicate at all, and as a result they do not understand each other. Sometimes it is important for organizational subsystems to uncouple, such as in the interest of security, but uncoupling is generally a less productive way to manage organizational relationships.

Loose couples and uncouples tend to predominate in the new work arrangements consisting of work-for-hire and contract relationships. The autonomy discussed earlier in this chapter is synonymous with uncoupled behavior, whereas the more traditional forms of work lean heavily toward the tight coupling of unequal partners.

However, the possibility exists that an entirely unanticipated form of work practice and management practice will develop as work coupling evolves further. As journalist and work historian Richard Donkin (2001) suggests, "Surely there will always be someone who calls the shots, someone who has the casting [*sic*] vote. But need it be the same person all the time?" (317).

In summary, the new work is intangible, knowledge-based, and portable and the new worker is fungible and disposable.

6

The Human Disconnect: The Impact of Isolation on Teleworkers

The female pigeon cannot lay eggs if she is alone. As a social creature, she must be able to see another pigeon in order for her ovaries to function. But if no other pigeon is available, her own reflection in a mirror will suffice. The pigeon's owner and a reflecting surface are sufficient to control the work and behavior of the pigeon, with little regard to the pigeon's emotional state or personal motivations.

But what happens to people when left alone for extended periods? Controlling the work of people is significantly more challenging than the management of pigeons, yet similar factors apply, and throughout history, isolation in its many forms has been a powerful tool for controlling human behavior.

"ALL ALONE BY THE TELEPHONE" (Irving Berlin, 1924)

What is Isolation?

Less than 50 years after the invention of the telephone, the device had gained so much control over people's lives that the image of sitting near the telephone and waiting for someone to get in touch had already become a familiar one, evoking loneliness and a sense of isolation. In this context, "isolation" refers to social isolation, a concept that is

This chapter is based on G. Vega and L. Brennan (2000), Isolation and technology: The human disconnect, *Journal of Organizational Change Management*, 13 (5), 468–481.

distinct from the privacy and solitude we may experience from being alone, but closely tied to four other and less pleasant characteristics. Isolation:

- Is imposed by others, rather than being mutually constructed or self-imposed (Diekema, 1992).
- Is not necessarily related to physical separation, but may occur when with other people, as at a party or at an event with strangers (Diekema, 1992).
- Is closely associated with the alienation that occurs when people are separated from personal control over their work (Erikson, 1986).
- In organizations, is linked to formal status for those with low status to begin with, such as workers performing repetitive tasks in customer service, data entry and manipulation, and similar activities (Miller, 1975).

What is known about telework and its potential effects suggests that we need to consider carefully the connection between social isolation and the virtual workplace.

Through Multiple Lenses

Because of the control over behavior that can be exerted through it, isolation is a compelling topic to people who value freedom. As is evident from the way criminals are isolated from the rest of the population and even from the rest of the prison population when they require additional "rehabilitation," we perceive involuntary separation as punishment. A brief look at isolation through the lenses we use in managing work processes and human behavior will help to clarify some social concerns related to telework, virtual workplaces, and other models of work in locations other than the main office, beginning with the smallest units of work and behavior.

Engineering. Although popular opinion would have us believe that engineers require less social interaction than others (according to cartoon lore, they would prefer to have little or no social interaction), the claim is ludicrous. One of the major concerns that researchers in engineering technology have is how to create sufficient social interaction to optimize performance (Caldwell, 1997, 298). The optimal level of social contact varies according to task, situation, and individuals involved. When social contact is limited without consideration of the other variables, the resulting performance will be subpar, the individual's sense of isolation will increase, and the work group as a whole is likely to suffer degradation in cohesiveness.

Psychology. Interpersonal isolation is one of the factors comprising the experience of loneliness (alienation, abandonment, and rejection). People are social entities and enjoy being around others, to varying degrees. Interpersonal transactions that provide affirmation and emotional content or information that leads people to believe that they are cared for within a network of friends can provide social support, reduce stress, and reduce feelings of loneliness (Rook, 1985). This theme has been consistent in the literature since World War II. Erich Fromm suggested that people do not really know what they want; rather, they know what they are supposed to want and "intense activity is often mistaken for evidence of self-determined action" (Fromm, 1941, 252–253). We live the illusion of self-determination, but actually feel powerless and alone; the more connected we become, the more alone we feel.

Management. A major concern of management theorists is how to communicate information effectively. The communication process consists of the following elements: (1) The sender formulates a message, selects the medium and method for distributing that message, encodes and sends it to the receiver; (2) the receiver decodes the message and provides feedback to the sender that indicates receipt and understanding. Each element of the process contains several components. For example, the encoding of the message must be done skillfully and accurately or decoding will suffer. If the message is in written form and spelling and grammar are faulty, decoding may prove difficult. If the message contains data in numerical form and the entry is inaccurate, decoding may prove impossible. Feedback differs according to the medium selected, and may include written response, oral response, body language response, and other cues. The quality of communication deteriorates as component elements of the communication process are eliminated. The essence of communication is involvement in the message, whether in the transmission or receipt of it. Technology can impede communication by focusing our attention on data rather than on the relationships that support the work of people. This concern has been evident since the earliest common use of computers at work: "The test, in particular, of the computer will be how much time it gives executives and professionals on all levels for direct, personal, face-to-face relationships with other people" (Drucker, 1970, 18).

Sociology. Total institutions, such as asylums, create barriers to social intercourse and keep people from their normal activities of "sleep, play, and work in different places, with different co-participants, under different authorities, and without an over-all rational plan" (Goffman, 1961, 5–6). Goffman's criteria for such institutions include the use of the same location for sleeping, playing, and working; the same participants in all activities; tight scheduling with one activity leading to the next; a plan that fulfills the needs of the institution; surveillance by supervisors; limited or restricted contact with the world outside the institution; social distance from others; the exclusion from knowledge about decisions regarding one's fate; and all of these in a nonvoluntary condition. The voluntary nature of the phenomenon aside, technology can, with alarming ease, create virtual institutions that fulfill all these characteristics. On the other hand, technology can create a sense of freedom in our work that makes the location of activity and its participants an irrelevant piece of the life equation. "Technology is the great leveler. Technology is handing us the capability of packaging our work in a way that suits us" (Donkin, 2001, 328).

Economics. Harking back to the heyday of millwork in New England, it became apparent that "with each worker fixed to a physical location in the production process, contact among workers virtually ceased" (Edwards, 1979, 114). Limited mobility also limits peer contact, and limited peer contact further limits the power of the worker to have control over the product. In this sense, isolation is a tool that can be used to limit the individual's power while increasing that of the organization's owners. Workers one century later, in the mid-1960s, became adamant about their right to control their own production by controlling the technology. As production methods moved from unit production (one item at a time or small batch production) through batch production (assembly-line large batch or mass production) to continuous flow processes (the equivalent of factories running 24/7/365), supervisory and social interaction among workers shifted in nature, in frequency, and in intensity. Within the unit and small batch production systems, relationships between task functions were direct and personal. Marketing, production, and development dealt directly with each other on daily operational concerns. Within both large batch and continuous process systems, the relationships between task functions became more indirect and dealt mostly with information transfer (Woodward, 1965, 128). This personal distance degraded the quality of communication and diminished workers' control over their production.

Welcome to dystopia.

ORGANIZATONAL FACTORS AFFECTING SOCIAL ISOLATION

The impact of technology and social isolation on individuals can be dramatic, associated as it is with a baker's dozen of organizational factors that exacerbate this impact. As indicated in Table 6.1, when the factors discussed here interact with one another, the effects on the

TABLE 6.1   Linking Organizational Factors with States of Isolation

Objective State of Social Isolation		Subjective Feelings of Social Isolation	
		Decreasing Likelihood	Increasing Likelihood
Imposed by others	1. External boundary control	Complete Choice	No Choice
Closely associated with alienation	2. Community integration	Integrated community	Separation and disconnection
	3. Organizational culture	Shared culture	No shared culture
	4. Meaningfulness of work role	Product/Process responsibility	Highly fragmented division of labor
	5. Degree of power	Mastery over events	No control
	6. Common ground	Common experiences	No shared experiences
Linked to formal status	7. Group norms	Group norms identifiable	No sense of group norms
	8. Group values	Understanding and commitment to group values	Misunderstanding and/or rejection of group values
	9. Authority	Access to authority	No access to authority
	10. Collegial interaction	Access to respected coworkers and peers	No access to respected coworkers and peers
	11. Meaningful feedback	Meaningful feedback present	Absence of meaningful feedback
	12. Artifacts of status	Possession of artifacts of status	No identifiable artifacts of status
Physical separation	13. Face-to-face interaction	Copresence	Completely off-site

Source: Vega and Brennan (2000, 479).

individual can be seen in both worker dysfunction and decreased organizational effectiveness.

External Boundary Control

People like to decide on their own who can have access to them or to their group. Unfortunately for workers, this organizational factor is the only factor that is actually imposed by the organization on the individual. "The regulation of [such] interpersonal access is considered one of the primary psychological tasks of successful interactions in social organizations" (Caldwell, 1997, 298). The contacts are conducted on a variety of dimensions, including the contact channels (touch, sound, vision), the type of contact made (emotional or task-oriented), and the intended results of the contact (goal coordination, social support, mutual understanding, information exchange). Caldwell defines the trajectory of this factor as extending from isolation (the undesirably low level of social contact yielding loneliness and alienation) through privacy (the ability of the individual to limit social contact to a desirable level in order to maintain psychological comfort and health), to invasion (an undesirably high level of contact). The organization that affords little privacy to the worker, whether personal or technological, is creating an environment that can become intrusive. By contrast, the organization that provides workers with few opportunities to open their boundaries on a voluntary basis is creating an environment that can isolate people from their peers and supervisors, and create psychological discomfort and stress. The way to remedy the imposition of isolation on distance workers is by relinquishing control over their boundaries to them.

Community Integration

The degree of community integration experienced by workers is controlled externally through organizational structure and systems. In traditional organizations, meetings may be held on the fly, in hallways, in lunchrooms, and at the coffee wagon—wherever people congregate. In virtual organizations, meetings may be held synchronously or asynchronously in chat rooms, via email threads, or by videoconference. The information transfer process is equivalent; what differs is the planned nature of the communication and the impact of formality on interaction. As one sociologist has claimed, "The sense of organizational membership that one experiences from continually taking part in virtual meetings, whether by email or conference calls, is not unlike the feeling of congregational membership one achieves from watching televised religious services" (Snizek, 1995, 17). Despite the use of emoticons, capital letters, asterisks, and acronyms, there is a significant lack of warmth and personal connection in electronically mediated communication. In addition, the delights of synergy and serendipity are absent when the workforce is distributed. The extremes of community integration range from a sense of total community to complete disconnection. Social isolation creates the latter.

Organizational Culture and Absorbability

Is the organizational culture such that new or existing employees can feel comfortable and embrace it fully? Organizations that encourage and support workers in off-site locations may experience difficulty in maintaining the culture that was developed prior to the influence of distance technology. Global businesses have long recognized that expatriate workers must be cycled back into the home office after a certain period abroad or they will begin to lose their national and organizational cultural connections. U.S. companies have acknowledged that sending American workers to other countries without sufficient training in the culture to be encountered and how to work effectively within it is likely to create more problems than it solves. The same problems can be experienced by teleworkers. How do new employees recognize the existing culture and learn how to be successful within it when the culture cannot easily be experienced from a distance? Is there one prevailing culture in the organization, or are there multiple cultures depending on work location and comfort level with technology? Transfer of the existing knowledge about international business can aid companies in avoiding potentially isolating effects of lack of cultural integration. Understanding the extremes of full integration (cultural immersion—through personal experience) and outsider status (second-hand experience) can make managers aware of the challenges faced by new employees working off-site and by existing employees adapting to a telework environment.

Meaningfulness of the Work Role

Everyone ascribes a sense of meaning or value to their daily labors; as individuals, we have all determined whether we are laying bricks or building cathedrals. The greater the meaning our work has for us (building cathedrals), the more joy we derive from the process. Social psychologist Kurt Lewin wrote about early Taylorism,

> The worker wants his work to be rich, wide and Protean, not crippling and narrow. Work should not limit personal potential but develop it. Work can involve love, beauty, and the soaring joy of creating. Progress, in that case, does not mean shortening the work day, but an increase in the human value of work. (Weisbord, 1989, 76)

This comment, made in 1920, continues to resonate today: the greater the meaningfulness of one's work role and appreciation of the work results, the lower the sense of alienation one experiences. When work is important and valued and the worker has responsibility over product and process, the tendency towards social isolation decreases. But when work is fragmented and passed along as discrete data captures, for example, it sustains the increasing likelihood of social isolation and worker alienation.

Power over Personal Production

The degree of power the worker experiences over the production process ranges from no control (with a high risk of total alienation) to compete mastery (with little likelihood of alienation). Historically, the power that workers were able to wield revolved around the skills they brought to the workplace. Highly skilled workers were more powerful;

apprentices were powerless. Today, this differentiation of power built on skills has disappeared, partly through the global process of deskilling that has resulted from the development of sophisticated technologies that perform both the simplest and the most complex work activities. People no longer need to either flip burgers or draw complex blueprints—computer-controlled machines handle both tasks more easily and efficiently. As our manufacturing and support service processes have increased in speed and dependence on technology, the need for workers with traditional skills has diminished. The skills that teleworkers bring to the table are more the innate capacities of emotional endurance and the ability to tolerate unusual working conditions than skills developed by training or education. The power of the worker is thus decreased, as the very nature of work removes the worker from a position of control and mastery into a position of subservience to an inanimate entity.

Common Ground

The search for common ground provides an opportunity for respite from a sense of isolation, when such ground is identified. The absence of common ground tends to increase both alienation and isolation. AT&T, a leader in U.S. telework, claims that only 7 percent of their teleworkers experience loneliness as a major problem because AT&T encourages people working outside the office to seek out interaction with others, even if that means doing their work in a coffee shop or the library (www.att.com/telework). Common ground can thus describe work relationships that are not limited to one's own employer but rather become inclusive of any worker for any company who is working away from the company's location. As we are enjoined by the changed social contract to maintain control over our own careers and depend less on our employer's management and direction (Pink, 2001, 11; Rousseau, 1995, 29), workers may be better off relating to one another and to their specific fields of endeavor regardless of employer than they are relating to coworkers in different jobs at a common employer. This definition of common ground can serve as a substitute for the water cooler, company cafeteria, and coffee wagon and create a sense of belonging that alleviates isolation.

Group Norms

The absence of identifiable group norms sets the scene for increasing social isolation regardless of organizational status, whereas clear group norms tend to reduce such feelings (Sproull & Kiesler, 1991). Group norms provide us with a sense of connectedness with others and with our organization; we learn how to fit in, how to succeed, and how to act under most circumstances by watching people in positions similar to our own. In many corporate cultures, when aberrant behavior becomes obvious, it also becomes potentially damaging, so most workers will do their best to read the semiotics of corporate culture and group norms. Even when such norms exist in abundance in the traditional workplace, some people have difficulty reading them. These people may become objects of ridicule ("bean counters," "pocket-protector wearers") and find their climb up the corporate ladder derailed by side issues. When pink slips are handed out, the "oddballs" may be first to go, followed closely by others who are not seen in public, explaining the rush back into the office of many teleworkers after the massive corporate layoffs of the third quarter of 2001 (Zbar, 10/25/01). Being obviously present and visible (like most of the employees) seemed a wise strategy to the otherwise hard-working but unseen teleworkers who were trying to meld with existing group norms. How much more challenging is it to remain aware of the subtle norms that groups devise to differentiate themselves from others when working in one's basement rather than at the corporate office?

Group Values

Acceptance and commitment to group values tend to be associated with a lower risk of social isolation, and the reverse condition tends to increase that risk. When working in remote locations without opportunity for face-to-face reminders, trust becomes the key value in worker relationships. Teleworkers need to depend on their on-site colleagues to share information, workers in the corporate office count on input from teleworkers, managers trust that people they cannot see are doing the job they were hired for, and everyone depends on someone else in a different location to do their part of the project and not let down the team. One of the operational challenges inherent to telework is our tendency to believe that conversations conducted by telephone are more compelling than conversations conducted in person. In our offices, we will frequently ask the person standing in front of us to "Wait just a minute while I get the phone," making it clear that the telephone takes precedence over the person. When the manager stops at someone's desk to request an adjustment to a report, no one thinks twice about it. When the same manager telephones a worker at home to make the identical request, the exchange takes on immediacy and an importance that the casual in-office exchange did not. The manager in the first instance is "managing by walking around," an accepted, positive characterization. The manager in the second instance may be accused of micromanaging, checking up on the out-of-sight worker, and controlling from afar. In remote relationships, "all of the team members have to strive for rich relationships within the group, the kind where a great amount of trust is the strongest bond" (Rosenwald, 2001, J1).

Access to Authority

The higher one moves up the status chain in an organization, the greater the access one has to authority and the concomitant diminution of feelings of social isolation. Information flow has historically been a top-down process, originating in those who controlled technology. This behavior has been traced back to the ancient Egyptian scribes who were the only ones who could read and write. Today's "scribes" are the technology gurus, the gatekeepers of information (Sproull & Kiesler, 1991). Logically, then, there are now two sources of corporate authority: the managers and the information technology group. Being close to the seat of power and authority filters a limited amount of knowledge and influence to those in the vicinity. Therefore, one may gain authority and influence if copresent at the work site or copresent in the information technology chain. This latter route is the only one available to teleworkers, whereas on-site workers may take advantage of proximity to both sources of authority.

Collegial Interaction and Electronic Socializing

Collegial interaction reduces the sensation of social isolation. Regardless of formal status, when people are isolated from co-workers, they experience stress and lonesomeness. The cartoon referred to in Chapter 4 appeared on bulletin boards and office doors all over the country in the 1990s, spurred by the growing popularity of the World Wide Web. The punch line of this cartoon: "On the Internet, no one knows you're a dog" (Steiner, n.d.). People need interaction so badly that status, gender, age, and even species differences disappear through technologically facilitated communication. Researchers and zoologists have been successful in teaching gorillas to use computers to communicate—it's a small step to Homo sapiens. As it stands, teleworkers already have the majority of their collegial interactions online rather than in person. True, the quality of online communication is thin when compared with face-to-face interaction, but either method can serve to fulfill some of our human need for socializing. Although the research that has been conducted in this area suggests that time spent on the Internet is time spent away from personal interaction (Nie, Hillygus, & Erbring, 2002; Putnam, 2002), to date no research has appeared that relates time spent on the Internet by teleworkers at their remote locations to decreased collegial interaction. Rather, it would seem apparent that the Internet facilitates increased social and professional interaction for distance workers, facilitating asynchronous conversations without regard to geographic or time boundaries.

Meaningful Feedback

The presence of meaningful feedback in relation to one's role performance is likely to reduce feelings of social isolation. The absence of such feedback can serve to intensify such feelings. Workers who are isolated geographically from their peers and supervisors or managers get less feedback than those who work under the organizational eye and therefore have less understanding of the big picture operation, as monitoring and feedback systems tend to be more refined at on-site than they are at off-site work locations. Forest rangers who work in isolated settings in the U.S. National Parks have indicated that they experience social isolation when out of communication contact with people, unrelated to their actual physical distance from others. U.S. astronaut Norman Thagard experienced the same effect during his stay on the Mir space station with several Russian cosmonauts. Unable to communicate properly with them due to language limitations and cultural differences despite training before his flight, Thagard suffered a lack of feedback analogous to that experienced by workers in more mundane jobs who do not understand or who have not been briefed on the interactions of their activities with those of unseen and distant workers in the particular work process (Caldwell, 1997). Disconnected sociotechnical systems with inadequate feedback controls can have a negative impact on the sense of inclusion and role satisfaction of remote workers.

Artifacts of Status

For workers with high status to begin with, the otherwise isolating tendencies of formal organizational structure can be alleviated through the use of identifiable artifacts of status (Miller, 1975). Although conventional wisdom would have us believe that "it's lonely at the top," artifacts of status such as the traditional corner office and the key to the executive washroom can make that isolation not only more tolerable but even desirable, especially to those who do not have it. Other artifacts of status are more subtle, often disguised as the necessary tools of production. People whose work depends on technology are likely to experience "hard drive envy" or envy of the larger capacity of another worker's computer system, peripherals, or office chair. The newest or most advanced equipment signals one's value to the company and visually advertises it to other employees. People who are working off-site do not have the benefits of this personal artifact of status and may, in fact, be using their own equipment or corporate cast-offs deemed "good enough" to be used at home (Vega & Brennan, 2000b). Although ownership of the means of production was approved by Karl Marx as a protection for the employee, in our twenty-first-century economy having to supply one's own equipment is an indicator of a lack of appreciation by the employer and devalued status in the eyes of colleagues, and the result may be continued marginalization of groups of workers with low status. Competition for organizational status requires that artifacts be provided that identify status accurately, or companies run the risk of further alienating their off-site workers. Workers who are unseen and devoid of personal advertising can easily experience diminished status as a factor that exacerbates feelings of loneliness and isolation in them.

Face-to-Face Interaction

When workers share the same physical location at the same time (i.e., collocate), they are less likely to experience a sense of social isolation within the group. Eliminating the opportunity for face-to-face interaction through distance in work location or work hours can increase feelings of isolation from the group in workers (Taha & Caldwell, 1993). It is for this reason that most companies require that their teleworkers appear on a more or less regular basis in the office, and that most teleworkers work at home only part of the week, spending some required time face-to-face with coworkers and supervisors. Computer aided communication does not supplant all physical connection as affirmed earlier, but we are often misled into thinking that it can do so. According to Wellman, Salaff, Dimitova, Garton, Gulia, and Haythornthwaite (1996), "Studies of virtual community, CSCW [computer supported cooperative work], and telework generally have not informed each other" (218). It is particularly difficult to determine the appropriate level of necessary face-to-face communication for work teams to operate efficiently and effectively. Isolation has been shown to be unrelated to physical distance (Caldwell, 1997; Diekema, 1992); it is common to feel most isolated when "copresent," such as at a party or on a commuter train when not part of a particular group of people. However, the impact of erratic presence at meetings and other organizational events is undocumented. We must consider the challenges inherent in appearing to drop in to the office where colleagues are spending all of their work hours, and maintaining a strong connection to the on-site work group without incurring excessive transactional costs (Ouchi, 1980).

CONSEQUENCES OF SOCIAL ISOLATION ON TELEWORKERS

Despite the long history of the knowledge worker in the United States, there has been little research done on the impact of technologically facilitated communication on worker effectiveness (Wellman et al., 1996). Even differentiating between what is "social" and what is "technological" has proven a challenging task (Brigham & Corbett, 1997). Keeping in mind the rapid growth of teleworking resulting from ease of access to enabling technologies and the reduction in their costs as the technology matures, many of the organizational factors listed previously appear likely to increase subjective feelings of social isolation in off-site workers.

Teleworkers operate predominantly off-site, have no identifiable artifacts of status, and may feel "out of the loop" because of limited feedback and visual cues. They may experience greater difficulty than on-site workers in identifying and participating in group norms and values because of their diminished opportunity for collegially shared experiences. The necessary logistic fragmentation of their work can easily limit their understanding and participation in the holistic work process.

Unlike the secondary effects that were designed into earlier, Taylorist management programs, the second order consequences of today's technological advances are often unplanned, unexpected, and detrimental to worker psychological comfort. It's difficult to imagine that the organizational factors discussed in this chapter can lead to positive worker outcomes over the long term, even if the short-term results are positive.

REDUCING THE IMPACT OF ISOLATION

Some of the negative impacts of isolation on workers can be avoided, alleviated, or eradicated by simple expedients; others may require more deliberate strategies.

- *Limit telework*. Instead of permitting teleworkers to work as much or as little as they prefer just as long as they meet their production goals, it can be healthier to limit the hours they work per week rather than losing themselves in a project and ignoring their physical, mental, or emotional needs. It would be wise to limit the number of days or weeks that teleworkers remain out of the office. Bring them in for meetings on a frequent basis to maintain their connection with the company and their co-workers.
- *Allow permeable boundaries*. Give up checking up on teleworkers when they are not in the office. These are mature, trusted employ-

ees who need to maintain personal control over the amount of privacy they want and need. Counting keystrokes is out, as is tracking visits to the Internet.

- *Delight in synergy*. Provide opportunities for synergetic interaction for employees, both through technology and in person-to-person social venues. Consider investing in video conferencing technology, in enterprise resource planning, and in collaborative process-management software so that workers can interact with each other easily (Zbar, 2/7/02). Encourage workers to check in with colleagues, to call instead of emailing, to seek out opportunities to speak with them and hear their voices.
- *Cultural immersion*. Develop a method of cultural renewal for teleworkers and nonteleworkers so that all remain on the same cultural page. It's easy for culture to slip. The problem lies not in the slip itself but in the lack of general awareness of the slippage until it's too late to recover. Sharing culture effectively may require annual retreats, semiannual daylong miniconferences, quarterly half-day corporate meetings, or some other type of company rally that clarifies values, goals, objectives, and corporate purpose.
- *Build cathedrals*. Make it clear to all workers that your company seeks to build cathedrals rather than cut stones or lay bricks. The mission and vision must be clear to all, and it must be transcendent and inspiring. When we are part of something larger than ourselves, the minor inconveniences of daily work as well as the major hassles of our jobs become less consuming while the work itself takes on meaning.
- *Value skills*. If what we value is emotional endurance, we must provide support and training for the further development of that skill rather than hope that emotional strength will be bred into future generations. If we need robots, we can build them. It is our moral imperative not to turn people into robots.

7

Unnatural Acts in the Workplace

American workers and employers have adopted telework far more slowly than had been anticipated by the early supporters of the program. There are many reasons for this reluctance to fully endorse remote work configurations, and I have selected ten frequently heard concerns about telework to discuss here. However, this list is not complete. We need to add to it the various personal fears that workers suffer regarding their family needs, employers' worries about inappropriate out-of-office behavior, resentment by non-teleworkers that can result in disgruntled and less productive employees, misunderstanding of the purposes of telework programs, potential effects on team or organizational culture and alliances, and the difficulties inherent to the quantification of the often qualitative results of telework programs.

The ten concerns presented here closely parallel the concerns that have appeared throughout the history of management and evolution of organizational approaches, and include one more often unspoken problem to the mix. That is, they tackle the bottom two thirds of the organizational iceberg—the irrational behavior that controls acceptance or rejection of organizational change—instead of being limited to rational and measurable operational concerns.

TOP 10 CHALLENGES TO THE ACCEPTANCE OF TELEWORK

10. The suitability of work to be done through teleworking processes
9. Balancing priorities
8. Changing technology
7. Security and privacy
6. Regulatory vacillation
5. Career path anxiety
4. The Stanislavski Syndrome
3. Muddy role description
2. The human disconnect
1. Unnatural acts

Let's look at each of these in turn.

Not All Work Is Suitable for Teleworking Processes

Not all work is suitable for telework. In particular, labor that is time- and presence-based rather than outcome-based is less likely to prove able to be completed from remote locations. Customer service, inbound or outbound telemarketing workers, and back office data entry workers are the exceptions to this general rule. Advances in technology have permitted workers who perform this type of unit-based work to fulfill their responsibilities seamlessly from a distance. A comparative look at the Bureau of Labor Statistics' employment records from 1988 and 1998 next to their projections for 2008 indicate steady growth in this employment sector over the 20-year period, decreasing slightly from 9.9 percent growth from 1988 to 1998 to 9.0 percent growth projected from 1998 to 2008.

What these figures do not tell us, however, is how the growth in the administrative support and clerical sectors compares with the growth in other employment sectors. Over the same 20-year period, professional specialties increased by 31.7 percent in the first decennial and are projected to increase by an additional 27.0 percent in the second decennial. Technicians and technical support increased by 27.6 percent, and an additional 22.2 percent is projected. The vast service sector increased by 21.5 percent and is projected to increase by another 17.1 percent by 2008. Executive, administrative, and managerial jobs increased by 19.8 percent, with another 16.4 percent projected (Kelinson & Tate, 2000; Bureau of Labor Statistics).

Table 7.1 shows the ten occupations with the largest job growth projected from 1998 to 2008. The occupations that are least likely to be conducted via telework are shaded: retail salespersons, cashiers, truck

TABLE 7.1   Ten Occupations with the Largest Job Growth, 1998–2008

	Employment		Change	
	1998	2008	Number	Percent
Systems analysts	617	1,194	577	94
Retail salespersons	4,056	4,620	563	14
Cashiers	3,198	3,754	556	17
General Managers and top executives	3,362	3,913	551	16
Truck drivers, light and heavy	2,970	3,463	493	17
Office clerks, general	3,021	3,484	463	15
Registered nurses	2,079	2,530	451	22
Computer support specialists	429	869	439	102
Personal care and home health aides	746	1,179	433	58
Teacher assistants	1,192	1,567	375	31

Source: Bureau of Labor Statistics, 2/9/00 [numbers are in thousands of jobs]

drivers, registered nurses, personal care and home health aides, and teacher assistants. These six categories account for 2,871,000 new jobs by 2008, compared with 2,030,000 new jobs for systems analysts, general managers and top executives, office clerks, and computer support specialists. Some of the latter group would be able to telework, at least for part of the workweek.

When we hear talk about the Information Age and the changes it brings, it is easy to be misled into believing that *all* work is changing, that *all* facets of our lives will reel from the impact of discontinuous change, that we will *all* benefit or be hurt by these changes. Nothing could be further from the truth. Much of our lives will be unaffected by the new economy and the new technology, and this includes employment for the vast majority of American workers. According to these Bureau of Labor Statistics employment projections, we will continue to truck our food and manufactured products across the country. We will continue to purchase consumer goods in retail environments requiring "live" sales personnel and cashiers. We will grow old and need personal care at home, or we will move into formal group living arrangements and receive our personal care there. Nurses will continue to ease pain, and students will benefit from teachers and assistants to teachers.

The new kinds of computer-related jobs that will prevail in terms of growth account for some 1,016,000 new positions. For these workers, it may well be sensible to require justification for their remaining in the office rather than teleworking, but workers with computer-related jobs are not among the majority. Even though all work is not suitable for telework, a significant segment of today's work can be conducted outside the traditional office environment. It is, perhaps, our own reluctance to take the risk of figuring out exactly *how* we can accomplish this transition that reinforces our reluctance to make the change.

Balancing Priorities

What is more important—retaining valued employees or keeping operating expenses low? There seems to be no easy answer to this question, as both priorities can be critical to the success, or even the sustainability, of a company in a volatile economy. After a decade of unprecedented stock market success and economic growth, the course of natural law (what goes up must come down) returned our investment feet to the ground and our business-model feet to the fire at the turn of the twenty-first century, leaving us feeling cornered by multiple demands.

Initiating a telework program properly—including designing a method for selecting employees and managers; training personnel on an ongoing basis; funding hardware, software, and support structure; providing dual real estate for workers; handling resulting issues of culture; establishing the infrastructure; and determining a system of output measurement and assessment—can represent a significant expense to a company interested in using telework as a retention or recruiting tool. However, a telework approach *is* effective and can be appealing, especially when high pay scales limit an organization's ability to hire needed personnel. It has become easier for government agencies, for example, to hire highly qualified and in-demand professionals, such as scientists, when offering telework as a benefit and as a competitive recruiting advantage (Vega & Brennan, 2000b).

The real concern when using telework as a recruiting or retention tool in the United States is that telework is meant to be a management option; it is first meant to have a business purpose, and only secondarily is it meant to serve as a lure or benefit for workers. That is the employer position in the policy manuals and agreements signed by federal teleworkers, as well as by many of those who telework in the private sector. Language such as "Teleworking at [agency name deleted] is a management option, not an employee right," "Teleworking is not an Employee benefit, but rather it is an alternate method of meeting the needs of the Department," and "[company name deleted] considers telecommuting to be a viable management work option that, when appropriately applied, benefits both the company and the individual" (West, 2000: Policy Pages, unnumbered) makes it clear that the primary benefit of telework must accrue to the organization, and the residual benefits to the workers involved. This is akin to determining which components of an item for sale are benefits and which are only features. It is possible that proponents have been trying to sell the features of telework for workers (reduced commutation, lowered stress, the ability to be at home when the kids return from school, etc.) as benefits (reduction of stress on the national and local infrastructure, lowered real estate costs, and similar organizational, institutional, and social goods).

Some of the avowed benefits are unlikely to have any positive residual effect on teleworkers. Indeed, part of the reduction of operating costs that accrue to organizations that encourage telework are simply shifted directly to the teleworkers themselves. Teleworkers consistently allocate a portion of their homes to their employers with neither compensation nor tax relief for it. When they seek to take an income tax deduction for this business-related space, they run the risk of "goading the IRS to audit" (Zbar, 8/23/01). It is curious that a company can use a management tool to its own benefit and then require that the worker pay for it. A visit to the IRS web site (www.irs.gov) provides clarification of this complex issue, as does consideration of the General Services Administration's Office of Real Property's "Cost per Person" model (www.gsa.gov/realpropertypolicy).

Working in conjunction with government agencies and private industry, the Innovative Workplaces Division of the Office of Real Property has designed a method of calculating the cost per person of maintaining office space for employees. This method incorporates the cost of real estate, telecommunications, information technology, and workstation furniture, as well as the cost of providing alternate work environments, such as home telework and the use of telecenters, on an average of two days per week. According to their 2000 findings, it continues to be less costly, at least in the Washington, DC area, to support workers at telecenters or at home than it is to provide central real estate for them. However, they caution the reader that telework ought not to be considered a means to attain the goal of reducing real estate costs, but should be seen instead as "an expansion and enhancement of the entire workplace environment" (GSA, 2000, 17). Despite this employer benefit, more than 10 million Americans would like to work at home "but do not believe their employers would agree to it" (Pratt, 1999, 4), suggesting to us that the expressed benefits are not at all clear to any of the parties involved.

A choice between reducing operating expenses and retaining employees is a Hobson's choice—neither option is acceptable. Instead of operating in a world of black-and-white, zero-sum choices, it pays to reemphasize the importance of recognizing the various continua upon which we live. A sense of balance and flexibility, a willingness to adjust to the changing environment, whether incrementally or in tectonic shifts, and a clear sense of organizational goals can assist us in making the appropriate contingent business decision.

Changing Technology

Technology costs money. And keeping up with changing technology requires continuous reinvestment of limited financial resources. Many companies are functioning with legacy equipment—existing hardware and software that is far from state of the art, but is perfectly functional under normal conditions. However, what is functional in an office environment with its on-site technical support and coworkers who can assist with problems may not be functional in a remote environment with support limited to a tech desk and an online manual or help screens.

Chapter 2 provided a full discussion of issues of changing technology and ways to address them. But the technological resistance to telework on the part of companies may tend to be based more in the general corporate reluctance to spend money on consumable resources during a period of economic volatility than on the difficulty of keeping up with the electronic Joneses. In the early days of telework, workers were often responsible for supplying their own equipment. As recently as 2000, some federal agencies were unable to devote sufficient fiscal resources to adequately support their home teleworkers, requiring the workers to provide their own computers or to use secondhand equipment abandoned by the agencies in favor of newer models. This created a two-tier system of employees: those who worked in the office with the most up-to-date equipment and support and those who worked at home, punished for their willingness to work in an alternate location by having to use outdated technology.

As it becomes more obvious that remote workers require, *at a minimum*, the same equipment as their on-site peers, organizations are becoming less reluctant to invest in the necessary equipment for teleworkers. However, the fluctuations in technology and the rapidity of change that demands continuous upgrades combine to create a pocket of resistance that can be overcome only by the open-ended commitment of fiscal resources.

Security and Privacy

Security and privacy are two sides of the same worry. The security side comes from employers whose responsibility is to keep their customer and corporate data away from the prying eyes of competitors and others whose interests are anathema to those of the corporation. The privacy side comes from the employees who are trusted to handle these data and to keep them safe, yet are at risk of losing their own privacy when this effort takes place outside the physical office environment.

Security and privacy in cyberspace can be hard to come by, requiring elaborate firewalls and multiple checkpoints that seem to be violable nearly at will by sophisticated hackers. An even more complex problem arises when companies implement powerful security systems and discover that they have a negative impact on the functionality of the software that allows them to do business in the first place. Effective security devices can produce increases in application response times, causing significant delays between data entry and display, limiting call completion when using IP telephony applications, and creating a generally sluggish electronic work environment (Tolly, 2001). In addition, the growth of the remote electronic storage industry, already strong in the later 1990s and fueled dramatically by the terrorist attacks of 2001, has become a costly and unwieldy business requirement.

On the flip side, 90 percent of workers in traditional offices surf non–work-related websites during working hours (Cohen, 2001), causing additional demand on bandwidth and infrastructure. It is reasonable to assume that workers in remote locations do the same at least as often. At the traditional work site, workers are aware that they are using the company connection to make personal purchases, write email, visit chat rooms, play games, conduct personal business, or generally wander around. It is clear that such activity is often monitored or, if not actually monitored, *can* be monitored quite simply. However, at home, it is less clear that one is using company resources for private activities on company time. The distinction between company time and personal time, company resources and personal resources, the company's business and "none of your business" is unclear. The availability and use of monitoring devices in workers' homes via the Internet comes perilously close to wiretapping, illegal under most circumstances (Hopper, 2001). And, such monitoring is certainly an invasion of the privacy of one's home.

Regulatory Vacillation

Are teleworkers at home? Or are they at work? Government confusion about the answer to this question has generated palpable response from all sectors of the working community. In November 1999, the Occupational Safety and Health Administration (OSHA) created a firestorm by declaring in a letter of interpretation that was later withdrawn that employers could be liable for federal health and safety violations that occurred in teleworkers' homes (Fairfax, 11/15/99).

Upon examination, it is clear that the letter, written to an employer who had inquired about certain safety considerations for employees working at home, was a sincere attempt to answer fully and completely the questions posed more than two years earlier by the employer. But the answers were devastating to a country of employers who had previously assumed no responsibility for the safety of the homes of their employees. The general interpretation of the letter was that OSHA required employers to vouch for the safety of the work environment, regardless of where that work environment was located. This good faith effort at clarifying issues succeeded only in raising others.

When the then-Secretary of Labor, Alexis M. Herman, withdrew the letter from Richard Fairfax, Director of Compliance Programs on January 5, 2000, the business community and telework advocates calmed themselves, reassured that teleworkers' homes would be safe from government oversight. In this respect, the OSHA position is one of protecting the privacy of employees and not limiting the ability of employers to permit alternate work arrangements without penalty. What this position also permits, however, is the existence of potentially unsafe working conditions in employees' homes, creating a de facto liability on the part of employers and a dangerous situation for workers and their families.

Many questions remain unanswered at the time of this writing. If an employee trips and falls over the computer cables while not on duty (if working specific hours), who is responsible? If the worker does not have formal working hours, who is responsible? If a circuit is overloaded and a fire results, who pays for the replacement of the home, the equipment, the possible medical expenses? These and similar problems are addressed in a situational manner, without regulatory support. This is an opportunity for the government to take a stand regarding the safety of the worker and a leadership role in the protection of its citizens. Until such a stand is taken, the wholesale adoption of telework without reservation is simply not going to happen.

Career Path Anxiety

Do you have to be there or do you have to fulfill certain responsibilities? This question is the one that drives much of the worker reluctance to telework. Perhaps originating in the concerns raised by the so-called "mommy track" of the 1980s (Rosener, 1990), nontraditional work environments, leadership styles, and career paths have been suspect by the more conventional (and majority) business leaders. For these people, face time is as important as demonstrable potential or a strong record of achievement. Some powerhouse industry leaders, such as EMC, refused as of September 2000 to permit teleworking, claiming that people had to be on-site in order to absorb the culture.

There is much to be said about being part of the culture of the organization that employs you. Being one of the guys has always shortened the route to success, whether in business or in community.

But the changing nature of the workforce makes being one of the guys difficult to achieve. Discretionary behavior based on gender, race, age, sexual orientation—or on visual markers—is illegal. Individuals are feeling less constrained than ever before by their needs to belong to a group and develop social capital (Putnam, 2000) and the requirement to build their careers at one company (Pink, 2001). Shifting loyalties and drifting allegiances have joined forces to create a work environment that encourages personal career development rather than corporate career development.

The person who is in the office is likely get the plum assignments just because she or he is visible. However, the person who is teleworking has the freedom to develop the skills and make the contacts that are necessary for individual success. Working in one's pajamas is hardly the major career benefit that teleworking provides; companies that want to retain qualified teleworkers will find a way to get those juicy assignments to the appropriate employee regardless of where he is sitting. Defined career paths may be relegated to the industrial past, but good management of valued employees can serve both the company and the worker.

The Stanislavski Syndrome

A leader in the great transition from the nineteenth to the twentieth century, Konstantin Stanislavksi left a legacy that transcends theater. The core of Stanislavski's philosophy led to the school of Method Acting—understanding the psychological motivations of the characters that the actors were playing. Characters were no longer to be considered unidimensional. Instead, they had real emotions and a complex internal life that the actors were responsible for demonstrating to the audience (Mills, 1995). Flat portrayals of stock characters such as the villain, the damsel in distress, the swashbuckling hero—all of these were relegated to the dusty closet of old costumes and light humor. In their place developed actors who were able to interpret the very human motivations and behaviors of real people. Do you remember Marlon Brando shouting "Stellaaaaaaa . . ." in *A Streetcar Named Desire*? The power of his performance derived from his personal interpretation of his character's motivation.

When we talk about teleworkers as a group of people, we have neglected to consider that teleworkers are individuals, each with individual needs, desires, and psychological demands. Why should workers telework? What is their motivation?

Kurt Lewin, Stanislavski's equally radical counterpart in the field of psychology, suggested that motivation is a contingent theory—that is, motivation is specific to an individual in a given situation. Motivation cannot be considered globally, only individually. He believed that we each act to resolve tensions in our personal lives, in our "subjective experience of situations" (Weisbord, 1987, 77). From the world of the hard sciences, Lewin adapted Force Field Analysis as a means to measure these tensions—the driving and opposing forces in our lives—and to adjust the existing equilibrium of these forces. The status quo can be changed by either increasing the driving forces or diminishing the opposing forces. Of the two options, reducing the restraints is the more effective because the process itself does not create additional restraints, whereas emphasizing the driving forces does nothing to diminish resistance, which may increase at an accelerated rate.

For this very reason, it is important to acknowledge the drawbacks of telework, both to workers and to managers. Without this acknowledgment, there is little hope of encouraging further experimentation and risk-taking in an emergent work environment. Once opposition is mitigated, support will carry the day. The opposing forces—numbering among them personal expense, loneliness, inadequate support from the office, home and worklife crossover, boredom, lack of access to necessary tools, sedentariness, loss of purposefulness, and others—must be combated, while the drivers (motivators) for *each individual* must be identified and reinforced.

Manager Role Description: Muddy

The role of the virtual manager is different from the role of the traditional manager. You will find a full description of this changing role in Chapter 8, but three questions have plagued virtual managers, their direct reports, and executive management since the inception of telework arrangements: Who am I? What do I do? How do I do it?. To understand this problem, we need to take a brief look at the differing demands made in the Information Age and the Industrial Age on employees at all levels.

In the Industrial Age, the goal was to eliminate guesswork about production capacity, the means of production, and the speed of production. Routine was idealized, guesswork eliminated, and repetition the activity of choice as early as 1751, as reported in Diderot's *Encyclopedie* (Sennett, 1998). In his description of a paper mill south of Paris, Diderot presents a model factory that separated the workplace from the home— a dramatic transformation of earlier work configurations. He believed that this "new work" style, where workers were paid directly for their labors and supported themselves on those earnings was a great improvement over the earlier apprenticeship/journeyman/master route. In addition, Diderot claimed that only by repetition could a laborer achieve excellence, take control of his destiny, and be at peace. Twenty-five years later, with the publication of *The Wealth of Nations*, Adam Smith refuted these idealistic statements and claimed that routine deadens the spirit; what was truly worth saving in Diderot's description was the principle of the separation of the workplace and the home as the most important of modern divisions of labor (Sennett, 1998). Despite his oft-cited pin factory experience, Smith understood that routine ultimately destroys human intelligence and keeps workers from having control over their own efforts.

Consider the workplace of the Information Age, where the goal is not the elimination of guesswork but rather the encouragement of serendipitous discoveries. Such discoveries are rarely made in an environment that requires routine, repetition of mindless activities, or overcontrol by supervisors. They are made in environments that cosset their creation and protect their development. For a full century, however, managers have been trained to squelch deviation from accepted procedures, to measure output and value output more than process, and to avoid surprises, even pleasant ones. "No surprises management" has been a watchword for several generations of managers—it should not be unexpected that asking them to turn in their tracks or veer from conventional wisdom results in confusion.

The Industrial Age manager focused on the quantitative measurement of efficiency as validation of his supervisory expertise and the workers' excellence and commitment. Frederick W. Taylor, the frequently maligned father of scientific management, was a leader in insisting on output measurement as a means of cost reduction, and rightly or wrongly his teachings have continued to influence American business. Each new management fad (and American business is always ready to accept the newest fashion) has provided a quantitative means for measuring fiscal improvement generated by the new trend. Fordism and the assembly line, Weber's rules and procedures, Roethlisberger and Western Electric, McGregor and Theories X and Y, systems theory and operations management, quality and statistical process control, to name a few, all focus on the quantitative measurement of efficiency to demonstrate effectiveness in aiding the agreed-upon goal of good management—an enhanced fiscal bottom line.

But the Information Age organization has a different focus. In this company, qualitative measures of effectiveness carry the day. The new business models are not always clear—enhancing the fiscal bottom line requires some mental stretching when an e-company seems to give away its product in lieu of selling it—and sometimes our unfamiliarity with the organizational goals of the Information Age company confounds our ability to adapt to these models. The reason for our confusion is that the new bottom line remains fiscally based while turning its focus outward, toward the greater community, with the goal of integrating its activities and successes with those of competitors, customers, and suppliers (Moss Kanter, 2001). Just as the Internet model of business focuses on customization and specialized, task-dependent products, so do successful Information Age companies focus on flexibility of work hours, job titles, and styles of employment, variability of motivation tools, incentives, and challenges, and willingness to create change while retaining valued employees. Moss Kanter reports on a 1999 study that provided the top 10 reasons employees stay with their current company:

> Affection for co-workers (71 percent), a pleasant work environment (68 percent), an easy commute (68 percent), challenging work (65 percent), and flexible work hours (54 percent). Among Europeans, the nonmonetary side of employment is even more striking. An aggregation of data from nineteen countries showed that job satisfaction, working relationships, and company identification topped the list of fifteen possible aspects of employment as being the most important to people while pay ranked at the bottom. (205)

If pay has been supplanted in value as a motivator for workers by other, more qualitative measures, corporate bottom lines need to have adjusted as well. And they have. The *Fortune* magazine list of "100 Best Companies to Work For" in the new century focuses on companies that provide congenial and flexible workplaces, a sense of social responsibility that infiltrates the whole organization from the top down, and family-friendly companies (Levering & Moskowitz, 1/8/01). The number one company on the list was the Container Store, located in Dallas, Texas. Entry level salary for production workers was $20,280, for professionals $26,500. "Enthusiastic employees (97% say that 'people care about each other here') recommend the place to friends; 41% of new hires came in that way last year" (148).

Industrial Age organizations existed through their commitment to linearity, the status quo, and standardization. But the Information Age organization lives by nonlinearity, transformation, and innovation, all of which require freedom, the freedom that is anomalous to Industrial Age management.

The Human Disconnect

Isolation plays an important role in management's ability to control workers. As indicated in Chapter 6 and for the purposes of this discussion, social isolation has four characteristics: it is imposed by others; it is not necessarily related to physical separation; it is closely associated with alienation; and, for those with low status to begin with, it is linked to formal status. As of August 2001, the average U.S. teleworker was an educated White male (65 percent) with a household income of from $50,000 (50 percent) to over $100,000 (17.9 percent), according to an IDC survey of 2,500 U.S. teleworking households (Zbar, 9/13/01). But that description is likely to change in the next decade.

As more and more workers opt to telework, the threshold of employee skills is driven downward from its end-of-century concentration on high-tech, highly paid and highly skilled White male workers to less skilled, lower paid women of various ethnicities. This raises a red flag for the potential to develop and marginalize a second-class workforce. Lower-skilled workers have already been marginalized. Women have been fight-ing marginalization for more than a century, and people of color have never been generally accepted in the American workforce. As these people are encouraged to work at home, suddenly the workers in the traditional workplace begin to look and sound more like the workers of the last century, the workforce with which we have become familiar. We no longer see the very people we blame for uncomfortable social change, and it is easy to marginalize people when we do not see them.

Another piece of the disconnect deals with our own motivations, whether as employers or employees. When employers encourage work-ers to telework for the good of the corporation yet shunt to the employee wallets some corporate bills for office space, electricity, and other shared expenses, they are using people rather than employing them. When workers request working at home with dubious motives in mind (child or elder care, for example), they are using their employers for personal ends. These kinds of transactional dealings are damaging to the long-term relationships that develop between workers and employ-ers, and create potential for strife with workers or worker representa-tives (Vega & Brennan, 2000a).

Even more damaging to the national psyche would be a trend toward working at home to avoid the dangers of dealing with the general public, of putting oneself in an exposed position in public places, and in general responding to fear of the unknown, fear of terrorism, and fear of personal harm. Fear is a powerful motivator, but it is not a healthy one.

Unnatural Acts

Both workers and managers in the traditional, hierarchical organiza-tions of the last century are being asked to perform what could be referred to as unnatural acts. They have been socialized one way yet are expected to perform in another. For a significant part of the 20th cen-tury, the goal of management was to maintain the status quo. "No surprises" was a respected corporate watchword through the 1970s.

The shake-up began with the recognition that the Japanese had captured the automotive industry, the symbol of American manufacturing might. By 1982, Peters and Waterman were decrying the old "rational" management, which operated under a set of beliefs that included an appreciation of large size, low cost, analysis, planning, doing it "right," controlling everything, providing monetary rewards, inspecting for quality control, the universality of business, the wisdom of top executives, and growth, growth, growth (Peters and Waterman, 1982). These guidelines built a strong IBM, a strong General Electric, a strong General Motors, a strong General Mills, but time ran out for this model.

Peters and Waterman (1982) suggested that the approach was antiquated, favoring cost reduction over revenue enhancement, leading to heartlessness through constant analysis. Rationality led to negativity and devalued creative thinking, leading to inflexibility and increasing complexity, while minimizing informality, prohibiting internal competition, and overlooking core values. The hidebound approach was finished, supplanted by idealizing the behavior of the supple and fast-moving entrepreneurial organizations that were flourishing while other more traditional companies were stagnating. The new guidelines focused on a bias for action—organizational fluidity, the elimination of bureaucracy via the use of multiple task forces (small is beautiful), appreciation of experimentation, speed, learning, and simplification— and got the organization "close to the customer," which was determined to be the key factor in attaining corporate success.

Tom Peters and Nancy Austin proposed a series of strategies in the 1980s, all leaning toward entrepreneurial activity, customers, and innovation. "Skunkworks" entered corporate mythology, and the origin of the 3M Post-It became one of the most celebrated and frequently cited product success stories, emerging as it did from an environment that sheltered creativity, that fostered experimentation, that permitted the agile development of unusual ideas. Big successes came from small beginnings (Peters & Austin, 1985).

Companies were expected to shift directions virtually overnight, with entrepreneurship taking the place of management and employees expected to take charge of their own destinies. This shift coincided with the explosive introduction of the personal computer for business and for home use, facilitating the growth of small businesses that, a decade later, proved to sustain the American economy in the face of reengineering, recession, and massive layoffs. By 1983, "the IBM PC became the most popular and influential personal computer," with 800,000 sold that year alone (Augarten, 1984, 280).

As early as 1989, management guru Rosabeth Moss Kanter was suggesting that the competing demands of high performance at work and high expectations at home were putting at risk the health of corporations and the health of individuals. These competing demands on the individual—invest in the future but maintain short-term paybacks, take risks but do not fail, do everything better while adding many new tasks to your daily quota, know all the details but delegate, dedicate yourself to a vision but be willing to change direction quickly, speak up and be a leader but cooperate and listen to others, throw yourself into your work but remain physically fit, and demand success while raising wonderful children—were clearly impossible to achieve. And the demands on the corporation—restructure and get lean and mean while offering employee-centered policies, encourage creativity but stick to your knitting, push for fast execution but take time to plan, decentralize into autonomous work units but centralize to capture efficiencies of scale—were equally unattainable (Moss Kanter, 1989b, 20–21). Superman and Superwoman were suffering burnout and, before they could find a way to recover, the stock market wavered and slipped in the late 1980s, creating widespread layoffs and corporate failures.

The sickening rise and fall of management theories, strategies, and processes progressed through MBWA, TQM, participative management, team-based production, One Minute management, and other alliterative acronyms before landing hard upon business process reengineering (Hammer & Champy, 1993) as a code word meaning cost reduction by flattening the organization and contracting out nonessential functions. According to the theory's originators,

> When a process is reengineered, jobs evolve from narrow and task-oriented to multidimensional. People who once did as they were instructed now make choices and decisions on their own instead. Assembly-line work disappears. Functional departments lose their reasons for being. Managers stop acting like supervisors and behave more like coaches. Workers focus more on the customers' needs and less on their bosses'. Attitudes and values change in response to new incentives. Practically every aspect of the organization is transformed, often beyond recognition. (Hammer & Champy, 1993, 65)

The results? Layoffs, particularly of the middle-class, white-collar worker—an unprecedented occurrence in America.

Downsizing struck hard, and workers had nowhere to turn but to themselves to create new jobs. They did so, building businesses out of the air, in their garages and basements, thanks to the availability of computer technology and skills learned in the corporate workplace. Those workers who were lucky enough to retain their jobs and who were not overcome by survivor guilt found that the corporate work environment had changed drastically. The traditional social contract between company and worker (you can count on retaining your job forever as long as you perform adequately) had vanished, replaced with a promise to employ the worker as long as that worker's services were needed. The worker became responsible for her own career, longevity in one company was no longer expected, and workers scrambled to get as much training as they could to enhance their own portability. The worker was set adrift, and companies—even those that had been recognized as industry leaders—became unstable.

By the time of the next movement—globalization and e-commerce—workers and managers alike were worn out; they were beyond burnout. New policies such as open book management and worker ownership seemed to lay corporate success or failure at the feet of workers, with management throwing its hands up in despair at its own inability to control the activities of workers or steer the course of economic stability. Worker loyalty having been destroyed along with the earlier social contract, both labor and management were in troubled waters. They had begun to confuse capitalism with democracy at work, with the results guaranteed to perpetuate their confusion. Guided by the expectation of financial reward (capitalism on a personal level), workers were encouraged to partner with their employers in an apparent measured equality (democracy on a personal level).

> In spite of all the talk of flatter hierarchies, the single-status workplace, and the bosses who call themselves colleagues, associates, or partners, and are on first name terms with their staff, the fundamental power base in most companies has not changed. There are still hierarchies supported by ambitious managers and formal reporting structures. Some of these managers, like Andy Grove at Intel, like to sit among their staff in tiny offices, sharing the work experience, but Grove is still the boss. (Donkin, 2001, 273)

The result? What Leon Festinger called "cognitive dissonance" (Festinger & Carlsmith, 1959), the inability of workers to reconcile their situation with their beliefs, the actual demands of the workplace with their ingrained and firmly socialized beliefs about what the workplace should be. Workers are being expected to perform *unnatural acts*. The concatenation of democracy and capitalism, coupled with the expectation that workers can be programmed to shift eagerly from one management approach to another, from one organizational design to another, from one set of social expectations to a vastly different set of them, is both unsettling and unrealistic. Changing the program on a computer is easy. Reprogramming a robotic device is straightforward. Writing machine code is a skill that can be learned. Logic and practicality guide these rational processes.

Neil Postman (1993) wrote a decade ago,

All of this may seem obvious enough, but the metaphor of the machine as human (or the human as machine) is sufficiently powerful to have made serious inroads in everyday language. People now commonly speak of "programming" or "deprogramming" themselves. They speak of their brains as a piece of "hard wiring," capable of "retrieving data," and it has become common to think about thinking as a mere matter of processing and decoding. (113)

Human change takes time. People are not like machines; they are irrational. They are not software to be guided by programming; people are hardwired to act on feelings, on emotions, on impulsivity, on personal needs and motivations. They can neither be programmed nor forced to function long in a dissonant environment, performing such unnatural acts.

8

The New Manager

The real goal of successful telemanagement is to make it look like nothing is happening, like it's all "business as usual," with workers in their cubbies, secretaries at the ready, the boss in the big corner office. Business as usual has not looked like this in the United States in several decades, yet we still cleave to the comfortable illusion of role separation by gender, seniority of position by age, importance or value to the organization by title, communication as necessary by verbal face-to-face processes, and measurement of individual performance by visibility and physical presence.

In the context of the traditional working environment, the selection of appropriate candidates for teleworking is paramount, well documented, and continues to stand as a challenge to the success of telework programs. However, a different selection process is often overlooked in the goal of expanding telework programs. That selection process has to do with picking the right person to *manage* teleworkers, field workers, and remote workers of all kinds. What are the characteristics of a good telemanager? How will the telemanager differ from the on-site manager? AT&T has been a leader in American telework since its beginning; we can learn a lot from the experiences of a telemanaging district manager.*

*Gregory T. Simpson is a district manager at AT&T who managed a team of teleworkers and telemanagers. The views expressed are those of the author and interviewee, and not necessarily those of AT&T. Parts of this chapter were published in "Please hold, I think my house is on fire," *People and the Workplace* (U.S. General Services Administration: Office of Governmentwide Policy—Office of Real Property, 2001).

In the not-so-distant past, the typical Bell System district manager could drive (or even walk) the full physical area for which he was responsible in a few hours. As third-line managers whose focus was upward, toward the higher reaches of the organization, district managers experienced little or no contact with the workers who reported to their "direct reports" (supervisors or foremen), and they liked it that way. Those days are gone.

BACKGROUND

AT&T has been a leader in advancing telework opportunities since the early 1990s, and more than a decade later the number of AT&T teleworkers continues to climb. By 2000, more than half (56 percent) of their managers teleworked at least one day per month, and 27 percent of all company teleworkers did so at least one day per week. Eleven percent of AT&T managers teleworked full-time, conducting their business in virtual offices at their homes or elsewhere. That increase was accompanied by a significant decrease (from 40 percent to 25 percent over two years) in formal, scheduled telework arrangements. Most of the increase has been attributed to corporate flexibility in terms of the creation of episodic, unscheduled telework options and informal arrangements that encouraged the creative use of time, space, and personal preferences. This trend corresponds with similar trends in the federal government, as documented by the Department of Labor.

Gregory T. Simpson, district manager of International Marketing within AT&T's Data and Internet Services organization, is a working example of the typical telemanager. Greg has worked for AT&T since 1992 when he joined AT&T as an account executive in the Manhattan Commercial Markets sales branch. Greg was hired initially as a virtual office employee and worked from an apartment on Manhattan's Upper East Side for over a year. He then joined AT&T's Global Services organization and was promoted into AT&T's International Network Services organization where he served as an offer manager, and later a marketing manager. Greg was subsequently recruited to serve as the executive assistant to a sales vice president in Manhattan who had branches reporting to her from Illinois, Texas, and Virginia. This led to his promotion to district manager in a customer care organization and later to an international marketing position in AT&T's Data and Internet Services group. Greg has maintained a functional home office throughout his tenure at AT&T and tries to work from home a few days each month.

In 1998, Simpson accepted a promotion to district manager in AT&T's Service Provider Markets Customer Care organization. His work included leading the ordering, provisioning, and maintenance centers, project management teams, a process engineering team, and a group of program managers. His team was located across the United States and, as a telemanager, Simpson had direct reports who were also telemanagers managing teleworkers. In this position, he had eight direct reports, each of whom also had up to a dozen people reporting to them.

FAIRY TALES CAN COME TRUE: BUILDING A GOOD TELEMANAGER

A misleading myth that has spread throughout the telework community is that, in a riff on Gertrude Stein's famous words, "A good manager is a good manager is a good manager." This could not be farther from the truth in the case of telemanagement. Traditionally, a good manager plays multiple roles (interpersonal, informational, decisional) and fulfills several functions (planning, organizing, leading, controlling). To perform these functions and play these roles, the manager needs to develop certain conceptual, human relations, and technical skills (Mintzberg 1972). According to management theorist Henry Mintzberg, a manager's roles can be deconstructed roughly as follows:

Interpersonal

1. Figurehead: represents the organizational unit in all matters of formality
2. Liaison: interacts with peers and others outside the organizational unit
3. Leader: provides guidance and motivation to the work group and defines the atmosphere of the workplace

Informational

4. Monitor: receives and collects information
5. Disseminator: transmits information within the organization
6. Spokesperson: disseminates organizational information outside the organization

Decisional

7. Entrepreneur: initiates change
8. Disturbance handler: mediates conflict, fills in for sudden departure of subordinates, handles special needs for customers

9. Resource allocator: decides where the organization will expend its resources
10. Negotiator: handles major nonroutine negotiations within and outside of the organization

These traditional roles are familiar, and some of them are, indeed, played by the telemanager. However, successful telemanagers handle these roles differently from traditional managers, using a different combination of the key conceptual, human relations, and technical skills. The job of telemanager requires an emphasis on a combination of five of the preceding roles: liaison, monitor/disseminator, and disturbance handler/negotiator. These roles are supported by highly developed technical and human relations skills.

Liaison

Making the team feel like a team. The earliest stage of team development—getting to know and accept one another—sets the tone for future interactions, and thereby plays a major role in assuring team success. Simpson's first goal in his new position was to meet his direct reports and shape this group of managers into a cohesive unit. Traditionally, this meant calling a meeting in the conference room, introducing yourself, listening to the introductions of others, and sharing your managerial philosophy. But a distributed workforce can make such meetings difficult to design, with one manager working in a cellar in Colorado, another in an attic in Florida, and a third in a room off her living room in California. Imagine having to meet and try to impress your new boss over the phone or to coordinate the new voices with the new names, differentiating between Sue and Suzanne, Jim and James, Bob and Robert. Where do you start?

The resulting teleconference bridge that was set up for the introductory meeting was only the beginning of a series of technological solutions that helped to cross time and space barriers. In order to ensure that everyone felt like they were part of the team, Simpson held weekly conference calls with his direct reports and required them to have weekly meetings with their own direct reports. He also set up a conference bridge for some celebrations such as birthdays that allowed remote employees to dial in and participate even though they could not attend in person and enjoy the cake.

Simpson hosted monthly conference calls/meetings with his entire district and brought them together twice each year for a face-to-face meeting that included training sessions. One of the challenges of the face-to-face meetings was to be able to have everyone travel to New Jersey for multiple days and still ensure that their work was being done and that client contact was not disrupted. This presented more problems than simply bringing everyone together in the conference room or auditorium. The solution was to extend the semiannual meeting by an additional day and provide the team members with several hours in the mornings and afternoons to do their work. Team meetings were held from 10:00 A.M. to 2:00 P.M. and again at 6:30 P.M. for dinner, leaving plenty of time for client contact in the morning and the afternoon.

Sometimes, it is about the technology. A collocated team ordinarily shares a voice mail system and thus has the ability to send broadcast voice mail messages to a distinct list of people or forward voice messages to one or more people. Initially, all AT&T teleworking employees were instructed to contact their local phone company for a voice mail service that callers could be sent to if the employee was either on the phone or away from the desk. As an unfortunate and unforeseen result, each team member had separate and isolated voice mailboxes.

In order to operate as a team, Simpson believed that his distributed team needed the same voice messaging capabilities as a collocated team would have. He worked with AT&T's technical support and arranged for all of his remote team members to have a voice mailbox on a single system in the building where he worked. He then instructed each of his remote employees to arrange for their calls to be sent to these remote mailboxes when they were on the phone or away from their desks.

This unique technical action gave his team the ability to send broadcast voice mail messages, but more importantly, it enabled them to forward actual messages left by customers, ensuring that information was received accurately. In addition, Simpson established email distribution lists so that he could target a specific manager and her team, his direct reports, or his entire district. The same lists were also used for voice mail broadcasts. The telemanager's ability to establish good lines of communication with remote workers is enhanced by a high comfort level with technology, and the telemanager's technical skills can shortcut the delays inherent in waiting on the line for tech support.

Monitor/Disseminator

A kick under the table. One of the advantages of having your team all sitting outside of your traditional office is that you can grab people from their desks if you need them. When a customer calls to find out something specific about an order, you can simply bring the person on your team who is responsible for the order into your office to speak to the client. This is not as easy when your team is spread across the country. The ability to leverage technology can help the telemanager to overcome this hurdle.

People who manage a project remotely spend a lot of time on conference calls, both internally and with the customer. What can be done when a manager calls someone who he knows is working from home and the person does not answer the phone? One method that Simpson used to reach remote employees while they were on conference calls was to send an email. Tied up on the conference call but sitting in front of their computers, Simpson and his team could communicate via email while remaining present on their conference call. This process is the modern day version of a kick under the table, whereby people can be told to stop speaking about a particular subject via email (or an instant message [IM]) without anyone else participating in the call being aware of the communication.

Making assumptions and orders of magnitude. The traditional manager can arrest mistakes in process, shortcut visible red tape, steer a co-worker clear of the business equivalent of pianos falling out of sixth floor windows. But when a manager does not see the conditions of a worker's workplace, it becomes difficult to protect that worker from egregious errors or obvious (to the manager) missteps. An employee who normally worked in the same office as Simpson opted to work from home one day in order to wait for a repairman. Not being experienced in telework and unfamiliar with wireless phone charges, he decided to dial in to the network on his home line with his laptop. This was fine because there was a toll-free number. He also decided that he could use his corporate calling card to make business calls and that would be free too, because he first dialed in to a toll-free number.

This would ordinarily have been an acceptable scenario. However, the worker did not have two phone lines in his house, so he used his personal wireless phone for the calling card calls. He was unaware of the fact that calls to toll-free numbers are not toll-free when dialed on a wireless phone. After spending the whole day talking on his personal wireless phone with his corporate calling card and using his home phone line for his laptop, he was quite proud of himself. He was less so when he received his wireless phone bill for that day and realized that he had racked up $350 in charges to the toll-free number for his corporate calling card. Clearly, some additional instructions from his manager, some sharing of information, would have helped. The informational role of monitor/disseminator requires that the telemanager accept responsibility for clarity and precision in communication prior to sending anyone to work at a remote site, in order to avoid just such costly and unnecessary errors.

Disturbance Handler/Negotiator

Why is my boss mad at me? People who work in a traditional environment see their managers who work in the same building, say hello to them in the hallways, meet them for lunch in the cafeteria, ride the elevator with them, and share the small events of life on a regular basis. In sharp contrast, often the only contact that a teleworker may have with her manager is a short email message that she sends or brief voice mail message. Therefore, managers of remote workers must make an extra effort to recognize the integral role that socializing plays in the manager-employee relationship.

When he first started managing his team, Simpson sent brief email messages to team members to ensure that specific items were being taken care of. After a short period, he began to hear rumblings from some of his employees who thought that he was angry at them. They were naturally confused because he did not seem displeased when they spoke with him—he was actually quite sociable. But Greg's non-chatty style was misinterpreted by teleworkers who were highly sensitized to the personal touch of collocated relationships and didn't relate easily to the electronic style of communication. This sensitivity to the brief, no-nonsense world of email communication has caused problems in many organizations, some of which have banned the use of email and moved to direct telephone calls when it appears that controversies are arising (Moss Kanter, 2001).

Simpson did not abandon email, but he changed his style when sending messages to remote employees. His work-related emails now begin with a personal reference ("How is your son doing?" for example) before getting down to business. This expedient has helped keep teleworkers' morale at the same level as those in an office who socialize with others throughout the day.

Close to the customers. One of the real benefits of having a geographically dispersed team is the enhanced ability to serve clients through local support. The challenge occurs when there are a disproportionately large number of clients in one region, but the team is evenly distributed across the entire service area. Client concerns about receiving support from a distant part of the country in a different time zone tend to increase congruent to the physical distance of the team from the clients' geographic location.

This fear can be overcome by showing them that the teleworkers do, in fact, complete several hours of work after the clients' business day ends or before it begins. Someone in the same time zone as the client can serve as an emergency backup person in case a problem arises when the designated support person is not working. In order to balance the workload, Simpson assigned a program manager in Colorado to support a client in Connecticut. The client in New Haven initially had some concerns that issues that arose early in the day would have to wait until the workday started in Denver, but this resistance was overcome when

Simpson assigned a program manager in New Jersey to address any urgent matters that arose prior to the start of the business day in Colorado. The emergency backup worked; the client never voiced any concerns thereafter about being unable to reach the appropriate individual.

IT'S THE SKILLS THAT MAKE A TELEMANAGER SUCCESSFUL

Clearly, the telemanager needs to develop a specific set of skills to support the roles just described. Instead of focusing on control, on finite projects, on monitoring behavior, and on the technical expertise of help desks and others as did the traditional manager, the telemanager's focus is on building trusting relationships, developing personal and professional creativity, creating a sense of comfort with ambiguity, being a clear communicator via several media, establishing a high level of technical competence in oneself, and maintaining as a primary goal the reciprocated interest that results from the growth and development of Direct Reports and their participation in big picture corporate goals. In fact, the telemanager resembles nothing so much as the project manager, a person who traditionally follows a project from start to finish. Some futurists have suggested that *all* managers will fulfill this role in the new economy (Pink, 2001).

How Can I Tell Whether They're Working?

One of the concerns that frequently arises among telemanagers is how anyone can be sure that the people working from their homes are in fact working and not napping, watching TV, or sunning themselves. Frequent articles in the popular press reinforce the impression that people who have business to perform outside the office are likely to be goofing off while the in-office worker is slaving away under the watchful eye of the manager (Coulacos Prato, 6/24/01). A sense of distrust and suspicion is fostered, destroying the delicate fabric of the team relationship and limiting the growth of social capital.

One answer to this concern suggests a revival of "management by objectives" (Drucker, 1954) where mutually agreed upon goals are set and performance against those goals is measured. MBO, although difficult to implement unless there is full support from the top of the organization and total commitment to annual review of organizational goals, has proven to be highly effective as a short-term measurement and evaluative process.

MBO is based on four behavioral principles (feedback, participation, reward, and reciprocated interest) that indicate a direct correlation between motivation to perform and performance levels. This suggests a developmental approach to appraisal, providing opportunities for feedback from the manager prior to the final appraisal for the year, the participation of the worker in establishing the performance goals for the period, a desirable reward at the successful conclusion of a year's objectives, and the design of personal, career-based objectives that mesh well with the corporate goals as determined at the head of the organization. Trust also plays a large role in this arena as well as knowing how much work you are asking someone to do and how much is actually getting done. It's no surprise that a great many team-building exercises involve blindfolds, falling, and trust in others. It is this trust that allows for the development of the relationships that create the social capital that is so crucial to the attainment of goals, especially in a remote environment (Lipnack & Stamps, 2000). A full discussion of social capital and organizational culture can be found in Chapter 11.

I Recognize the Voice but Can't Place the Face—Promotion from Afar

An additional skill that telemanagers must learn is how to develop others. It has been accepted within the arena of global management for more than a decade that successful global managers make recruiting, training, and developing talented workers a priority (Bartlett & Ghoshal, 1992). The management of workers transnationally does not differ to any significant degree from the management of a remote workforce within one country. The identification and development of skilled and talented employees is a essential factor in the long-term viability of a telework program.

It is not uncommon for people to move up the ladder within a large office of a traditional organization because they have worked closely with other people and have been exposed to managers other than their own. It is not always possible for teleworkers to have such networking opportunities, and they may therefore be overlooked when it comes time for promotions or other opportunities, especially if they are located in an area where the company does not have any offices. One of the workers in Simpson's district took matters into her own hands. She reported to one of Greg's managers, who seemed uninterested in helping her develop her career, so she called Simpson one day and asked him, "What are you going to do to get me promoted?"

This was an intrepid move for someone that Simpson had never spoken to before nor had had any career discussions with. The traditional district manager, or "district manager past," would have been shocked by the boldness of this action, as it violated the sanctity of the chain of command and the scalar relationships that are so beloved of traditional organizations. But telemanagers need to learn how to relate to people both several levels up and down within the organization on a less formal basis. After he was able to determine the worker's qualifications and her career goals, Simpson was able to help her. The worker, located in Oklahoma City where AT&T does not have a large presence, was frustrated by her apparent lack of career opportunities. After speaking to one of his peers who managed a product management district in New Jersey, Simpson learned that his colleague was having difficulty filling positions that had opened as a result of other workers' having taken advantage of the voluntary retirement program, creating a shortage of qualified people at headquarters.

Simpson's colleague, like many others in New Jersey, was not intending to fill any of his open positions with remote employees. However, after talking about the benefits of hiring someone for a product management position who had experience implementing his product, he saw the benefit of promoting the Oklahoman. This teleworker could offer good value to the company even if she was in Oklahoma City while the rest of his team was in New Jersey. This manager now has a few other members of his team who work remotely as well.

Dealing with Realities

The traditional manager need know nothing at all about the personal lives of her direct reports, but the telemanager often knows more than she wants to. The development of a high comfort level with knowing "too much" about events that are occurring outside the office is a valuable skill for the telemanager. One evening, Simpson was on the phone with one of his virtual office employees when she mentioned that she smelled smoke. The worker was not terribly concerned, because her high school-aged daughter was upstairs in the kitchen.

As Simpson and she chatted about business, the worker indicated that the smoke smell seemed to be getting a little worse. She shouted up to her daughter from her basement office to see what was going on and returned to the phone in a panic, asking Greg to hold because her daughter was not answering and she thought that her house was on fire. She set the phone down and Simpson heard her continue to call for her daughter as she ran up the stairs. All he could think of was whether he should call 911. Before long, the worker was back on the phone with the full story: her daughter had started to make macaroni and cheese and then went into her room to listen to music. She forgot about the pot on the stove and could not hear her mother yelling over the CD player. Luckily, the fire was not serious, but it could have been worse if the mother were in a traditional office, miles away from home instead of in the basement. And Simpson himself had to be prepared to respond to this potential emergency from another state. Knowing your employees has taken on a new definition in the virtual organization—there is little that can be classified as "too much information" if it helps to build a trusting and lasting relationship.

Counterintuitive Problem Solving

As in most large companies, at AT&T supplies are purchased centrally in order to ensure volume discounts and cost-effective purchase of commonly used office products. Pallets of printer/copier paper are purchased at a substantial discount by the central purchasing department. When dealing with a distributed workforce, however, such traditionally successful strategies work less well—it may cost more to ship a ream of paper to a remote employee than the ream of paper costs. Creative thinking is required to solve problems that run up against the wall of tradition. By the simple expedient of bypassing the standard procedure, Simpson installed a new process by which teleworkers and remote employees could gain approval to purchase supplies on their own from approved vendors and avoid the added shipping expenses.

People who work in small organizations or in nontraditional, organic business structures may smile at the simplicity of this solution, but for those who work in large, extended, formal, traditional businesses, solutions like these are not easy to implement. They require that the telemanager not be bound by what has been acceptable in the past, but find a way to creatively adapt appropriate existing processes to handle the needs of a changing work environment while working within the confines demanded by the size of the organization.

At the end of the day, bypassing traditional methods, rules, and procedures may be the appropriate behavior of telemanagers committed to improving the effectiveness of their direct reports and the efficiency of their organizations. MBO can help to establish personal guidelines for action for both the telemanager and his staff because, according to the original intent of Drucker's philosophy of management by objective, all objectives are managerial by nature.

And, at the beginning of the new day, all managerial objectives need to have a component that empowers workers to do their jobs wisely and effectively. According to Rosabeth Moss Kanter (2001), "The 'stickiest' work settings (the ones people leave less frequently and more reluctantly) involve opportunity and empowerment" (206). Opportunity and empowerment provide a framework on which to hang a series of motivational tools that focus on a bigger picture than the traditional carrot and stick served to support. Moss Kanter (1989a) suggests these five: helping people believe in the mission; allowing high performers to select their own projects; providing opportunities for learning; publicizing people's successes to enhance their reputations; and sharing in the value created by their own efforts. All of these tools require that the manager respect the needs of the workers as well as the needs of the corporation.

SUCCESS BREEDS SUCCESS . . . OR DOES IT?

As we have seen, the telemanager acts as linchpin in a delicate balancing process and is clearly the key to a successful remote work environment. We noted in the beginning of this chapter that the goal of effective telemanagement is to make it look like nothing unusual is happening. But something is happening, and we would wisely pay attention to it.

What is happening is this: The telemanager is running smack up against internal and external resistance, resistance that can easily upset the delicate balance established through the development of trusting relationships, professional empowerment, clear communication, appreciation of creativity and innovation, and technical expertise. Without conscious effort at maintaining stability in the face of a changing work environment, the unnatural acts described in the previous chapter can derail the telemanagement process.

Peter Senge has been a leader in popularizing managerial understanding of systems theory, a full discussion of which appears in his book *The Fifth Discipline* (1990) as well as in Chapter 5 of this volume. The telemanager can readily apply lessons from systems theory to understand the balancing process inherent in managing remotely. Senge (1990) says,

> Whenever there is "resistance to change," you can count on there being one or more "hidden" balancing processes. Resistance to change is neither capricious nor mysterious. It almost always arises from threats to traditional norms and ways of doing things. Often these norms are woven into the fabric of established power relationships. The norm is entrenched because the distribution of authority and control is entrenched. Rather than pushing harder to overcome resistance to change, artful leaders discern the source of the resistance. They focus directly on the implicit norms and power relationships within which the norms are embedded. (88)

Examine the elements of resistance identified in Chapter 7. Each of the top ten causes of resistance to telework has its origins in the threat of shaking up the status quo, changing the way we live and work, and upsetting the balance of power with which we have become familiar after more than a century of modern business. Successful managers regularly address the challenge of introducing something new into their environments. Teleworking provides them a new opportunity to exercise their creativity in facilitating change.

9

Telework and Families

The impacts of telework on the social fabric of our lives and on our family/work balance raise some red flags of concern for social scientists. Research in public sector and private industry has indicated both positive and negative implications of telework for individuals and for families, although the bottom line impact of telework for companies has always been positive (Pratt, 1999). Despite the best intentions of government and business human resource specialists, blurring the boundaries between work and home can have a significant impact on families. The loss of control over personal space, diminished human interaction among workers, and the creeping and ever expanding universe of work that may impinge on the personal lives of workers threaten widespread acceptance arrangements, even among its supporters.

Demographic and social changes have dramatically altered the composition and needs of today's workforce. The notion of the family-friendly workplace has evolved as a response to these changes. Telework is often included as a component of such workplaces. In common with any technology-enabled innovation, telework has the potential to result in both benefits and costs. The challenge remains to ensure that the benefits accrue to both workers and their families as well as organizations while the potential downsides are recognized and minimized. This chapter seeks to highlight the mixed outcomes that currently ensue from teleworking arrangements.

THE FAMILY-FRIENDLY WORKPLACE

We are living in a new world—a world driven by technology, dominated by access to information, and connected by electronic relationships. This 24/7/365 world presents great opportunities for achievement and frightening potential for individual malfunction. The extension of the workday and blurring of the home/work division, the rise in employment of women resulting in the prevalence of the two-income family, and a general fascination with electronic technologies and access to information via the Internet, facilitated by inexpensive, improved bandwidth have created a home life without privacy, a business life without downtime, a social life without quiet, a life of universal availability that is the natural result of our devotion to connections.

In 1994, President Clinton issued a directive to all federal agencies to establish a "family friendly" workplace that would aid in recruiting and retaining an effective workforce for the government. The family-friendly workplace would serve as a leveling mechanism to make federal employment competitive with private sector employment, despite the lower wages associated with the former. This occurred as the economy was soaring upward, taking workers to higher income levels with it.

The essence of the family-friendly workplace can be expressed as the development of programs that make it easier for workers to integrate the needs of family with the demands of work. Such programs include flexible work schedules and locations, leave programs, job-sharing or part-time employment, employee assistance programs, on-site child care, elder care, referral and informational services, and, of course, telework (www.workandfamily@opm.gov). Many of these programs had been accepted by the private sector over the preceding decade as appropriate additions to enhance the quality of work life (QWL) and to retain the services of the ever more demanding high-tech worker and ever more stressed baby boomer with aging parents and school-aged children.

Since the 1970s, futurists have warned about the potential social dangers associated with uncontrolled economic growth and purely econocentric national policies (Toffler, 1970). Toffler reported with sorrow about the lack of " 'social indicators' to tell us whether the society, as distinct from the economy, is also healthy. We have no measures of the 'quality of life.' We have no systematic indices to tell us whether men [sic] are more or less alienated from one another" (455). National surprise and concern resulted in a set of reforms and innovations in the workplace that addressed Toffler's fears. Recommendations for autonomous work groups, integration of support functions, challenging job assignments, job mobility and rewards for learning, facilitative leadership, lowest-level decision making, self-government to the greatest extent possible, and the minimization of differential status symbols were designed to improve society's health (O'Toole, 1973). In addition, the normalization of the single parent family, one of the legacies of poorly implemented but well-meaning social policy, created a series of unanticipated economic and social consequences for subsequent generations. We have not moved much further in a quarter of a century to solve these problems.

Fifteen years later, the Hudson Institute emphasized that "a thoroughgoing reform of the institutions and policies that govern the workplace [is needed] to insure that women can participate fully in the economy and that men and women have the time and resources needed to invest in their children" (Johnston & Packer, 1987, xxv). They further suggested that improvements in health care, pensions, and unemployment insurance that address the issues of dynamism in an aging workforce, and in reconciling the demands of women, work, and families through "flexible hours, the use of sick leave to care for children, more part-time work, pregnancy leaves for mothers and fathers and other . . . necessary changes in the structure of work that will accommodate the combination of work and family life" should be the top priorities of the nation during the last decade of the twentieth century.

Quality of work life. When we talk about quality of work life (QWL), we are talking, in part, about a response to the foregoing suggestions, which were taken very seriously both by government and by industry. Quality of work life originated in the theory of sociotechnical systems (STS), developed by Eric Trist and Fred Emory. Trist, a British researcher in the United States, used the term sociotechnical systems to describe "the interaction of people (a social system) with tools and techniques (a technical system)" (Weisbord, 1987, 143). Critically, the interaction was deemed intentional, not accidental, and spoke directly to choices made in the context of economic, technological, and human values. These choices both describe and define our society today, just as they did in the 1970s. The original research that stimulated the development of this theory was performed in the South Yorkshire coal mines after World War II. The thrill Trist experienced in discovering the existence of self-regulating work teams and leaderless groups in the mines facilitated by rapidly advancing technological improvements was duplicated in other locations and by other research teams, all of which held similar value sets in esteem. They all focused on the concept of teams, of group work, and of the benefits of community.

But times change and values change. Fifty years later, our social values reflect less interest in community and a much greater focus on the individual. Sociotechnical designers sought "to broaden each person's knowledge of social and economic consequences, and to encourage each worker in developing a range of skills needed to get results. They treated the work system, rather than discrete tasks, as the unit of analysis. The work group, not each person, became the focus for change. Sociotechnical principles called for internal regulation, each person monitoring and helping achieve group goals" (Weisbord, 1987, 154). Some sociologists and social commentators of the early twenty-first century are decrying this loss of community, "Indeed, of all the domains of social and community connectedness surveyed in this book, systematic long-term evidence on workplace-based connections has proven the most difficult to find. Many of us today have friends at work, but it is unclear whether we are more likely to have friends at work than our parents did" (Putnam, 2000, 87). Others are applauding it as a response to the overfocus of the past on the demands of the workplace: "And since no position is permanent—but other positions are usually available and destitution is not around the bend—you might as well enjoy what you do. Produce quality work that's a genuine reflection of who you are. Use your freedom to accept responsibility for your work. Decide for yourself what constitutes success. And if you're not having fun—at least some of the time—you're doing something wrong" (Pink, 2001, 83). The concept of "fun in the workplace," although endemic to American culture, cannot be considered a universal value, or even one to which most workers can aspire.

More than thirty years ago, Peter Drucker (1970) described three quarters of the U.S. workforce as knowledge workers, and in the intervening years we have seen these workers use technology on an ever-increasing basis. And many of these workers are in production-style jobs that masquerade as "knowledge" work. The increase in the use of advanced technology in today's workplace and the rise of the two wage-earner family generate not only the need for more flexible work styles and work schedules, but the ability to provide them as well. These two elements come together in the telework configuration, a concept that seems an ideal match for the new worker.

The U.S. federal government has endorsed various forms of telework for government employees (Vega & Brennan, 2000b), and new legislation has been proposed to support expanded efforts to encourage federal workers to participate in the telework movement. In February 2001, the Office of Personnel Management instructed department and agency heads to remove barriers to telecommuting, identify positions that would lend themselves to telework, and to offer employees in those positions the opportunity to work from an alternate location. The goal was to "ensure that 25 percent of the federal workforce is participating in telecommuting programs at least part of the time by April 2001" (Ballard, 2001). Representative Frank Wolf (R-Virginia) has emphasized the importance of telework to federal employees and to their families on numerous occasions, claiming that "telecommuters are more productive, are happier and are spending more time with their families."

In the late twentieth century, QWL came to refer primarily to the amount of time workers could obtain away from the job, rather than the intrinsic pleasures of developing on-the-job relationships that sustain us away from our families. In the twenty-first century, work itself has become ever more integrated with our family lives, bringing with it the potential impact of disintegrating the life of the family.

THE EVOLVING AMERICAN FAMILY

The American family of the twenty-first century is smaller and less common a living arrangement than it has ever been. Since 1970, the traditional family consisting of married couples with children has decreased from 40.3 percent of the population to only 24.1 percent of the population in 2000, during an increase in total U.S. households over the same period from 63 million to 105 million. The greatest loss in household numbers (a household is the one or more people who live in a housing unit) was in the largest households, those with five or more people (from 21 percent to 10 percent), and the greatest gain in household numbers was in the smallest households, those with one person or just two people living together (from 46 percent to 59 percent). Perhaps most telling of all, households with children under age 18 decreased from 45 percent of all households in 1970 to only 33 percent in 2000 (Fields & Casper, 2001).[1]

During this same time frame, single-parent families began to thrive, with single-mother families increasing from 3 million in 1970 to 10 million in 2000 and single-father families from under 400,000 in 1970 to 2 million in 2000. Married couple families with children declined from 87 percent in 1970 to 69 percent in 2000 (of a total of 37 million family groups).

In 2000, most of the married couple families lived in the suburbs (55 percent), the overwhelming majority of which (82 percent) owned their own homes. In contrast, most of the single-father families (52 percent) and single-mother families (56 percent) lived in the central cities and significantly fewer owned their own homes (58 and 49 percent). The married couple families were older than the single-parent families and, not surprisingly, had higher educational attainment, with 29 percent having graduated college compared to 13 percent.

Why are these things so?

[1] All population data in this section are from the same source at the U.S. Census Bureau.

You can blame it on the women. As we were warned in the 1970s and 1980s, women were to have a significant impact on the workforce and society of the future. Several factors contributed to this impact: women's legal control over procreation allowed them the autonomy to plan family size, and the consequent smaller families made fewer home life demands on women (Reich, 2000), or at least made the demands over a shorter period of time. In addition, trailblazing women have opened up challenging and interesting jobs for other women, creating a series of new markets for college educated workers. More women than ever are enrolled in colleges, increasing the pool of available workers and limiting the time those workers have to heed the demands of their biological clocks. Consequently, women's options have expanded dramatically over the 30-year period, and women have recognized that in order to "have it all," they must postpone certain activities while pursuing others.

And you can thank the women for it. At the same time, the movement of American society from a production focus to a service economy created a decline in income for blue-collar American men. Unwilling to live "deprived" lives, their wives went to work in great numbers, albeit at lower salaries than the men, in an attempt to fulfill the promise of the American dream—a standard of living that meets personal expectations (Reich, 2000). This promise of a higher standard of living and being able to participate in achieving it decreased the appeal of remaining at home, even among those women who preferred the more traditional housewifely life.

But traditional roles shift with time and practice; what was radical in 1950 became old-fashioned in 1970. What was revolutionary in 1990 will become traditional by 2010.

Continuing debates. These changes have revived and inspired discussion on three ongoing debates: the needs of individuals versus the needs of families; the needs of families versus the needs of business; and the needs of business versus the needs of society. Curiously, these components of life are often portrayed as hostile relationships rather than cooperative partners. There has been little suggestion of the creative tension in these relationships that could offset the natural, second-order consequences of change.

The increase in satisfaction of the needs of individuals, such as single parents or women seeking self-actualization through career challenges, has created stresses on the traditional family that have been part of the shift to smaller living groups. These smaller living groups then find that they are unable to find the time to both work at their demanding jobs and fulfill all the maintenance tasks of the earlier family model, including child care, elder care, cooking, and cleaning. These tasks are out-sourced to external providers (baby-sitters, agencies, assisted living communities, restaurants, cleaning services), relieving the family heads from their responsibilities and creating growth in service industries (Reich, 2000).

This is good for business and for individuals, but bad for society, inasmuch as the new jobs tend to be low skilled and poorly paid. The workers in this segment of the new economy have little opportunity to self-actualize, let alone support themselves and their own families above the subsistence level. As a result, it has become harder and harder to find workers to fill the service jobs, and other solutions have been sought by business to solve the "problem" of the family. Flexibility has been seen as the solution—flexibility in workplace, in work hours, in technology, and in workers themselves.

Twenty years earlier, the suggestion had been made that 15 percent of the workforce would be employed part- or full-time at home, in the "electronic cottage."

> In some houses, perhaps the majority, we might well find couples dividing things up more or less conventionally, with one person doing the "job-work" while the other keeps house—he, perhaps, writing programs while she looks after the kids. The very presence of work in the home, however, would probably encourage a sharing of both job-work and housekeeping. We would find many homes, therefore, in which man and wife split a single full-time job. For example, we might find both husband and wife taking turns at monitoring a complex manufacturing process on the console screen in the den, four hours on, four hours off. (Toffler, 1980: 233)

Toffler proposed other configurations as well, including couples holding two different jobs, each spouse working separately in the home, or a couple holding two different jobs in the home and sharing both by alternating shifts. Any of these arrangements was destined to improve spousal relationships and family structures by increasing commitedness, the core of successful relationships. "Love Plus, the combination of sexual and psychological gratification plus brains . . . plus conscientiousness, responsibility, self discipline, or other work-related virtues" (235) was destined to shake the world, as illustrated by this gentle, self-mocking poem:

> I love your eyes, your cherry lips,
> the love that always lingers,
> your way with words and random blips,
> your skilled computer fingers. (235)

Real life has not worked out exactly this way; instead of sharing all the work (both housework and job-work), we have chosen to outsource and downsize. But, our belief about the core value of relationships remains the same —families are still committed to one another, spend considerable time under the same roof, reproduce, and support one another (Reich, 2000). And, at least one study has suggested that teleworkers manager their family lives "better" than traditional office workers (Pratt, 1999).

MIXED BLESSINGS FOR FAMILIES

Telework is one manifestation of this major social transformation and has been greeted with great enthusiasm by companies and workers, and with somewhat abated enthusiasm, tempered by concern over changing roles, by managers. Technology has rendered location both flexible and static—transactions can be conveniently and accurately completed via email and other electronic media from virtually any remote location, and advances in technology have incubated new work designs and have supported alternative work arrangements. Place is no longer viewed as playing a significant role in work process, and the impact of distributed work (as opposed to collocated work) is proving a mixed blessing for workers.

On the positive side of the ledger, we can count the following:

- Telework promotes employment in remote areas. Although statistics indicate that most teleworkers live in urban areas (www.workingfromanywhere.org), nonetheless many people in rural areas have significantly improved their quality of life and employability through work-at-home programs. Putnam Investments, America's fourth largest fund group (Healy, 2001), has maintained a telework program since 1990. As of 2001, more than 700 employees are working at home in a variety of positions. Many of the newer employees live in remote regions of Maine and Vermont, far from central cities with employment opportunities. For these workers, working at home is more than an option—it is a necessity. They often have a life style that does not permit for the extensive travel that would be required for steady work, yet they need a stable income to help level out the seasonal income earned through the fishing industry, agriculture, or craft/trade endeavors. They receive their formal training in a college near to their homes and never come into the main urban offices. The program is so popular that over 1,500 people applied for the first 50 jobs made available in Maine. Chapter 15 provides a full history of the development of Putnam's telework program.
- The U.S. federal government employs individuals all over the country, and, in many cases, the distance they must travel on a

daily basis in order to complete their tasks is formidable. Specifically, engineers and inspectors, coordinators and investigators, and others in similar jobs cannot perform their work without visiting sites that are often far from both their offices and their homes. The process of teleworking can allow them more efficient use of their time as well as preventing stress on both environment and individuals. Availability of telework arrangements is seen as a recruitment and retention benefit by the public sector, providing them a way to compete with private industry for talented and skilled personnel.

- Telework provides a sense of freedom to those members of the workforce whose work hours are circumscribed by needs of family. One worker interviewed in Putnam's Maine workforce described it like this: "Well, the main reason [I came to work here] was their work at home program because I am a mother of four children and I home school them as well. I really need a job that had flexibility and this position had great flexibility in that I work . . . that I start my job early in the morning at four and I work flexible hours and typically I'm done by between 9:00 am and noontime or so."

- A project manager at R.F. Weston, an international environmental engineering firm, made similar comments in an interview on his cell phone while he was pumping out his basement after heavy rains created flooding in his area. He had taken advantage of the flexible working arrangements to deal with this home-related problem and to be closer to the hospital where his mother was recovering from an illness. Despite these personal needs, he was able to continue his project management responsibilities, including supervising his engineering team and coordinating a project several hundred miles away.

- Teleworking may provide more autonomy for workers, especially women, than do traditional work environments. As indicated by a study conducted for the book *Ask the Children* and reported to the U.S. Department of Labor (Galinsky & Kim, 2000, 256), two related benefits of telework for parents are the provision of "relatively more autonomy for mothers and relatively more learning opportunities for fathers." This study is based on a survey of both parents and children of teleworking and nonteleworking parents, and had some surprising findings, as reported later.

- Work itself may mean something different when performed in a telework environment. Instead of being paid for hours on the job, many teleworking positions reward workers for output and for task completed. This change is likely to create a sense of satisfaction in the work itself, which is often absent from technology-supported employment (Casimir, 1999).

On the negative side, telework presents some significant debits to the personal balance sheet.

- Perhaps the gravest concern for teleworkers themselves is the way in which the existing literature treats benefits to teleworkers. In nearly all the academic and practitioner studies that have been produced in this field, the benefits to teleworkers are defined in terms of the benefits to companies, assuming a reciprocity of interest that may not exist. Actual benefits to the workers themselves are provided in a throwaway style that degrades their importance to the overall movement and treats worker needs as a necessary adjunct to business success rather than as a prerequisite of acceptable employment practices.
  - One 43-page paper details the benefits to employees as follows: "The employee-related benefits of telework that we consider include those benefits an organization receives as a result of having more satisfied employees. These benefits result from the improved work-life balance that telework provides employees and the benefits teleworkers receive (reduced commute time, lower stress, more time with family, ability to meet family care needs, better ability to meet work demands, etc.)" (Kunkle, 2000, 21).
  - Another paper suggests that reduced absenteeism is a benefit of primary concern to workers, and "because of telework, employees can manage their work and family lives with greater flexibility than if they could not" (Pratt, 1999, 26). Of course, these things are true, but do the benefits accrue to the employee or to the employer?
  - The year 2000 Telework America study claimed, "For the most part, teleworkers indicated that the availability of telework would be very to extremely important if they were to seek a new job. The only area in which this was less the case was for teleworkers with 6 months or less experience. . . . Job satisfaction is related to these answers. Although the great majority of home-teleworkers replied that their job satisfaction was unchanged or improved, a few noted decreased job satisfaction since they began teleworking" (Nilles, 2000, 34–35), proving only that people can get used to any working arrangement if they must.
- Telework tends to blur all boundaries between work and home, but most obviously the physical boundary. Most home offices are spaces carved out of the family room or some other location that was originally shared space. When computers, telephones, fax machines, and other technologies are supplied by the employer for use at home by the employee, these machines are generally off-limits for personal or private use. The space that was family shared

space becomes working space for Mom or Dad, the den becomes an office, doors get closed, confidential materials litter home surfaces, and the phone rings at odd times during the day or night. A typology of work spaces presented by WorkSmart 1996 shows a 10-step evolution of modern offices, as follows:

- Fixed offices and the bullpen
- Integrated systems furniture (egalitarian cubicles)
- Universal plan (cubicles of varying standardized sizes)
- Home-based telework
- Telework centers (community based)
- Non-territorial offices (hoteling)
- Found alternative workplaces (coffee houses, hotel rooms, cars, etc.)
- Designed alternative workplaces (office clubs, copy shops, etc.)
- Team offices (movable office configurations to accommodate teamwork)
- Integrated workplace strategies (integration of all the preceding models to optimize performance) (Kunkle, 2000).

It would appear that many organizations have reached the final step and have determined that it is in their best interest to use the homes of employees as satellite offices, with the result that "home is no longer a haven from paid work; the border between the two is vanishing. . . . Sometimes [workers] travel so much, they have no settled place of work but only temporary 'hot desks' in a variety of locales" (Reich, 2000, 100).

- Children may become unwitting coworkers of teleworking parents. Although children of teleworking mothers do not feel shunted aside by their parent, children of teleworking fathers feel that their father puts work ahead of family more often than children of nonteleworking fathers. Both teleworking mothers and fathers put more hours into work per week than their nonteleworking counterparts (over 50 hours per week for both mothers and fathers) (Galinksy & Kim, 2000). The charming picture of days gone by of little Jane or John pulling threads near the sewing machine as mother or father put in long hours at piece-work is less charming when drawn with today's child coloring pictures on discarded printouts near the home computer.
- Workers become particularly alert to the perception by coworkers of being off duty when they are supposed to be on call, of talking to customers while wearing nonbusiness attire, of being controlled by their work. One manager commented that he "knows people who roll out of bed, turn the computer on, decide to respond to 'just one e-mail' and, before they know it, it is afternoon and they have not showered, eaten, or stopped working since they started

at 6:00 am. . . . [It] often happens to diligent workers that the work pulls them in, engages them, and they work harder and harder, driving themselves relentlessly." Although another manager in the same company has said, "As we move into the information age, it seems telework is actually a return to a more organic way of balancing work and family . . . blurry lines aren't bad" (Allenby, 2001), nonetheless there is significant evidence that blurry lines easily create abusive and intrusive work/home imbalances. Stories abound of workers who carry their cell phones into the bathroom or out to the mailbox lest supervisors think they are not working when they do not answer the phone. To be fair, there is little difference in the telework environment from the office environment when it comes to the case of overwork. Internet companies are likely to have a culture of "office as home," where work never ends, there is always something happening, and people may sleep on a couch in their offices. In this case, "the office is a place to live as well as work" (Moss Kanter, 2001, 50). Offices like that of Abuzz provide all the comforts of home—music, food, space for pets, community events, opportunities for service. Why go home?

- The loss of control over personal space may result from home telework environments. When workers agree to sell their labor in an isolated, technologically facilitated environment located in their own homes, they may forgo (often without being aware of it) their privacy and their autonomy. They accept a set of expectations that are designed primarily for corporate convenience and that often permit the interchangeability of employees described by function but undifferentiated by individual skills or needs (Vega & Brennan, 2000a). Their own needs may become overlooked; they become fungible in their positions and more malleable by managers and corporate interests. So insidiously has this factor entered the telework equation, that upbeat and otherwise clear-thinking individuals have endorsed the concept of fungibility by calling it "free agency" and making it a virtue rather than a drawback: "Instead of laboring in loneliness, free agents across America are inventing an array of new groups to replace the workplace communities many have left behind" (Pink, 2001, 124).

- In the case of public employees (and some private sector employees as well), they are not reimbursed for the use of their personal space for business work, nor can most employees deduct this space from their income taxes. In fact, some states have been billing teleworkers for state income taxes if their home is in a different state from their employer's location. New York State billed one worker $5,357 in state income taxes for working from his home office in Maine (Deibel, 2001). Expenses are borne by the worker in the public sector, and organizational savings are simply costs transferred to the employee. The U.S. General Services Administration Office of Governmentwide Policy Office of Real Property has designed a "Cost per Person Model" that helps government and private industry determine how much can be saved by using alternate work sites, including workers' homes, although they clearly state that "[T]elework is not in and of itself a means to the end goal of reduction of floor space and subsequent savings in rent bills" (2000, 17). In the 19th century, unions protected workers against such abuses; in the 21st century, no such protections exist. Workers are made to feel grateful that they are allowed to conduct someone else's business in their own homes and be monitored while they do so. This suggests the removal of workers' simple human dignity and their right to privacy.

- Devotion to the needs and commitments of the organization has a natural sociological origin in the work ethic that drives the American economy, as well as the economies of other countries where telework is increasing rapidly, such as Finland, the Netherlands, and Sweden.

However, at least in the Netherlands, some realistic precautions are taken by teleworkers to avoid such spillover. "Working at home aggravates the feeling that the work is never done. . . . While working at home, household tasks impose themselves upon the teleworkers. The dishes are sitting on the kitchen sink, asking to be washed, the laundry is waiting for treatment. . . . To get enough work done on the one hand and to guard themselves against too much work on the other, they [the study participants] write down the exact amount of hours worked, use fixed time schedules and fixed place to work. . . . Thus telecommuters reproduce the traditional labor division between paid and unpaid work. . . . Segmentation is used by career oriented families to prevent the private sphere to intrude into the work sphere, and by family oriented households to keep the work outside the private life. Segmentation is not only useful for the telecommuter him- or herself. It makes clear to others when this person is working, which means that it is also clear when he or she is free" (Casimir, 1999, 281–282).

- The creeping and ever expanding universe of work that is facilitated by technology may impinge on the personal lives of workers. Beepers, cell phones, fax machines, and other intrusions of business life into our homes and vehicles can leave us forever on call. It is the unusual individual indeed who is able to hear a telephone ringing and not answer it, even at dinnertime. Our desire to remain connected creates its own disconnection with our families and our sense of personal space. As social space and workplace begin to meld, work becomes indistinguishable from the rest of our lives and all sense of work/rest separation disappears. This connectedness is seen as a virtue by those who provide blanket endorsements of virtual workplaces, to wit: "Since it is physically impossible to be in two places at once in the face-to-face world, access to new places also used to mean that you had to leave old places behind. The electronic era suspends the Newtonian laws of motion. In cyberspace, people do not have to desert old places in order to access new ones. You can simultaneously be in numerous online places, join new groups while weaning yourself from old ones." (Lipnack & Stamps, 2000, 105). A certain frenzy is created that keeps us from ever resting, sitting still long enough to think, or appreciating the moment as it is.

The difficulty of knowing when to say "enough" to the demands of work, the development of methods of extricating oneself from the constant stimulation of electronic connection, and the personal strength to "pull the plug" when the workday is done are the new protections that teleworkers must develop. Balancing the intrusion of telework technology into our private lives with providing the opportunity to support our families, finding meaningful work, and protecting the environment is a compelling set of social challenges for the twenty-first century. The expansion of new methods of work, the development of new ways to combine family life and the provision of the necessities for that family life, can be the most crucial role played by technology today, moving such technologies from the debit side of the social ledger firmly to the credit side, worldwide.

10

Telework, Organizational Culture, and Institutional Learning

It has become trite to say that we do not like to change. Trite, but it is nonetheless true. Change demands that we examine our current behavior (our "theories in use"), and it is change that generates learning (or shifts in our "espoused theories"). According to Chris Argyris and Donald Schon (1974), developers of this concept:

> The complicated and difficult task of constructing (their) theories-in-use depends on simultaneously overcoming and altering the dynamics of the group in which (they) are trying to learn. No wonder that attempts to help individuals construct their theories-in-use evoke reactions ranging from bewilderment ("What *are* you asking us to do?") to dismay ("How will we ever create such a model?") to embarrassment ("I'd feel stupid saying it that way") to fear ("You're asking us to change the basis of our life") and to astonishment ("You mean you're asking us to redesign our culture?"). (1974, 38)

HOW WE LEARN

Learning has been the topic of numerous treatises in the area of education, psychology, neurology and other hard sciences, and management theory. We are fascinated by the concept of learning because it seems so mysterious: How is it that one day we do not know something and the next we do? The trip from total lack of awareness to the ability to analyze, create, and evaluate (Bloom, Mesia, & Krathwohl, 1964) is worthwhile examining if we want to understand the cultural changes that may be required as a secondary effect when telework programs are implemented.

Individual Learning

It is generally accepted that learning means, at the very least, the acquisition of knowledge and, at the next step, its application to solving problems. Therefore, we can consider that learning is a means to a specific end—we learn something in order to apply it rather than simply learning it for the sake of learning itself. In the world of education, students learn primarily in order to demonstrate that they have learned, justifying both the cost of their tuition and their absence from the world of work. When they do enter the working world, their approach to learning must change from passive to active, from learning in order to prove that they have learned to learning in order to perform their jobs more effectively and get raises and promotions, and the like. The learning environment becomes more challenging and less forgiving, and the academic learning skills that the learner has developed may not be effective tools in the acquisition of knowledge in the new environment.

The process of learning at work requires the ability to learn experientially, that is, to carry out an action, observe the effect of this action, reflect upon the action and its effect, recognize the general principle that governs the effect, and apply the action under a new circumstance (Kolb & Fry, 1975). This process repeats itself, each time improving the quality of the action taken. The result is learning. It works for technical problems: writing code, testing the program, considering how well it runs and deriving a standard protocol, and then testing again in a different program. It also works for human interactions: delegating a task, observing how it has been handled, reflecting on the effectiveness of the delegation, deriving a general rule for delegating that incorporates appropriate changes, then, delegating again in different circumstances.

Where it does not work, we can assume some problem in the environment itself. Perhaps failure is not an option in the specific learning environment or, more insidiously, perhaps success has become too appealing. In such a case, we may see an individual's first step down a path that becomes a series of subsequent actions that puts one's job, one's self-image, or one's psychological comfort at risk. When the stakes are this high, people are less willing to take risks; however, if they do not take risks, they cannot learn. They will have no opportunity to examine their espoused theories against their theories-in-use, or to consider whether their goals are congruent with the goals of their organization.

Espoused Theory. Our espoused theories, or our "theories of action," describe what we believe or what we say we believe about the way we act. Espoused theories tend to be politically and socially acceptable, well articulated and carefully thought-out. They tend to present us in a good light, perhaps a better light than we really merit. When asked about how we would behave under specific circumstances—such as "What is the impact of an applicant's attractiveness on your hiring decision for an office job?"—we are likely to insist that personal attractiveness plays no role in our wise and sensitive hiring practices. However, study after study indicates that personal physical attractiveness plays a significant role in hiring, and that people who are easy on the eyes tend to get hired quicker, get paid more, and get promoted faster as well (Nykodym & Simonetti, 1987). When asked about the amount of television we watch, we are likely to say that we watch the news, we watch a couple of special shows per week, and that's about it. However, Nielsen Media Research studies show that Americans watch 3 hours and 45 minutes of television each day. This surely accounts for more than our claim of occasional viewing can support. When questioned about our eating and fitness habits, we may insist that we eat healthy food like fresh fruit and vegetables—maybe even claiming that we ingest the U.S. government suggested five portions daily—and that we exercise on a regular basis. Why, then, are Americans in the worst physical shape they have ever been in? Why are we more obese than ever before? (See Satcher & Watkins, 1999).

Is it because we are incorrigible liars? No, these disconfirmations are the result of conflict between our espoused theories of action and our theories in use.

Theories in use. Theories in use describe the way we actually behave; when confronted with the examples just presented, we do discriminate in our hiring practices; we do watch television for many more hours each day than we estimate; and we eat fast food in enormous quantities and with depressing regularity, often while pursuing our sedentary pleasures.

It is pointless to ask people to describe their theories in use. The only way to determine what these theories are is to observe the behavior of the individual or group in question. For example, in Chapter 8 of this book I mentioned a popular suspicion about teleworkers and their tendency to goof off because no one is watching them. This attribution of behavior (a guess about the theories in use of teleworkers as a group) is far off the mark. In fact, telemanagers have reported cases of extreme conscientiousness, of teleworkers getting lost in their work and spending much more time at it than on-site workers normally do (Jackson, 2002; Pink, 2001; Vega & Simpson, 2001).

As in this example, when theories in use run counter to espoused theories, learning becomes problematic, and our ability to acknowledge the need for change is limited, as is our own awareness of our participation in this resistance. It is difficult for us to recognize our own theories in use because of the difficulty in articulating them. Looking at our behavior, we are likely to offer excuses, reasons, and rationalizations to account for the lack of congruence of our theories in use and our espoused theories; we are unlikely to reflect upon our actions and derive theories inductively from them. We may even try to fool ourselves as a protection from the admission of our own potentially misaligned behavioral responses. Although we may have tacit knowledge of our theories in use, we still encounter problems in making that knowledge explicit.

Institutional Learning and the Impact of Telework

If there is a real trick to learning, it is the ability to discuss our actions publicly, submitting them to the analysis of others and to our own time-distanced reflections. This process requires group involvement and openness in a protected (or safe) environment. When implemented in the prevailing organizational structures that value rationality, winning, and control, group discussion and self-reflection are likely to result only in single-loop learning—learning that reinforces existing relationships as well as "competitiveness, withholding help from others, conformity, covert antagonism, and mistrust, while deemphasizing cooperation, helping others, individuality, and trust" (Argyris & Schon, 1974, 83).

In contrast, when we are successful in double-loop learning, we succeed in changing the rules of the game rather than in reinforcing them. When the rules support the competitive type of actions described ealier, there is something to be said for overturning them and building a new set of precepts on which to base our behavior. In institutional settings, this common reluctance to confront theories in use and adapt them appropriately to new situations can easily inhibit organizational learning and can have a negative impact on productivity. Because it is human nature to reinforce one's own position and tend to discredit that of others, the various stakeholders dig in their heels and argue their position simply for the purpose of maintaining control, winning the argument.

An organization that engages in telework has provided evidence that it is willing to participate in double-loop learning—changing the rules of the game when they no longer seem to work to benefit the organization. Because telework itself creates a substantive change in the rules of engagement, of social intercourse, discourse, organizational communication and trust on all levels, the teleworking organization is likely to be a learning organization. In fact, even the consideration of the implementation of telework into the organizational structure requires us to open our minds to new methods, new goals, and new patterns of behavior. It requires us to cross system boundaries and closely examine organizational interactions, one of the powerful laws of the Fifth Discipline (Senge, 1990).

Ford Motor Company provides a good example of organizational learning generated by telework. Despite being the leader in automotive innovation in the early years of the automobile industry, and introducing several notable innovations over the course of three quarters of a century, Ford had a well-deserved reputation as a stolid, traditional, bureaucratic manufacturing organization. This old-economy company faced serious staffing problems during the mid-1990s, and traditional solutions proved ineffective in the face of employee requests for scaled-back hours, educational opportunities, and their desire to spend more time with their families.

A proposal was made for flextime, transitional work, and telework, and a pilot project was put into place in 1998. An automobile manufacturer supporting telework? Sounds ridiculous, self-defeating, and unlikely to gain senior management support, but based on the results of the yearlong pilot program, CEO Jacques Nasser approved the initiative. According to Ford's spokesperson, "Our upper management recognizes there are different ways to get work done than the traditional 9-to-5 or 7-to-midnight in the office. Now the focus is not on the means to the end, but the end, the objective" (Zbar, 8/30/01). Institutional learning was "forced" by telework, and the success of this innovation encourages openness to other new ideas in the future and to new ways of changing the rules. According to the experts, "long-term effectiveness depends on the possibility of double-loop learning" (Argyris & Schon, 1996, 96), so this indication of Ford's willingness to engage in double-loop learning speaks well of its future potential. But that potential is unlikely to be realized without sufficient social capital.

SOCIAL CAPITAL

Social capital includes all the resources that people bring to the table "through personal and business networks . . . information, ideas, leads, business opportunities, financial capital, power and influence, emotional support, even goodwill, trust, and cooperation" (Baker, 2000, 1). Of these, many claim that the most valuable are trust and cooperation or commitment (Grantham, 2000; Lipnack & Stamps, 2000; Putnam,

2000), often referred to as "generalized reciprocity," a transactional approach to communal relationships. It reflects a diluted version of the Golden Rule—we do something for others with the understanding that others will do for us when needed. Trust grows naturally in a society that looks out for the needs of others and subscribes to the moral norms of loyalty, dependability, and honesty (Fukuyama, 1995). The existence of trust in a society reduces the costs of doing business or of performing other transactions, because it reduces the drag on progress that suspicion generates. Therefore, even if only on a purely transactional level, trust is a critical commodity in the pursuit of organizational goals. An investment in the development of trust through the accrual of social capital accumulated from the social networks discussed in Chapter 4 can yield formidable returns.

The Impact of Telework on the Acquisition and Use of Social Capital

An individual's accretion of social capital depends, in large part, on the ability to be in touch with others, to be available for use, to stand ready to reciprocate. Nothing has been more instrumental in putting people in touch with one another than the telephone. As telecommunication methods become more sophisticated, the impact of the technological revolution that started with the operator-assisted telephone has connected each of us with more individuals that we could have imagined only fifty years ago. In our often idealized version of a simpler life style and idyllic reminiscences of relationships past, we accept without question that social ties were stronger then, friends were more dependable, and community life was bedrock firm. People lived in small neighborhoods, in close proximity to those who cared about them, in a self-contained universe of reciprocity and caring. Yet, the *Book of Home Building and Decoration* (1912) states unequivocally,

> There is probably no single form of modern convenience that has become as much of a necessity as has telephone communication between the home and outer world. In city, town, suburb, village and the open country, communication by telephone once established in a neighborhood quickly attests its claims to convenience and necessity and even the most skeptical are ready converts, after a short introduction to its wonders—for wonders they are even to those who are constantly in touch with the telephone. . . . Every progressive housekeeper fortunate enough to be able to afford a telephone, by which she may communicate with the trades people at any minute, realizes what a blessing this servant of electricity has become to mankind. In cases of illness, in troubles of any kind, aid and friends are so easily summoned that fear seems almost a thing of the past. (Stern and Gwathmey, 1994, 58)

From its very origin, the telephone was identified as a facilitator of relationships, and lauded as such. Jokes abounded about the number of hours spent on the phone by housewives, and later teenagers. These same jokes are updated today and focus on the number of hours spent surfing the Internet. The impact of the two activities seems to be similar—we connect with others in any way we can, and we seek this connection both urgently and compulsively. However, studies conducted in the late 1990s (Kraut, Lundmark, Patterson, Kiesler, Mukopadhyay, & Scherlis, 1998) suggested that the hours spent surfing the Net posed serious psychological threats to those who did so excessively. These threats included the inability to conduct normal social relationships and the subsequent limiting of personal interaction to computers and technologically mediated processes.

Although some of these concerns have been alleviated after several years' further observation, the question remains as to the type of relationships that are developed in electronic environments. Are people developing weak ties or strong ties (see Chapter 4), and what is the impact of telework on the acquisition of social capital? The current research in this area suggests that virtuality impedes the development of social capital, at least in work environments (Prusak & Cohen, 2001).

Social capital is created through shared values—that is, "social capital cannot be acquired simply by individuals acting on their own" (Fukuyama, 1995, 27). Values are shared through common interests, and common interests are expressed through personal association (Fukuyama, 1995: Putnam, 2000). This happens in local communities, in professional associations, in social groups, and at work. According to Prusak and Cohen (2001), "Social capital grows when team members meet face-to-face and work side-by-side" (88). Companies that make the effort to design ways for people to physically meet with each other are more likely to develop larger banks of social capital that can be invested in organizational learning, in attaining group goals, and in creating positive change.

Software has been developed that breaks the either/or mold of working in the office or losing control of your desk space when you work elsewhere. Web-based reservation systems allocate resources and office space on an as-needed basis for seamless communication (Weinberg, 8/27/02), and some companies have even designed "Touchdown Sites" to permit teleworkers to reserve their own physical spaces for meeting, working, and collaborating with others at the office (Zbar, 8/15/02). These physical structures help to generate the social structures that increase social capital (Orlikowski, 2000).

An interesting corollary to the commitment to developing strong social ties that will result in the social capital available for organizational improvement is competing research that suggests that strong ties inhibit creativity and stifle the very innovations that a learning organization is trying to foster (Florida, Cushing, & Gates, 2002). According to this research, the more connected we are with each other, the less able we are to expand our networks to include newcomers who may have different perspectives from ours. As a result, creative people avoid areas with strong social ties and seek out less cohesive locations that will permit them to pursue innovation. This suggests that the weaker ties developed through electronic communication can serve as incubators for the protection and expansion of creativity.

An organization makes this happen through change.

CREATING CHANGE

According to renowned psychologist and management consultant Edgar H. Schein, "The evidence is mounting that real change does not begin until the organization experiences some real threat of pain that in some way dashes its expectations or hopes" (Coutu, 2002, 105). This claim explains a great deal about the difficulty of creating positive change in organizations. Simply stated, it hurts.

Seventeen organizational factors that are inimical to change have been identified in the context of the public sector (Sugarman, 2000), but these are equally valid in the private sector. These factors get in the way of the organizational learning that is critical to the change process. They include:

- Blaming and finger-pointing occurs when errors are made.
- Failure means failure, rather than an unsuccessful risk.
- Attention to stakeholder interest allows external stakeholders the power to micromanage internal affairs.
- People dig in their heels and refuse to change, waiting out the current urgency until it passes.
- Senior managers micromanage operations.
- Dysfunctional organizational structures are frozen into the core of the business.
- Poor worker performance is neither censured nor improved.
- Accountability is weak, and workers feel helpless.
- Workers feel abused and taken advantage of.
- Workers doubt the expertise and dedication of their managers.
- Worker vision is limited and narrow.
- Information is not shared in a timely way.
- The mission is not accepted by all.
- Workers are not clear as to what their jobs entail.
- Customers feel they have no recourse for poor service.
- Competing stakeholder interests splinter organizational focus.

- Rapid turnover creates discontinuity and volatility.

We have encountered some of these factors before. For example, volatility has been coupled with virtuality as a key destroyer of social capital (Prusak & Cohen, 2001). Too much change too fast creates as many problems as too little change too slowly. Lack of accountability in the higher levels and pervasive fear in the lower levels of the organization run directly counter to the ability to learn, which requires risk and failure (Argyris & Schon, 1974). Lack of clarity in terms of mission and goals, job responsibilities, a fuzzy vision of the future, and perhaps most importantly, doubt about management's commitment and sincerity impede learning to such an extent that organizations that lack empathy find themselves at a severe disadvantage in global business relationships (McGill & Slocum, 1992).

Getting people past the pain of change is the responsibility of the organizational leadership. This process requires that the leader design, institute, and support appropriate learning processes that foster individual growth and personal mastery for all employees (Senge, 1990, 345). It also requires that the leadership develop a mission and vision that is clearly understood and can be accepted by all. Policies and strategies must be founded on a solid core of values, yet must remain flexible and adaptable in the face of global volatility. And people must take responsibility for their own actions. Telework can both facilitate and impede progress toward this ideal.

Telework as Impediment

One of the irksome byproducts of learning and change is the personal embarrassment felt by those who take public risks and fail, sometimes spectacularly. We look at those failures from our positions of safety and are relieved we did not [select from the following]: design that marketing campaign, hire that incompetent bumbler, write the code that caused the server to turn belly-up, erase the only copy of the annual financial report while trying to change the font, or something similiar. Yet all these errors are opportunities for personal and organizational learning—we amend our hiring practices, we institute new safeguards, we proofread more carefully, and we study the demographics more before we commit significant funds to publicity efforts. When distance separates coworkers from the results of their actions and from the well-meaning derision of their peers, however gentle, learning slows down. Telework can, thus, inhibit both the incremental and discontinuous changes that signal growth in an organization by protecting workers from direct constructive criticism. It even inhibits those not directly involved in a particular situation from becoming aware of it, eliminating tangential as well as direct learning.

Telework as Tool

I began this chapter with a statement from Chris Argyris and Donald Schon about why people think that learning is hard to do and why change is so threatening. In short, it's because change is confusing, overwhelming, embarrassing, and it promises the loss of dearly held ideas and convictions. This attitude is engendered by membership in a group that reinforces fear and the behaviors that accompany fear. Many organizations unwittingly thrive on fear, so much so that W. Edwards Deming (1986), well known as an advocate of the total-quality movement, included among his famous "14 Points" this reminder: "Drive out fear. Create trust. Create a climate for innovation."

Expelling fear from the workplace is not mere rhetoric; it is an urgent and vital task that should take first priority in the organizational agenda. This expulsion must be accomplished in a top-down manner; leadership must be committed to the adoption of safe space for failure without fear of retribution. The oft-repeated story about Thomas Watson, Sr., of IBM and his reluctance to fire the maker of a massive error still serves to remind us that an investment in individual learning and development is only the beginning of the process—the balance requires practice before we can anticipate a payoff. The requisite practice will (yes, *will*) result in failures—after all, learning takes place after reflection upon failure, not after basking in success. Taking a risk means taking a chance on failure, and taking a chance on learning. An organization that takes that risk risks becoming successful.

The dynamic of any work group is likely to reinforce the predominant organizational attitudes because "individuals find themselves locked in not only by their own behavior but also by the group dynamics that these behaviors produce" (Argyris & Schon, 1974, 38). In order to alter the ability to learn, the group dynamics must change. If people are kept from developing groups that encode nonlearning behaviors, it automatically becomes possible for learning to take place.

Here is where telework and its accompanying technologies can be excellent resources. When an organization implements telework, it indicates a commitment to alternative electronic communication methods and a focus on task time over speed of completion. Thus, reflection upon action becomes possible and creativity can be expressed without fear of derogation. Experimentation with ideas makes possible innovation, failure without blaming, collaborative conversation, and information sharing (Farson & Keyes, 2002)—all of which are prerequisites to learning and change.

Instead of privileging aggressiveness and competition, remote communication privileges expertise and thoughtfulness. The result is likely to be organizational learning, openness to change and, as we see in the next chapter, the potential for significant competitive advantage.

11

Telework as Competitive Advantage: A Constellation of Challenges

The stakeholder analysis in Chapter 3 showed the competitive advantage that telework provides in several key business functions. In terms of human resource management, telework provides employers an advantage in recruiting and retention, primarily because of the desirability to workers of second shift availability, reduced commutation time and expense, and improved quality of work life, as well as perceived increase in "free" time. Overall, the balance of work and home life is improved through telework.

Telework also provides a financial advantage to employers in terms of cost reduction and increased productivity and effectiveness, leading to increased profitability. The profitability advantage appeals to many of telework's stakeholders, including employers, equipment suppliers, telephone companies, and consultants. This chapter focuses on the ways in which the competitive advantage of telework has been measured, and examines how much of telework competitive advantage is perceived and how much is reality.

PERFORMANCE MEASUREMENT

Performance measurement is one of the thorniest challenges in the telework constellation. When work is traditional—that is, work that can be counted and quantified, performance measurement is a straightforward task. Numerous protocols have been developed that count quantity, speed of production, quality of output, and efficient use of resources per hour (or week, or minute) of work time for each employee or employee group. These are then analyzed using financial data, costing inputs, amount of rework, and other variables. The field of operations management is devoted to such counting measures as the foundation for production departments and quality initiatives. The development of quantifying metrics for supervisory management began with Frederick Taylor (or, some would say, with the Egyptians and the building of the pyramids) and has continued profitably through innovations in management science to today's sophisticated statistical process control practices. The process of performance management depends on our ability to agree upon definitions of certain terms, such as "performance," "productivity," and "quality." Although there are generally accepted definitions of these terms in the arena of manufacturing, there is little or no agreement on these terms in the arena of knowledge work. Knowledge workers and their tasks differ significantly from manufacturing workers and tasks. What must we measure about telework to determine its contribution to organizational profitability? And how shall we measure it?

The Balanced Scorecard approach can help, but it is far from the final word on quantifying the intangible. The concept of the balanced scorecard (Kaplan & Norton, 1996) derives from early connections with the gauges on the bridge of a ship at sea. The ability to monitor at a glance all the functions of the ship's systems made piloting safer because the pilots could be more responsive. The same idea is believed to help guide the organization through its daily trials and quarterly tribulations. However, measuring a ship's progress is not really comparable to measuring the success of a business initiative. The goal of the ship in question is typically to make port safely, offload its cargo, load a new cargo, and make for another port. This is a series of concrete endeavors with beginnings, middles, and endings. Telework is not an endeavor per se; rather it is the embodiment of a philosophical and humanistic movement. In this case, the quantification of telework may result in the violation of the very philosophical foundation of the movement. Telework's philosophy has to do with empowerment. Measurement has to do with control.

Performance Measurement and Intangible Results

One of the tenets of the balanced scorecard is that everything can be monitored and measured. The trick is to determine what to measure and how that measurement relates to organizational goals. It is important to determine the strategic goal that is being addressed or we run the risk of situating telework as a solution in search of a problem.

Commuting and the environment. Telework was originally framed as a way to lessen commutation strains on our infrastructure and to lower the environmental impacts of pollution from emissions. A full discussion of telework's effectiveness in this area appears in Chapter 13. In brief, regional and state programs have shown that telework does reduce the environmental impact of commuting as well as the impact on the local highway infrastructure. These effects were determined by measuring vehicle miles traveled (VMT) and associating them with auto emissions, air quality, and number of commuters who have shifted to telework status at least one day per week. Results were dramatic.

Social benefits. A secondary consequence was the set of social benefits that accrued to teleworkers. Social benefits have been measured primarily on an anecdotal level. "People" say they have more time for their families. Workers "prefer" to be at home when, for example, the children return from school. That oxymoronically named group, "working mothers," can work odd hours while the children are asleep without leaving the house. Some of these benefits are dubious and are very hard to measure. For example, how important is a "preference?" Is my preference the same strength as yours? Is the potential for isolation discussed in Chapter 6 outweighed by the potential for "free time?" These social impacts are ancillary to the main goal, which relates to environmental impacts.

Organizational impact. It is only a tertiary benefit that competitive advantage derives from reduced costs to the employer, increased access to a broader workforce, and possible increases in productivity. Some of the reduced employer costs pertain to recruiting and retention. According to Telework America 1999, companies that implemented telework attained a 63 percent savings in the cost of absenteeism and increased employee retention (Pratt, 1999). This extraordinary finding was self-reported, rather than the result of figures maintained by participating organizations and, as such, is less powerful than would be a similar concretely documented statistic.

Other studies relating to the impact of virtual teaming, similar in many ways to teleworking, show positive results but are cautious about generalizing their claims. For example, gaining access to skilled and specialized workers becomes easier and less expensive when the company is willing to allow telework. Some projects cannot be conducted at all without remote access for specialists. The participants of one case study were reluctant to make broad claims, but "[M]ost members did, however, express the view that their particular teamwork would have been impossible without the ability to regularly connect with distant members" (DeMarie, 2000, 11). In fact, virtual teaming is rarely possible without telework, but quantifying the benefits proves elusive. It was not possible for the researchers in the aforementioned case to determine accurate estimates of cost savings or quality improvements. In fact, they were far more able to identify disadvantages and to measure them than the positive results.

Yet, industry gurus and supporters insist that there are significant business benefits to be derived from telework. Focusing on the agile workplace, supporters continue their emphasis on the business case, especially on the "anywhere, anytime" component that pleases both workers and employers. But a survey conducted by the U.S. General Services Administration (GSA) of workers in government and in private industry showed that telework had no impact on worker satisfaction or on worker intention to change jobs or accept a job, which finding seems to eliminate, or at least significantly reduce telework as a factor in worker retention (Vega & Hanlon, in press).

Productivity Patterns

It is the claim of increased productivity that casts the longest shadow on the credibility of telework supporters. Where is the evidence of the productivity improvements? What is being measured? The same study that claimed 63 percent savings realized in retention and absenteeism indicated that telecommuting increased productivity in the firms surveyed by 22 percent. The following year, the Telework America 2000 survey suggested that productivity increases resulting from telecommuting were 22.5 percent, also self-reported (Nilles, 2000). How do these measures relate to organizational outcomes?

Knowledge work might include measurement of the following:

- The attitude of the worker vis-à-vis project assignments
- The amount of "waste" accrued during the creation process
- The amount of rework necessary
- Willingness to assist coworkers in other departments
- Effective use of technology
- Ability to work independently
- Willingness to collaborate

The same measures could be used to address teleworker performance, as long as it is clear that the measurements must relate specifically to the growth of the business rather than to the public good or for any other reason. Unfortunately, it is the rare nonmanufacturing company (I have not encountered any) that monitors or measures any of these seven items. Any organization that were to focus so intensively on the productivity patterns and performance of workers in a nonmanufacturing environment would likely be spending more time and resources on measurement than on production itself.

There are some companies that have formally measured improvements in productivity as a result of telework. For example, a survey of the call center industry in 2002 indicated a 12 percent increase in productivity in their remote workforce over their in-house staff. In addition, the remote agents were more experienced than the in-house agents (27 percent of remote agents had more than five years on the job, whereas only 12 percent of in-house agents had more than five years). The remote agents were also more educated than the in-house agents— 42 percent of them had a college degree, compared to 17 percent of in-house agents. Thirty-nine percent of the call centers surveyed planned to use teleworking agents within the near term—two years from the date of the study (Kistner, 5/7/02).

But these companies measured the productivity of the knowledge equivalent of assembly-line workers. Call centers are notorious for their employee turnover and poor working conditions, with each call timed and random calls monitored. Bathroom breaks are often limited, and quotas are steep. The length of an agent's tenure is directly related to the ability to accept constant rejection and frequent verbal abuse. It's hard to imagine that anyone would find such work desirable; the ability to work at home might make it tolerable.

A more credible claim of productivity increases comes from the Texas Workforce Commission. The state of Texas has aggressively sought out ways to develop telework programs and has sponsored numerous pilots in state agencies to test out the claims of savings and increased productivity, as well as to comply with the Federal Clean Air Act. Two agencies in particular noted dramatic improvement in productivity among their teleworkers. The General Services Commission saw an increase in productivity of 25 percent among teleworkers over the course of their three-year pilot. More importantly, the Texas Workforce Commission Appeals Department evidenced an increase in the timely processing of caseloads from 48 percent to 76 percent. This figure is particularly striking, since the workers in question are without doubt knowledge workers—68 percent of those teleworkers were attorneys (Texas Comptroller of Public Accounts, December 2000).

The figure is also striking because the processing of caseloads is measurable but does not require micromeasurement or continuous monitoring. It has the benefit of being outcome based, rather than process based and thus is both sensible and oriented toward attainment of organizational goals.

The U.S. GSA Office of Governmentwide Policy has introduced a "productivity payback model" that is designed to help organizations determine the potential payback in productivity from the introduction of various investments in the people, in their work places, and in the tools that they use in conducting their work. The measurements in the payback model are based on desired organizational outcomes and calculated on the specific average compensation of the workers whose output is being considered. The real payback, claims the GSA, is in worker satisfaction and its natural result—improved productivity and lowered turnover (Productivity in the Workplace, 2001).

Certainly, productivity can be monitored and measured electronically (Kistner, 9/11/01), but unless productivity has outcome-based measures and results in a contribution to improved attainment of organizational goals, it is difficult to justify claims that telework provides competitive advantage through enhanced performance. In a knowledge economy, such outcomes could be the artifacts of knowledge, such as reports, patents, Web site design and maintenance, publications, development of code, grants, or conferences. Or, outcomes could reflect enhanced capacity to conduct intellectual activity, such as networking models or online collaboration resulting in sharing knowledge such that improved decisions are made.

Joe Roitz, AT&T's Telework Director, claims, "Virtual work is such a powerful way to run an enterprise. You don't have all these visual perceptions to get in the way. You remove that lens and bias and you're left with pure knowledge." AT&T's employee survey indicates that employees produce 10 percent more work on teleworking days, resulting in $65 million in increased output from those workers (Zbar, 9/12/02). Roitz's perception seems to be accurate in terms of internal productivity measures that relate directly to AT&T's goals, providing evidence that the eye of the beholder may be nearsighted when it comes to secondary impacts, but that it is possible to measure increases in productivity that relate directly to telework.

Organizational Structure and Value Creation

One of the challenges in organizational design is the difficulty in aligning corporate design with organizational strategy. It is the strategy that should inform the decision about including telework in the design as a productivity tool that can lead to competitive advantage. A series of acid tests have been developed that can help to facilitate this decision in terms of "fit" and generally good design principles (Goold & Campbell, 2002). These nine tests can be used as benchmarking devices to help clarify the likelihood of telework's providing competitive advantage in a specific organization.

The market advantage test. Will telework provide a positive contribution to organizational marketing strategy? This requires an analysis of all market segments, and who is responsible for handling them. Are all segments being covered adequately? Is there satisfactory collaboration across marketing groups without changes? How are complex problems addressed?

The parenting advantage. Can telework improve upon the way corporate value is developed within the organization? Where are the weaknesses in corporate value creation? Can they be addressed through telework?

The people test. Will telework engage your best workers adequately and take advantage of their strengths? Who will you lose through the implementation of telework? What is the impact likely to be on the organization?

The feasibility test. Is the inclusion of telework possible in the organization's industry? Will the organization be able to service its stakeholders via telework? Are there cultural constraints that limit the likelihood of teleworking success?

The specialist cultures test. Can telework be incorporated into certain areas of the organization and not in others? Are there specialist units for which telework would provide benefits and others for which telework would be detrimental to success?

The difficult-links test. Will telework improve or damage internal organizational communication? Is it likely that collaboration and communication will suffer?

The redundant-hierarchy test. Does the corporate hierarchy have so many levels that the inclusion of one more internal structure might cause it to implode? Telework does require an additional reporting/operational/support component—is that component likely to make the hierarchy too steep to be functional?

The accountability test. Is it possible to measure the performance of the members of the unit that is teleworking? Is the existing control process fuzzy before the implementation of telework? If so, telework will not make this simpler.

The flexibility test. Will telework allow the organization to pursue innovation and to become adaptable to change? Can the organization overcome the impediments to change that have been identified through this analysis? Will the managers accept it, endorse it, and welcome it?

Once these tests have been carefully considered, the decision to include telework as part of the organizational competitive strategy will be, at the least, well reasoned.

OTHER CONSIDERATIONS

The difficulty of determining competitive advantage is exacerbated by several veiled factors. The foremost of these is the general loss of differentiation among companies that imitate the advantages of their competitors. Over time, concepts, best practices, and innovations by market leaders are copied by market laggards, and these concepts cease to have a significant impact on challengers. According to researchers James G. March and Robert I. Sutton (1997), "The result is the progressive elimination from net effect of organizational factors that are clearly relevant to performance advantage or disadvantage. . . . The basic idea is that any feature of organizational practice that might provide major competitive advantage is ordinarily adopted by all competitors" (699).

If telework were universally adopted, benefits related to competitive advantage would dissipate in direct relationship to the improvements in performance and productivity experienced by its practitioners. As with any innovation, the competitive advantage it provides is ephemeral.

A second factor that confounds our ability to ascribe direct linear advantage to the implementation of telework in a company is our human tendency to shade our experience through a haze of positive retrospection (retrospective bias) and through our desire to make sense of and give meaning to the stories of our work lives. Objective statistical methods that measure improvement and impact are difficult to establish; how much more difficult it is to measure such changes subjectively and qualitatively. When we "tell the story" of telework, it is not possible to separate the affective and the objective—both are part of the account. The story will be told from the perspective of the teller, and the self-interest of the reporter (whether employer, employee, consultant, vendor or supplier, or member of any special group) will further color the narrative. Recounting revisionist history is the temptation in the path of all who participate in retrospective analysis because it is easy to manipulate memories and tell the story we want to tell.

Crisis Management

Some telework specialists tell the story of a remote workforce in terms of the competitive advantage of crisis management. We are all aware of the temporary rise in the numbers of teleworkers in the immediate aftermath of September 11, 2001. Those temporary teleworkers disappeared as quickly as they came on the scene, once their normal office routines were reestablished in new locations. This is not meant to disparage telework in any way; rather this indicates a clear advantage provided by it. Any company that ignores viable methods of disaster planning is running risky business.

The potential disasters can cover events far less sinister than terrorist attacks. Bad weather, disrupted travel patterns, personal emergencies that keep workers at home but still able to work, and erratic levels of worker demand are all valid uses of organizational teleworking, and all are represented in the success stories told about the phenomenon of remote work.

Flexibility

As the economy improves and companies recover, corporate success will depend heavily on agility and the ability to move fast. Telework provides both by creating leaner organizational structures staffed by confident, independent, skilled, and adaptable workers. Teleworkers tend to be problem solvers, people who spend less time talking with others and more time focused on task. If what is needed is a task orientation, telework can provide it easily.

The major technical impediment to broader use of telework is the lack of general availability of sufficient bandwidth to satisfy the needs of workers outside the office and the expense of such bandwidth where it is available. As such bandwidth becomes widely available and affordable, companies are likely to find a renewed interest in encouraging their workers to "go home and go to work."

12

Dueling Banjos: Values in the Virtual World

The toe-tapping bluegrass banjo duet, theme song of the movie *Deliverance,* describes the battle for prominence of two competing musicians, each with his own tone, instrument, and focus. First one banjo player takes the lead, then the other wrests it away and picks up the pace. Back to the first, then the second, back and forth several times until the joyful conclusion that incorporates the ideas, themes, and perspectives of both. The competing themes of privacy and access, electronic monitoring and civil liberties, and work life and home life take on a similar sound in the virtual world. The pull of competing values and objectives leaves many confused and uncomfortable even when they embrace either position. We have not yet been able to find an ethical Tao of the virtual world that combines the extremes and supports an evolving set of life principles in harmony with the impacts of technology on the community of work.

PRIVACY

Privacy, the bulwark upon which our personal freedom and safety are based, becomes a flimsy guardian once it encounters technology. We have become accustomed, as civilization and urbanization have thrust us closer together physically, to protecting our psychological space and our personal distance from others. Rooms within our homes have doors, windows are covered. At work, we lock our desks or lockers. We perform our ablutions in private. Our purchases are hidden in plastic or paper bags, or delivered in the plain brown wrappers that disclose nothing about purchase, purchaser, or sender. On the surface, we are a private society.

Private, that is, until we remember show all-tell all television shows, magazine and newspaper articles, and our obsession with knowing every detail of every aspect of the lives of public and private figures alike. Private until we discover that our employer knows our entire medical history, our family tree, our appointments with the personal trainer. Private until we learn that our purchases in the plain brown wrappers are not hidden from public view any more than is the number of the credit card that made the purchase. And our ally in this frenzy of snooping? The very technology that facilitates our private and public lives.

Voluntary and Involuntary Surrender

According to the *New York Times*,

> Employers can listen in to your phone calls. They can read your e-mail—even if your message is marked "private." They can listen in to your voice mail. They can monitor what is on the screen of your computer and what you have left on your hard drive. They can install software that monitors the number of keystrokes you perform per hour, and measures the time you are way from your workstation. They can make you urinate into a cup to test for drugs. They can read your credit reports, and look at your medical records. They cannot give you a polygraph test, but they can probe your innermost thoughts with psychological tests. They can share information about you with creditors and government agents. (cited in Sykes, 1999, 137–138)

In addition, keystroke loggers that keep track of the actual keys typed, not just the number of keystrokes, can be installed. Because anyone can be a creditor, anyone can access these reports. And we let them do this.

Access and availability. One reason we surrender our privacy through technology is our need to be connected, to be in contact with our coworkers, customers, and supervisors at all times. In order to combat the enduring image of the disheveled teleworker in bunny slippers, casually sipping coffee while the "real" workers slave away in the office, many who work at home feel obligated to be more responsive to requests, emails, telephone calls, or other electronic contacts than their in-office peers. Continuous availability strips away the personal space created by distance, and invites unseen electronic eyes and ears to observe our activities.

In addition, in order to be effective at their jobs, teleworkers require the same access to company files and databases as in-office workers. The technological advances described in Chapter 2 are what permit the kind of access needed by teleworkers. As a minimum, teleworkers require Internet access to retrieve data from the central work location or distributed locations in not only a one-to-many relationship but also in a many-to-many relationship. This may mean file downloads or database searches. It may mean emails or retrieval of filed email messages. It may mean instant messaging (IM) communication. These methods facilitate remote work and encourage individual responsibility for whole tasks, rather than the piecemeal work processes that often result in poor product quality. The problem with this is that the data links go both ways. According to the Privacy Rights Clearinghouse, "There are virtually no online activities or services that guarantee an absolute right of privacy" (www.privacyrights.org).

This is true for the simplest online connections. As the allure of technology increases, it becomes more possible to create home network environments that can communicate with office network environments. The result—workers can check their offices while at home and their homes while at the office (Schonfeld, 1998). This dramatic escalation of privacy invasion makes it possible for teleworkers to access office printers and for employers to have a real-time virtual picture of the activities being conducted by the teleworker at any time.

Confidentiality. Confidentiality no longer exists. Every time we post a message to a public newsgroup, it is archived and made available to anyone who requests it. These postings are part of the public record, along with our names, email addresses, and information about our service provider. In addition, exemptions to federal law permit the ISP systems operator to view and disclose our private emails if there is reason to suspect that we are trying to damage the system or harm another system user. These exemptions also permit the disclosure to a third party of our private emails if the recipient consents or we consent. If the email system is employer-owned, the employer has the right to view any messages on the system (www.privacyrights.org).

Even if we are careful in our emails not to disclose personal information, our computers themselves are sharing our secrets. When we browse the Internet or the World Wide Web, we leave an electronic trail of our visit that is collected and stored by both our ISP and the systems operators of the site we have visited. The process of surfing also leaves deposits, called "cookies," on our hard drives that record the locations we have accessed, making it easier for us to return at a later date and also making it easier to market products to us that are matched with our individual interests. When we visit Internet sites from our offices, the cookies are left on our work network systems, further disclosing personal information about us to our employers. When we surf the Web in our home offices, if we are teleworkers using equipment and/or access provided by our employer, that data is also available to our employers, along with our emails and personal files. Our emails are archived for varying periods of time, depending on their content. Emails with human resource management content must be archived to the same extent that hard copy would be, from 1 to 30 years (www.lindquist.com). As a secondary impact, routine electronic maintenance that includes periodic system backups creates a long-lasting record of confidential corporate communications, rendering irrelevant the Enron/Anderson paper shredding incidents as a result.

Firewalls and sealing wax and other fancy stuff. Some companies have invested in virtual private networks (VPNs) to create a form of internal confidentiality by decreasing the risk of unauthorized access to corporate systems. These VPNs provide secure remote access for corporate file sharing, database usage, group messaging, and other telework applications over the Internet. VPNs protect files and records of clients from prying and hackers. The ISP acts as interface between the corporate network and the users behind the firewall, with VPNs even providing encryption services to further secure data.

Encryption (usually done via software) scrambles email messages or files so that they are unreadable to the uninformed. Private information that is so encrypted truly is private; it cannot be read by the systems operator or anyone else unless they have the key. As of 2002, encryption is not illegal in the United States even though it inhibits access by law enforcement agencies to material that would otherwise be available to them (www.privacyrights.org).

Monitoring On-Site and Off-Site

Workers have the right to a reasonable expectation of privacy. That means only that employers must give fair warning to workers in order to monitor them. Such fair warning can consist of a disclaimer that the employee signs upon hire permitting monitoring of telephone calls and email records. It might be written in the employee handbook. It might consist of signs posted within the office environment that remind workers that they are under video surveillance. It might be simply the repeated message (for the benefit of the customer) on a customer service representative's telephone line, "This call might be monitored for service quality." Whatever form it takes, once given, it provides tacit acceptance of surveillance.

Most large companies conduct some level of monitoring or surveillance of the activities of their employees. According to the AMA (American Management Association), "more than three quarters of U.S. firms now monitor their employees' e-mails, Internet activities and computer files" (AMA 2001 Survey on Workplace Testing—www.amanet.org), and such monitoring is virtually unregulated. Employers are permitted to monitor telephone calls, but are supposed to stop monitoring when they realize that the conversation is a private one (www.privacyrights .org). If the worker is wearing a telephone headset, even conversations with the co-worker at the adjoining desk may be monitored when such casual talk is picked up by the personal microphone. A record is made of every telephone call, and this record can be accessed by the employer without special requests for it. Employers can install software on computers that counts keystrokes, monitors Internet usage, provides remote entry into files on hard drives and on computer terminals, and that keeps track of employee idle time. Email and voice mail messages, even when deleted, are likely to remain on the system, backed up for safety purposes onto tape or other storage media (www.privacyrights .org).

These forms of surveillance and monitoring are commonplace in offices, but telework has now brought electronic surveillance into workers' homes. Mini Web cameras allow a supervisor to track a teleworker's movements at home, monitor bathroom or coffee breaks, and "watch" a worker even in the privacy of her home. The same software that monitors workers in the office can be installed for remote computer-monitoring purposes. This constant surveillance can place a heavy toll on workers, especially those whose work hours are less defined and highly flexible. A "peek-a-boo, I-see-you" arrangement in the office may be tolerable, but at home we continue to expect a measure of self-determination and personal space.

American workers spend approximately one third of their lives at work. When work takes place in the office, two thirds of their lives remain for home, commuting, or other activities, including sleeping. This time remains free from view by the employer. When we work at home, at least two thirds of our lives may be spent in contact with the technology that invades our work lives and makes us subject to external scrutiny. Research has shown that people who work in physical isolation from others are likely to feel the most stress when being monitored at work (Aiello & Kolb, 1995). Stress naturally reduces productivity and has a negative impact on quality, as well as increasing absenteeism and decreasing retention. Bringing work stress into the home would appear to be a nonproductive move (see Chapter 9).

The Constitution and the Bill of Rights

> The right of the people to be secure in their persons, houses, papers, and effects, against unreasonable search and seizures, shall not be violated, and no warrants shall issue, but upon probable cause, supported by oath or affirmation, and particularly describing the place to be searched, and the persons or things to be seized. (Fourth Amendment to the U.S. Constitution)

Americans' right to privacy from government intervention rests on the Fourth, Fifth, and Fourteenth Amendments, which have created in us a sense of perfect freedom to do whatever we choose to do unimpeded in our own homes or private places. In addition to performing all the decent activities in which we normally participate, we have felt free to tinker with explosives in our basements, to view pornography in our bedrooms, to plan nefarious acts in our living rooms and on the telephone, and, in certain states, to tape conversations relating to extremely private matters without informing the people who are being taped. We cherish our individual right to privacy and have protected it at great expense to society at large through the course of our history. Some of this protection has led to well-publicized abuses of the public trust on a grand scale, and some has led to the violation of individual rights at the microlevel. Some claim that the American respect for privacy is what permitted the terrorism of September 11, 2001. But, whether large-scale or small, electronic advances have redefined our private space and our private rights.

Our private space may now include the entire virtual world, accessible over telephone wires, via satellite and other wireless communication, and any connection to the Internet or World Wide Web. Some feel that limits on Internet access and privacy would constitute the limitation of personal freedom; some feel that the Internet is a public place where privacy is not guaranteed. This debate will not be resolved any time soon. However, the broad outlines of it have a direct impact on our ability to perform work at remote locations while still maintaining the confidentiality of the data that we manipulate, the privacy of teleworkers in their own homes, and the sacrosanct protection of our civil liberties.

Government eavesdropping. Much has been written about the effectiveness of electronic surveillance (Sykes, 1999, 156–166), and wiretapping (its common name despite the frequent absence of actual wires) is a highly regulated process. It requires the initial authorization of a Department of Justice official before local U.S. Attorneys apply for intercept authorization. Intercept authorization orders are filed with federal district court judges, who limit the surveillance to specific federal felony offenses for a period of not more than 30 days per intercept order. In order for authorization to be granted, the application must clearly indicate probable cause, a specific telecommunications facility or place to intercept, a description of the type of conversation to be intercepted, and the identities of persons anticipated to be intercepted. New exceptions were made for the FBI following the terrorist acts of September 11, 2001, and these change periodically. The original requirements were meant to prohibit "fishing"—and so, intercept authorizations were granted only in cases of ongoing investigation. Federal wiretap laws have been in effect since 1968 (Title III of the Omnibus Crime Control and Safe Streets Act), with modifications keeping the FBI up to date with changing technology. In 1986, ECPA (Electronic Communications Privacy Act) clarified how the existing wiretap legislation applied in cyberspace and set boundaries for citizens' online privacy from government interception. By 1994, CALEA required carriers, including ISPs, to cooperate in federal investigations.

Four years later, in 1998, roving wiretaps became legal, as long as they only "remembered" emails for a specific subject. Carnivore, a packet sniffing software installation, was the FBI's technological innovation to meet the official requirements for wiretapping described earlier. Packet sniffers are able to identify specifics within email communications and can ignore other communications not relevant to ongoing investigations. "This is a matter of employing new technology to lawfully obtain important information while providing enhanced privacy protection" (www.fbi.gov/hq/lab/carnivore/carnivore2.htm).

Not all constituencies believe that Carnivore is an innocuous innovation, however. On March 25, 2002, EPIC (Electronic Privacy Information Center) filed a Civil Action (No. 00-1849) in U.S. District Court—District of Columbia against the Department of Justice, claiming that the FBI performed an "inadequate search" for material related to and explaining the legal and policy implications (not simply the technical specifications) of Carnivore and Ether-Peek (another similar device). The concern of opponents to Carnivore and other electronic monitors is based on the existing lack of controls on the Internet and the inherent freedom of all participants to express themselves fully and openly, without risk of government intervention or suppression.

The rights of employers. The right to workplace privacy is less straightforward and even more complex than the laws surrounding government wiretapping and constitutional law. The right to privacy that we ordinarily refer to in relation to employment derives from common law and states rights, which vary from location to location.

Under the circumstances of normal activity, the employer's legitimate interests prevail over the personal interests of the employee

(Sykes, 1999). An employer's legitimate interests include productivity, company liability in cases of harassment or threats of violence, the use of company resources for conducting personal business, and conflicts of interests in which the company is at risk, such as solicitations, chain letters, selling personal items, or making personal gain on company time. An employee's interests may not coincide with these, and, as a result, appropriate balance must be established between the two sets of potentially conflicting interests. Many states permit employers to read employee emails and to monitor employee telephone calls, which seems reasonable when in the office, where the employee is using equipment owned by the company, on company time. The rules get a little muddier when teleworker privacy rights are at issue.

If a teleworker is using company equipment and company-supplied-and-paid-for Internet access, even if the equipment is at a location other than the office, the same standard applies—the employer has the right to read emails and monitor telephone calls. According to Lewis Maltby, president of the National Workrights institute in Princeton, NJ, "Everywhere is a workplace today," and company issued computers or electronic access do not have to be used in the office in order to be scanned by packet sniffers or monitored by systems operators (Jesdanun, 1/6/02).

But what happens when teleworkers are employed by companies that do not provide equipment and access? They must then use their own equipment and pay for their own ISP connection and attendant expenses. The natural assumption would be that under these circumstances, the employer does not have the right to monitor electronic activities. However, if the worker uses personally owned equipment to connect with the workplace's network or email system, that equipment may be subject to the same sniffers and other surveillance software used on company-owned equipment. As a result, two of the real benefits of telework to the workers themselves, unstructured work time and performance- or project-based evaluation, may go by the wayside. The attempt to protect the integrity and confidentiality of company-owned materials, knowledge, or intellectual property rights results in a violation of the privacy of the individual. This ethical balancing act increases the tension between the already competing values of work/family, individual rights/corporate rights, haves/have-nots.

IS TECHNOLOGY VALUE FREE?

In *Modern Times,* the classic film featuring Charlie Chaplin and his encounters with technology, we are treated to scenes of chaotic factory work, lack of concern for workers, dangerous working conditions, and the complete breakdown of privacy for those workers. Entire walls turn into talking heads, and workers are subject to indignities that, in their extremism and sheer lunacy, are laughable. The laughter continues with Lucille Ball in the candy factory, a continually speeding-up assembly line, and cheeks bulging from chocolates that never got wrapped. We do not laugh as hard when we consider the indignities visited upon "real" factory workers, as described in *Rivethead*, by Ben Hamper (1991), however.

> We stood there for forty minutes or so, a miniature lifetime, and the pattern never changed. Car, windshield. Car, windshield. Drudgery piled atop drudgery. Cigarette to cigarette. Decades rolling through the rafters, bones turning to dust, stubborn clocks gagging down flesh, another windshield, another cigarette, wars blinking on and off, thunderstorms muttering the alphabet, crows on power lines asleep or dead, that mechanical octopus squirming against nothing, nothing, nothingness. (2)

Is the closely monitored teleworker in store for the same dismal fate? Does technology spell doom to workers?

Defined by Our Work

We Americans love our work. We must love it, considering the amount of time we spend doing it. We know who we are based on what we do. Our casual meetings, now known as networking occasions, invite the question "What do you do?" rather than the "How do you do?" of days gone by. The answer guides the subsequent interaction according to an evolving hierarchy of career choices, culminating in anything having to do with telecommunications and technology. In the 1970s, my husband worked for New York Telephone—Ma Bell, as the company was fondly nicknamed. His answer to the question "What do you do?" was a guaranteed conversation stopper. "I work for the telephone company" ended any further discussion of his "unfortunate" career choice. Today, working for anyone in the telecommunications industry generates excited conversation and sharing of technology stories. Electronic bonding, reminding us all that we are what we do, leads to other, less compelling topics, like family, hobbies, and personal interests.

"Increasingly," Kay S. Hymowitz (2001) suggests, "we view work not just as a way to pay the rent and the orthodontist but as an end in itself. . . . Knowledge workers in all fields are working like mad, as are young singles in general: the Families and Work Institute found that 73 percent of today's 25- to 32-year-olds work more than 40 hours per week, compared with 55 percent in 1977." She further suggests, "Many Americans now expect their job to feel as if it were an emanation of their own desires and on their own time."

We are our work; our work represents our personal worth. When we have a job that carries inherent status, we feel good about it. As others make assumptions about us based on what we do, so do we make similar attributions about ourselves and others. We can tolerate indignities relating to privacy when our work is high profile, highly paid, or recognized as highly professional. Celebrities can scarcely venture out in public without being accosted by autograph seekers. Athletes shower and dress in full view of others in common locker rooms, as do physicians and surgeons. Politicians have handlers and entourages that permit them little freedom of movement. It is, therefore, no surprise that the ordinary wage earner is subject to some manner of monitoring and control.

The Push toward Efficiency

The motivation for all this monitoring is a simple one: At base, we are a production-oriented society. The expectation is that we are getting paid to do a job and that is exactly what we are supposed to do during our working hours. It is unacceptable to use the hours from 10:00 A.M. to 2:00 P.M., for example, the bright middle of the day, for our personal business. That is the core of the workday and we should be working. How will we ever complete our assignments, make the necessary contacts? Even knowledge workers have succumbed to the production mentality: Write one more report, do a bit more research, turn out one more proposal, write 50 more lines of code. Just to make certain that we are sufficiently motivated to work hard every moment of every paid hour, we willingly surrender to the electronic invasion of our privacy. After all, we were comfortable with the Gilbreths and their time and motion studies, and we still want to believe efficient means better, faster means better, and more means better. What have we sacrificed on the altar of efficiency?

WORKING AT HOME—INTRUSION OR RECONNECTION?

The blurring of boundaries between home and office, between private and public, between civil liberties and economic controls has generated personal and political fallout that demands our attention. As work technology encroaches on the private lives of Americans, it becomes apparent that several sacrifices have been required.

One sacrifice—privacy

One sacrifice—confidentiality

One sacrifice—human dignity

In order to obtain the best and broadest access to the electronic world, we inadvertently expose ourselves to monitoring and tracking by electronic voyeurs. Working at home increases our exposure in cyberspace, and we pay for the pleasure. We subsidize private industry by underwriting satellite offices in our spare bedrooms and accept a set of expectations that are designed primarily for corporate convenience. Organizational savings are costs transferred to workers, and these same workers are made to feel grateful that they are allowed to conduct someone else's business in their own homes and to be monitored while they do so.

"The pull of work accelerates the tempo of home. The push of the outside world competes with domestic priorities" (Jackson, 2002, 23). When interviewing one worker for a study about communication processes, a respondent talked to us on her cell phone in her car, transporting her children to dancing school. She seemed to feel it was perfectly appropriate to be conducting an interview on her employer's behalf while driving her children to an activity, on her own time. This devotion to the needs and commitments of the organization has a natural sociological origin in the work ethic that drives the American economy, as well as the economies of other countries where telework is increasing rapidly. This work ethic lends itself to putting company before family, work before home, effort before leisure, the public before the private, concern for others before personal dignity.

Life is hard for the majority of people in the world, and one of our human responsibilities in the conduct of our normal lives is to remove as many hardships as we can from others. But when our "normal" lives are conducted within an environment that idealizes work, values information over relationships, and privileges corporate interests over human process and needs, we confront a series of hard-to-resolve challenges. Humanist social concerns may be overlooked, including the basic human rights of individuals to personal and family autonomy, the maintenance of private property, and time for rest from labor. Eliminating the possibility of escape from one's labors and retreat to family peace makes a mockery of success through efficiency and hard work. Technology can easily dehumanize individuals and deny them the ability to separate work from home, to protect privacy, and to restrain the blind commitment to valuing organization needs over individual needs. The government plays an important role in protecting the individual from the group, as we see in the next two chapters.

13

Telework in the Public Sector

> The only orthodox object of the institution of government is to secure the greatest degree of happiness possible to the general mass of those associated under it.
>
> —Thomas Jefferson (1812)

PUBLIC DRIVERS

Why would people voluntarily allow themselves to be governed by others? From earliest history, people have gathered together and established some form of organization that we call "government." This government was meant to control the actions of the members of the community, protect them from harm, and establish methods of dealing with miscreants. The goal was to prevent entropy, or the fall into chaos that results from lack of organization. In 1776, the rebellious founders of the American republic claimed that government had several other purposes, among them to ensure the right to "life, liberty, and the pursuit of happiness." This optimistic perspective has typified the positive side of the governmental ledger, with the less optimistic but more realistic Hamiltonian perspective tempering it: "But what is government itself, but the greatest of all reflections on human nature? If men were angels, no government would be necessary" (Hamilton, 1788).

The first 150 years of American democracy were marked by a small federal government that interfered little in the affairs of the member states, assuming that life, liberty, and the pursuit of happiness were best served by the smallest possible unit. When the impact of one individual was too small to be effective, town meetings served. When they proved insufficient to the task, representative government on the city level, then the state level filled the gap. The federal government maintained a hands-off policy in terms of the activities of states and the welfare of individual citizens. That changed dramatically with Franklin Delano Roosevelt's New Deal administration's response to the Great Depression. In short order, the states became dependent on the federal government to provide for the needs of their individual citizens through a series of alphabet agencies meant to support and sustain a failing economy and an ailing citizenry.

This pattern of heightened focus on federal control repeated itself periodically over the following fifty years, culminating with the Clinton presidency. Much like Roosevelt, spurred by the economic challenges of early 1990s, Bill Clinton instituted a formidable level of federal engagement in the lives of Americans. By that time, the legacy of federal control via fiscal arm bending was well accepted into the American mind-set. The proliferation of agencies dedicated to protecting the rights of individuals attested to that. On July 11, 1994, Clinton issued a directive requiring each federal agency to establish a "family friendly workplace" to aid in recruiting and retaining an effective workforce and to "enable federal employees to better balance their work and family responsibilities . . . increase employee effectiveness and job satisfaction, while decreasing turnover rates and absenteeism." The race to employee happiness, mandated by government, had begun, and telework was part of it. The following timeline provides an overview of the development of federally supported telework.

A Timeline of Federal Initiatives: A Decade of Support

1990. We can date telework in the federal sector to the implementation of "Flexiplace" in 1990. Flexiplace was a government attempt to improve the quality of work life for federal employees, expand the ability of the federal government to recruit and retain talented workers vis-à-vis the private sector, and to reduce federal operating expenses. The program overall had a slow start; by 1993, only 700 federal employees across 13 agencies were involved in the Flexiplace pilot programs (Joice, 1993).

1993. Undaunted by limited participation, the U.S. Office of Personnel Management (OPM) officially endorsed the use of the telework by federal agencies, and the U.S. Department of Transportation (DOT) was able to publish initial findings describing the implications of telework on transportation. These findings were positive, indicating that telework had a significant favorable effect in reducing dependence on the transportation infrastructure, environmental pollutants, and over-all commuting time.

1994. President Clinton's memorandum created a sense of urgency among federal agencies and established the government as a player in the game of getting and keeping valued and talented workers. By the following year, several agencies (Association for Commuter Transportation, U.S. Department of Commerce, Environmental Protection Agency, General Services Administration, Department of Transportation) had joined together with AT&T to establish Telecommute America, now known as Telework America. This public/private partnership served as the springboard for further legislation and was ready to act nearly concurrently with any governmental programs.

1996. The National Telecommuting Initiative, implemented by the President's Management Council, established a five phase plan to increase the number of federal teleworkers to 60,000 by the end of fiscal year 1998. At the time of the plan's inception, there were an estimated 3,000 to 4,000 federal teleworkers in formal telecommuting programs. Uncounted, and estimated at a much greater number, were those in episodic or informal telework arrangements. According to the Action Plan, the increase in teleworkers to 60,000 would generate savings to the government of $150 million annually in facilities alone, excluding the ancillary benefits of increased productivity, better service to the taxpayer, improvements in transportation and health, and other dividends.

The Action Plan encouraged four different kinds of telework: home-based telecommuting, community-based telecenters, mobile/virtual offices, and the U.S. General Store. The goal of the program was to employ the appropriate type of telework to match the needs of the agency and individual. Home-based telecommuting was designed for a worker who "spends time in both the traditional office, as well as using information technology and communications packages to perform work from home." The community-based telecenters are "remote office arrangements shared by multiple workers in the same geographical area but distant from the central office location." Mobile/virtual offices "enabled 'road warriors' to function in multiple locations or environments, including customer sites, hotels, cars or even at home." The U.S. General Store was designed as an "accessible, one-stop service center . . . as a way of centrally locating government services" (PMC, 1996).

The ambitious proposals put forth by the President's Management Council challenged the ability of agencies to engage in the activities necessary to involve their staffs while maintaining their existing level of productivity and funding. The five phase implementation program required that within a period of three years, agencies accomplish the following:

- Perform a survey of the status quo, including inventorying existing arrangements and identifying positions potentially eligible for telework.
- Provide logistical preparation that included the development of training materials and facilities analysis.
- Promote the initiative through federal, state, and local contacts as well as through public-private partnerships.
- Implement the program by developing agency goals, selecting strategies and participants, and initiating the programs.
- Evaluate the program by developing a database of participants, sharing best practices, and preparing reports on telecommuting success in attaining national goals.

The federal government endorsed the growing telework philosophy of "work anywhere, anytime" that had become the mantra of Telework America, encouraging Americans to disregard place and time in favor of individualizing "how" one works, and accommodating those needs. Endorsements and recommendations aside, however, the federal workforce was not rushing to engage in the variety of telework options.

According to the Office of Personnel Management, there were a total of 24,889 telecommuters in the federal workforce by October 1998 (*Review of Federal Family-Friendly Workplace Arrangements*). This accounted for less than half of the goal of 60,000 teleworkers that was established in 1996 and generated a series of studies, conferences, meetings, and research papers dedicated to determining why government workers did not want to leave their offices. A series of impediments to telework were identified, including insufficient budgetary support that resulted in technological scrimping, the lack of training for teleworkers and their managers, an unwillingness to entertain change, and a general misunderstanding of the role of management in the new economy. Later initiatives addressed some of these barriers.

1999. Public Law 105-277 required agencies to make at least $50,000 annually available to pay for telework at telecenters, and a series of hearings were held by the House Workforce and Education Committee to determine why telework was not more widely used by federal agencies. Desultory compliance with this law resulted in an increase in telecenter usage from 337 federal employees in 1999 to 405 federal workers in telecenters in 2001. In the three years, a total of only $798,718 was spent by 14 of the 20 agencies covered by the law, out of a possible $100,000,000 available for the project. It seemed clear that telecenters were not to be the primary avenue for telework, especially after the results of the hearings were presented. More than half the responding agencies cited cost as the primary reason for not using the telecenters, followed by employee inconvenience and lack of employee interest as explanation for the low participation. Working at home was considered preferable to commuting to a telecenter.

2000. After five years of gently promoting telework, the federal government got serious about its commitment to propel agencies into participation. Secretary of Labor Alexis Herman called a symposium to discuss the future of telework and the American worker. Participants in the symposium, a cross section of public and private interests, academic and practitioner focus, and macro- and microperspectives, met to discuss the evolution and economics of telework, telework and organizational behavior, and the cultural and social implications of telework. The symposium set the stage for the passage of Public Law 106-346, Section 359:

> Each executive agency shall establish a policy under which eligible employees of the agency may participate in telecommuting to the maximum extent possible without diminished employee performance. Not later than 6 months after the date of the enactment of this Act [by April 2001], the Director of the Office of Personnel Management shall provide that the requirements of this sections are applied to 25 percent of the Federal workforce, and to an additional 25 percent of such workforce each year thereafter.

This law sounded like it meant business, but the wording was so confusing that strict compliance would have resulted in nothing beyond the establishment of policies; no additional people would be required to telework. Clearly, the spirit of the law was to encourage more telework, but the language of the law had no teeth. No quotas were established, and no penalties exacted. The results were negligible; as of December 2001, 4.2 percent of federal employees were teleworking at least one day per week, in comparison to the October 2001 ITAC survey results showing 20 percent telework participation in the private sector (*The Status of Telework in the Federal Government,* 2001). The big numbers were still to be attained, despite policies having been submitted by 63 of 65 responding agencies.

2001. A new administration underscored the importance of continu-ing the emphasis on telework, this time focusing on the greater use of alternative work sites to increase the employment of people with dis-abilities. The New Freedom Initiative asked Congress both to establish a fund to help the disabled purchase equipment to make teleworking a feasible option, and to encourage the purchase of such equipment by employers through tax credits.

The events of September 11, 2001, created an environment in which telework was the option of choice for federal employees with offices in the World Trade Center, the Pentagon, and other locations in the New York City and Washington, D.C. areas. In a homey, reassuring website posting, the U.S. General Services Administration and the U.S. Office of Personnel Management suggested the cautious use of telework for federal workers suffering traumatic response in the aftermath of the terrorist attacks (www.telework.gov/recovery.htm). They warned agencies to balance the benefit of easing the commute and recovery from trauma through giving workers "more time with loved ones" with the dangers inherent in not separating "anyone for long periods of time from a place where they have experienced a traumatic event." Part-time telework hours were suggested, citing the wisdom of "the old saying about 'getting back on the horse that threw you.' " Over the six months that followed, most of the workers who had been displaced from their offices had established new office locations, as was the case in the private sector. Telework had proven itself useful in disasters, even if it had not captured the imagination of the traditional, commuting federal worker.

Some Notable State-Initiated Programs

Across the nation, states climbed on the teleworking bandwagon, typically as the result of pressing requirements in specific areas. For example, several states joined with private industry in partnerships geared to meeting environmental goals and reducing traffic congestion in an attempt to meet guidelines for The Clean Air Act, a program where failure to comply may result in the loss of federal highway funds.

One particularly successful program has driven more than 15 percent of Arizona's state-employed workers to teleworking at least one day a week (Zbar, 7/11/02). Spurred by the threat of the loss of critical federal highway funding, Maricopa and Pima counties, designated as "non-attainment" zones for meeting Clean Air Act guidelines, participated in the Governor's Telework Partnership and achieved record participation in the program.

Arizona had been a leader in telework, having introduced its pilot program in 1989 in partnership with AT&T. The pilot showed that teleworking reduced travel while increasing productivity, efficiency, and job attitude. Endorsements flowed in from teleworkers, their supervisors, and their nonteleworking colleagues alike. Such feedback from the last group is particularly meaningful, as one might think that on-site employees might fear extra work could accrue to them due to the absence of their teleworking peers. However, 77 percent of the nonteleworkers indicated that the program should be expanded, 82 percent believed that telework did not impede office routine, and 67 percent offered to telework if given the opportunity. These results go beyond polite acceptance; they indicate overwhelming support. Following a formal program and development phase, the mandated program phase began in 1996. After having attained the earlier 15 percent goal as of 2002, the mandated program phase continued with the participation goal increased to 20 percent.

From its inception, the Arizona program had the benefit of gubernatorial, legislative, and private sector support. The web site devoted to this program (www.teleworkarizona.com) makes it eminently clear that telework offers solutions to some of Arizona's most pressing problems—traffic congestion, air pollution, energy consumption, the cost of office space, organizational effectiveness, and employee turnover. Teleworkarizona estimates that the nearly 100,000 Phoenix area residents who telework just one day per week save over 900,000 miles of travel and more than 16 tons of pollution per day. As part of the program, the Arizona Department of Health developed the mobile/virtual office for six environmental laboratory consultants and saved $11,102 in office rent the first year alone. Travel time was reduced by 14.4 percent (5,623 hours) by the Department of Weights and Measures over a 12-month period, saving more than $55,000. Arizona's telework program has won awards for excellence every year since 1991, four of them from the Clean Air Campaign.

California was an even earlier presence in telework. In 1983, the California State Energy Commission sponsored a study by Jack Nilles about the energy impacts of telework, and by 1987 the state went forward with a pilot project that crossed several agencies and engaged some 230 telecommuters. In 1990, telecommuting was established by the governor as a mandatory option for every state agency to reduce travel and prepare for potential disasters (Nilles, 1998). Early adopters of telework, its potential was apparent to California agencies. California's goals were not only to alleviate the negative impact of commuting miles on air quality and to limit energy expenditures, but there was the added need to mitigate the problems created by California's geographic disaster potential. To many, California is synonymous with earthquakes, smog, mud slides, and forest fires. The 1989 earthquake destroyed bridges and throughways and kept workers from commuting to their jobs, but those who were teleworking continued on through the disaster and afterwards. Subsequent frequent earthquakes have not interrupted teleworkers and have allowed the business of the state to continue despite freeway closures. Each major tremor rekindles a sense of urgency in Californians to move toward the alternatives to commuting provided by telework.

By 2002, more than 3,500 California state employees were teleworking. A telecommuting unit in the Department of General Services has been established that leads a multiagency telecommuting advisory group (TAG). In 1994, each state agency was enjoined to investigate its operations and identify areas in which telecommuting may be beneficial to the organization, supported and assisted in this duty by the Department of Personnel Administration.

Similar programs exist in most states with comparably positive results, both for state employees and for workers in private industry. One creative initiative comes out of Virginia, which in 2001 launched the Telework!VA incentive program. This program "reimburses companies for equipment, services, and training costs incurred in the pursuit of telework" (Kistner, 6/11/01). The program was developed to overcome resistance to telework based on the cost of providing the services, and provides up to $3,500 per employee in equipment lease and training costs.

Other imaginative efforts have been proposed, such as the e-village project in Madera County, California. This novel planned community, a joint project of California State University, Nortel Networks, and the Property Development Group, was designed as a dedicated telework community 180 miles from the heart of Silicon Valley. The goal was to make modestly priced housing available in an environment that supports distance workers. The 30,000 single family homes that would sell for $120,000 in Madera County (compared to the $1 million they would cost in Silicon Valley) would be equipped with high-speed video, voice, and data networks—10 M bit/sec Internet connections, multiple phone lines, wireless LANs, online PC backup, and videoconferencing would all be part of the amenities provided to each house. Although one year after the announcement of the project no work had yet been done, exploiting opportunities such as this one creates true public/private partnerships that can benefit all.

Regional Efforts

Many of the individual state efforts led to natural collaborations in regions. Metropolitan areas in the East and entire states in the West joined together in the effort to shorten commuting time, reduce environmental impacts and improve the quality of work life for municipal as well as private industry employees. There are no provisions for tax incentives that can be made by these collaborative groups. Instead, they have had to design creative enticements to increase telework in their areas. The Telework Collaborative is one such program. Established in 1993 by Arizona, Oregon, and Washington, it was joined by California and Texas shortly thereafter "to accelerate the acceptance and adoption of telework programs in public and private organizations by better understanding and addressing the needs of employers, managers, supervisors, co-workers and the teleworkforce" (www.teleworkcollaborative.com). The Collaborative has turned telework into a moneymaker by selling its programs and materials to other states, agencies, and private organizations. As of 2002, organizations in 26 states and 14 foreign countries have availed themselves of the programs and consulting services of the Telework Collaborative.

Another significant regional effort arose in Washington, DC. The metropolitan Washington region has the second longest and most costly commute in the nation (West, 2000). The Washington Metropolitan Council of Governments forecast a 44 percent increase in vehicle miles traveled by 2020, compared to a highway capacity increase of only 11 percent. The future looked bleak for commuters, residents, and businesses (including the federal and local government) in terms of pollution, delays, and personal impacts. In response, the Council of Governments set in motion a five-year plan to have 20 percent of the region's workforce telework by 2005. They designed an eight-step plan to increase telework participation and offered free one-day seminars to help businesses in Washington, DC, Virginia, and Maryland start or expand their telework programs. Coupled with initiatives from the entire region, their efforts began to show results. By the time the "2001 State of the Commute" survey was completed, 15 percent of the regional workforce was telecommuting on an average of 1.5 days per week, up from 12 percent in 1998.

In October 2000, WACOT (Washington Area Conference on Telework), sponsored by the Metropolitan Washington Council of Governments, Fairfax County, Virginia, and ITAC brought together proponents of telework, politicians and government representatives, academics, the press, practitioners, and the curious to share their experiences, identify best practices, and offer solutions for overcoming management barriers to telework. Held in conjunction with Telework America Day, the conference was successful in generating further interest in telework among the various constituencies. The second annual conference was cancelled after the events of September 11, losing some of the momentum generated by the first conference.

LIMITS ON INITIATIVES

Although over time some barriers have been overcome, there are still unique constraints on telework that are faced by the public sector. At the symposium on telework mentioned previously, some of the challenges to successful implementation of telework programs were highlighted. These included a management culture in the government that resists change and a worker culture that resists giving up a permanent workstation or moving into a boundaryless organization such as that demanded by an emphasis on telework. In addition, facilities management is complicated by the inconsistent absences created through telework, and double overhead can be the result. Existing policies and regulations may get in the way of rapid implementation of programs, and the difficulty of measuring the positive impact of telework may retard the needed policy and procedural changes (Joice, 2000).

We can, of course, view some of these "challenges" as decoys—public agencies are limited in their actions by many regulations as well as by a strong union presence, but these regulations do not prohibit the positive actions that would invest the American public sector worker with enthusiasm for telework. Teleworking ventures that have proven successful have arisen from the same cultures described as inimical to emergent work structures, and this has happened for several straightforward reasons. The successful programs have in common some cultural and organizational design characteristics that have facilitated the development and implementation of these emergent work forms. These characteristics have typically included the following:

- Work groups whose task assignments lend themselves to off-site production, such as surveyors, lawyers, and investigators
- Technical employees and/or workers in self-managed positions (Grade 12 and higher)
- The fortune or misfortune to be located in an area with either extreme congestion (like Boston's Big Dig area), severe pollution (such as certain CDC programs in Atlanta), or great distances to be traveled to a central workplace (such as OSHA offices in Texas or Colorado)
- Extraordinary budgetary constraints to be met that force consideration of alternative solutions or new directions or, alternately, surprisingly deep pockets that permit the extensive hiring of experienced outside consultants and the purchase of excellent portable equipment
- A method of rewarding rather than penalizing entrepreneurial behavior

These have acted as stimuli for the creation and acceptance of new work designs, regardless of a national federal work culture that has been described in less agreeable terms. The large bureaucracy that is the heart of the federal organizational structure has been superseded, in the successful telework programs, by a sense of agility that is unexpected and therefore all the more effective.

Instead, what has proven a limitation restraint on the widespread acceptance of telework in the public sector has been resource driven, or rather, lack-of-resources driven. Some of the successful government programs share a characteristic not often found in public sector circles—access to deep pockets. Dollars can provide both technical expertise (in the form of consultants and facilitators from outside the government who are not tied to yesterday's solutions or to a career path dependent on the government's grade system) and actual equipment—laptops, modems, and the like—that keep workers on the same virtual page as their in-office colleagues.

There is little as inimical to business success as inadequate tools to perform required tasks. Workers who depend on electronic technology for accomplishing their jobs should not be required to use antiquated computers. However, most federal agencies cannot afford to purchase duplicate equipment for workers. In fact, simply upgrading existing equipment is beyond the fiscal ability of some. Many federal teleworkers are required to use either their own home computers or to use equipment that has been handed down by their departments when they upgrade. One of the most successful tactics undertaken by private industry has been to recognize that workers out of the main location need *more*, not less, support, and they have reallocated their resources accordingly. Done skillfully, this one action can have greater impact than many of the more obvious, visible managerial support interventions and certainly has more universally positive impact than do mandates (Vega, 2000).

Additional stumbling blocks to public sector success included the standard concerns of effects of telework on career trajectory, difficulty of measuring productivity and monitoring performance, perceived inequities in selection processes, and lack of training at all levels. Recommendations were made to develop a tracking system that would provide a clearer picture of the extent of participation in telework programs, to provide training for managers and workers alike in all facets of telework implementation, to nurture an overall culture change that would embrace the positive effects of telework, to develop systematic methods of allocating resources where they are needed, and to improve communication between the various constituent interests in the programs (Stough & Bragg, October 2000; Vega & Brennan, June 2000b).

Several of these recommendations were put into practice. One subsequent study contracted by the GSA focused on issues of technology, previously identified as an impediment to widespread adoption of telework. The main finding of the study was that "today, no single information technology barrier is preventing or impeding telework implementation" (Booz Allen Hamilton, 4/5/02). The study identified the need to involve IT management in decisions that relate to telework and to establish less idiosyncratic selection and acquisition criteria for home-based telework technology, as well as engaging IT training staff in providing appropriate preparation, training, and ongoing support to potential teleworkers.

According to the researchers, "More than half of teleworkers use their own printers and personal computers for telework" (ES-6), and "over 75% of teleworkers are using dial-up connections to connect to their agency networks" (III-5). This substantiated earlier findings of significant use of personal equipment being used for government work. The successful programs that were reviewed all had several things in common: They were supported from the beginning by senior management who were able to mobilize the necessary support from a variety of departments to make the projects proceed in a timely and effective way, budgeting and funding of implementation were consistent and centralized, and IT training was provided for teleworkers. Overall, this report confirmed that issues of both funding and management need to be resolved before there can be any hope of expansion of telework in the public sector. It also confirmed that this sort of good management, if applied to any work model, can create success.

Government reflects the society of which it is a part. In some ways, the use of telework in government mirrors the opportunities and benefits discussed in relation to the private sector. The challenges that government faces, however, are different and more difficult to resolve than the challenges faced by private industry when initiating new projects such as telework. Limited budgets, a regularly changing management team based on political interest and motivated by besting the opposition rather than finding workable solutions, and the tendency to confound democracy with capitalism sets up roadblocks to success that require the commitment and ongoing support of shifting incumbencies and constituent interests.

14

Telework around the World

GLOBAL TRANSLATIONS

Building alliances while eliminating barriers to trade has created an international work environment that is dependent on technology, mediated by cooperation-based competition, and conducted, for the most part, in English. New work structures that function in a 24/7 mode around the globe have challenged governments and human resource departments to find ways to make work suit the needs of workers and to help workers fulfill the needs of business. In the United States, telework was initially motivated by a need to conserve resources. In a curious reversal of motivations, telework in other countries has been sponsored primarily by business interests in aid of cost cutting and competitive productivity.

Since the mid-1990s, telework has grown rapidly in acceptance and has earned the status of accepted work model in Europe as well as in other regions around the world. In the United Kingdom, telework has increased at an average of 13 percent each year since 1997, in sharp contrast to the 1.6 percent annual growth rate for all employees (UK Labour Force Survey, 2002). In the overall European community, telework is perceived as an important enough trend to require protection of the citizenry. The social partners of the European Council passed a resolution in July 2002 covering the treatment of teleworkers that differs in many ways from the less formalized teleworking relationships that exist in the United States. Their *Framework Agreement on Telework* is direct in stating the goals of telework: "The social partners see telework both as a way for companies and public service organizations to modernize work organisation, and as a way for workers to reconcile work and social life and giving them greater autonomy in the accomplishment of their tasks."

Further, the emphasis is on the voluntary nature of telework, both for the worker and for the employer. The teleworker's privacy is guaranteed, the employer takes full responsibility for protecting corporate data (although the teleworker is expected to follow the rules set up for this purpose), and all liabilities, costs, and maintenance of equipment are clearly defined at the beginning of the telework relationship. There are no ad hoc decisions to be made and, presumably, no uncomfortable surprises to be discovered. The worker is treated like a professional and given control over production: "The teleworker manages the organisation of his/her working time." There are also opportunities for promotion comparable to those of on-site workers: "Teleworkers have the same access to training and career development opportunities as comparable workers at the employer's premises and are subject to the same appraisal policies as these other workers."

A survey by the Gartner Group that is frequently quoted predicted that there would be over 137 million global teleworkers by 2003. Regardless of the system used to count teleworkers, that figure is highly inflated. Nonetheless, it has an impact on the activities of telework associations throughout the world and creates a sense of urgency that encourages the further development of telework processes.

NATIONAL STATUS—IN BRIEF

We have no generally accepted definition of telework in the United States. The rest of the world shares our lack of precision, but focuses more on the technology that facilitates the work than on the specific location of the work. European Telework Online (ETO), a telework clearinghouse that bills itself as "The Internet portal for teleworking, telecommuting, and related topics," operates with the broadest possible definition and includes home-based telework, mobile telework, telecenters, telecottages, functional relocation (such as employing people in another part of the world to perform both front and back office processes electronically), outsourcing, and virtual teaming in its description of telework: "Information and communication technologies (ICTs) are applied to enable work to be done at a distance from the place where the work results are needed or where the work would conventionally have been done." No minimum time out of the office is required in this definition.

Other parts of the world determine telework using different standards. For example, in Australia, the desire for precision in assessing the prevalence of telework and eliminating from the total "staff who use some form of information technology to undertake work tasks in their own time," has led to the exclusion of "contract workers; employees working at sites other than their homes; employees augmenting their normal work routine by working form home; and employees working less than one day per week from home" (Lindorff, 2000, 7). Naturally, this has lowered the Australia estimates significantly in comparison with Europe and the United States.

The difficulty of defining telework is reflected in the challenge of estimating the number of teleworkers, for without the definition the count in meaningless. The collection of statistics internationally is as flawed as it is within the United States, colored by enthusiasm and optimism. On the same Web page, two sequential but conflicting articles indicate that as of 2000 there were 23 million teleworkers in the EU nations (private sector), accounting for 16 percent of the workforce and, by 2005, over 16.2 million (or 10.8 percent) of the European workforce will be involved in teleworking in "one way or another" (www.ivc.ca /studies/European.html).

Table 14.1 provides a general estimate of the magnitude of the teleworking trend outside the United States based on the most recent available figures, ranked in order of percent of population. A discussion of the teleworking situation in several of these countries or regions follows.

Germany—Telearbeit in Deutschland

Germany takes the first place among percent of teleworkers because it counts all teleworkers in the country, including "occasional teleworkers" (those who telework less than one day per week). This somewhat misleading statistic "is due to independent staff in small businesses and office workers taking work home" (Flutak, 10/9/02). Based on these figures, the three-year growth among teleworkers is remarkable—in 1999, the same research group indicated a total 2,132,000 teleworkers in Germany, 6 percent of the workforce, the European average at the time (Korte, 1999).

Telework is a more recent phenomenon in Germany than in many other countries, becoming acceptable only in the late 1990s. It continues to be an urban phenomenon, with a younger average worker (38 years old compared to 48 years old in Sweden), male, and either self-employed, a professional or manager. As of 1999, only one quarter of German firms offered telework as an option, but that low penetration was forecast to increase rapidly. The more recent statistics indicate that

TABLE 14.1   Number of Teleworkers as Percent of the Working Population

Country	Number of Teleworkers	Percent of Working Population
Germany**	6,000,000	18.0%
United Kingdom*	4,000,000	15.0%
Japan***	2,460,000	16.5%
Finland*	300,000	13.6%
Norway*	50,000	11.4%
Sweden*	400,000	10.3%
United Kingdom++	2,200,000	7.4%
Canada*	1,000,000	7.1%
France*	300,000	1.3%
Low Countries*	140,000	1.9%
Ireland*	40,000	2.9%
Germany*	800,000	2.4%

*Source: L'Institut Allemand de l'Economie, 2000
** Source: Bonn Empirica, 2002 (includes "occasional teleworkers")
***Source: Japan Telework Association, 2001
++Source: UK Labour Force Survey, 2002 (people who work at home at least one day per week)

it has, at least in part, overcome the major barrier to telework as described in the ECaTT (Electronic Commerce and Telework Trends) report: "Also quite a few organizations have doubts as to the productivity of teleworkers and sufficient quality of their work results. Problems with the trade unions and an expected resistance from the workforce are negligible. Slightly different to other countries German decision makers seem to show some more conservative attitudes since the reason 'We do not need telework, everything went well so far and we do not expect this to change' ranks second" (Korte, 1999, 41–42).

United Kingdom

The UK Labour Force Survey (LFS) is the source of the firmest data that are available for the United Kingdom. The LFS defines teleworkers as people who use both a computer and a telephone to work in their own homes at least one day per week. This includes "occasional teleworkers," "home-based teleworkers" and "teleworker homeworkers," but excludes those who are based in telecenters, the "mobile warriors" who are not based at home, and those who work at client sites rather than at their company office. As a result, the impact of telework on the British work force is underestimated vis-à-vis the U.S. workforce estimates, which include all of the above categories.

Telework has gained wide acceptance in the public sector—26 percent of all teleworkers are public sector employees. Self-employed individuals predominate among private teleworkers, comprising 43 percent of the teleworking workforce (as compared to 11 percent of the overall workforce), with the remainder being mostly managers and professionals or technical workers. The gender breakdown of teleworkers is consistent with traditional role separation, that is, significantly more men than women telework, especially among government employees (67 percent of government teleworkers are men; 53 percent of the entire workforce is male). It is anticipated that considerable growth of telework in rural areas will occur as the wireless broadband network is established in the remote areas of the Western Isles (Smith, 8/19/02). Significant public funds are being devoted to this initiative. A survey by British Telecom (BT) of its "workabout" group, at 5,000 strong, the largest such group in the United Kingdom, indicated continuing interest and general approval of various flexible work arrangements, telework among them (Hopkinson, James, & Maruyama, 2002). Findings of this study were remarkably congruent with the findings of similar studies conducted by parallel organizations in the United States, including mixed responses in terms of longer working hours coupled with improved quality of work life and work/life balance.

Growth in telework in the United Kingdom is dramatic, evidencing an increase of between 65 and 70 percent between 1997 and 2001. Even at a total of 7.4 percent of the working population, this is a trend to watch.

Japan

The changes that have rocked work life in the United States have not left Japan unaffected. Similar challenges have been experienced in the two countries, with the changes in Japan following by a half decade. Japan's policy of lifetime employment began its decline toward the mid-1990s, while the U.S. was still pointing to Japan as a leader in quality, productivity, and efficiency. In 1996, Japan counted fewer than 1 million teleworkers among its extensive workforce, and defined such teleworkers as employees who, "in spite of their company having a head office, work at home or satellite offices regularly or irregularly" (www.japan-telework.or.jp).

Japan has been a late starter in telework due to a set of social circumstances that limits working at home. These circumstances include a preference for management by time rather than management by objective (which is the rule of thumb for managing remote workers), the importance among workers to feel like they belong to a company rather than simply have a job, the lack of space in Japanese homes for home offices, and despite wide use of personal computers and mobile telephones, Internet access has not been readily available. As a result, there have been few pilot programs from which to gather data (Sakai, 1999). According to Dr. Sakai, "The corporate survival is a much more important matter than creating a comfortable working environment for each employee. The companies' greatest interest of today is in how to come up with a measure which reduces office costs, raises labor productivity, and distributes surplus workers to other areas of business" (3).

A major barrier to telework for the Japanese is the difficulty of managing and evaluating the productivity of remote workers. However, based on the need to raise labor force mobility to counteract the labor shortage occurring around economic recovery, Japanese companies have begun to use telework in earnest, leaping from 4.2 percent of the workforce in 1996 to 16.5 percent of the workforce in 2000 (www.japan-telework.or.jp).

Finland

Finland is the European leader in many electronic initiatives. It is home to the largest percentage of mobile phone owners in Europe (57.8 percent of the population in 2000), has the largest percentage of teleworkers if all categories of telework are included, and has the highest percentage of firms offering telework opportunities to employees (Nupponen and Vainio, 2000). It has the second highest percentage of at home PC users and is second in the use of email. Overall, Finland represents the self-effacing European telework leader.

Technical requirements for telework have been met in Finland but, as in the rest of the world, organizational preconditions are still lacking. There is still managerial reluctance to apply telework broadly. This exists, according to Nupponen and Vainio, because companies are still operating on the old paradigm that limits worker independence and focuses more on control than on effectiveness. Teleworkers are not differentiated from the rest of the workforce, either by legislation or by union mandate. In Finland, work is work regardless of location. Their categories of teleworker include home-based teleworkers who work from home at least one day per week, using a personal computer and a telephone, and are either in salaried employment or are self-employed; permanent teleworkers who perform the above activities more than 90 percent of the time; alternating teleworkers who work at home more than one day per week but less than 90 percent of their time; mobile teleworkers who work at least ten hours per week away from their home and from their main workplace, using online computer connections; and self-employed workers whose main place of work is at home. If all these categories are included in the calculations, Finland led Europe in 1999 with 16.77 percent of the workforce teleworking.

Supplementary telework, working from home less than a full day per week using computers and telephones, is a growing trend in Europe, led by Finland. One quarter of European companies offer supplementary teleworking; in Finland, almost 50 percent of the companies do.

Finland has succeeded in encouraging the growth of telework through a combination of governmental and educational initiatives designed to improve working conditions and organization. The focus on learning organizations and innovation create the conditions for acceptance of new work formats and structures.

Sweden—Distansarbete

Sweden is the grandmother of European telework, with a significant population of individuals who have been teleworking since the late 1980s. In a report sponsored by ECaTT in 1999/2000, more Swedish companies than any other in Europe offered telework opportunities (62 percent). Email usage in Sweden was the highest in Europe at 40 percent compared to the European average of 18 percent. Fifty-eight percent of the population had home access to Internet and half the population (4.6 million Swedes) had mobile telecommunications access. As early accepters and leaders in telecommunications technology and telework opportunities, a series of national strategies to support and encourage additional telework was established in 1996:

- To use ICT (Information Communication Technology) in an active way to create growth and employment that makes Sweden competitive as a nation,
- To protect everyone's equal right to use ICT as a tool for higher skills and capability, democracy and justice,
- To make use of both women and men, according to experiences and competence, in developing ICT,
- To use ICT to develop the welfare state and to increase the citizens' quality of life,
- To use ICT to support groups with special needs in the society,
- To create a broad access to information to make people more involved and for progressing the level of proficiency and skills,
- To keep up and develop the Swedish language and culture in a more and more boundless world,
- To use ICT to increase the efficiency and quality in the public sector, and to improve the services towards citizens and companies. (Pitkanen & Thorslund, 1999)

These goals reflect the Swedish approach toward work and society and highlight the attitudes that govern Nordic telework. As a result, it is no surprise that 72 percent of the workforce desires to telework and that the main barrier to telework is data security rather than managerial practice.

A Swedish Gallup poll conducted in 2001 indicated overwhelmingly (75 percent) that telework provided advantages to companies and near half (45 percent) offered employees the opportunity to work remotely with access to company data. Of those teleworking firms, 47 percent claimed increased productivity among their remote workers. The follow-up poll in 2002 showed that, once supplied with broadband connections, 55 percent of the survey respondents claimed to be teleworking more than they did with dial-up service.

Canada

Canadian participation in telework appears to be low, but that perception grows out of the apparent lack of data regarding the number of Canadians who are engaged in this work phenomenon. As long ago as 2000, 69 percent of Canadian households owned a computer and more than 50 percent had Web access, according to a Nielsen survey, far exceeding U.S. figures. In addition, Canada can boast of the world's cheapest Internet access—$20 per month at a time when the United States was paying $28 and Germany $74 (www.ivc.ca). The country's very low population density (7 people per square mile), high computer usage, and cheap access create a telework environment that is poised to explode. Supported by many studies that provide anecdotal evidence of the human resource benefits of telework, large Canadian employers such as Nortel, IBM, Bell Canada, Digital Canada, AT&T (where 55 percent of the managers telework), Hewlett Packard, Xerox Canada, and Intel encourage increased participation in telework for existing and prospective employees.

In addition, with reports of workers from developing nations offering their services for free on a trial basis, Canadians feel sharply the competition between their workforce and an international workforce that is no longer isolated by distance from employment opportunities, according to the Canadian Telework Association. This threat is likely to encourage more rapid and broader acceptance of telework than any positive opportunities have thus far afforded.

France—Teletravail; Spain—Teletrabajo; Italy—Telelavoro

Once hailed for its innovative technology—for example, Minitel—France has since lagged behind in the European race to an information society, along with Spain and Italy. In terms of telework, penetration was only 2.9 percent of the French workforce in 1999, and major changes have not occurred as of this writing. There continues to be resistance to formalized telework initiatives in these Latin countries, and working at home occasionally is not considered telework by French workers or employers (Baudoin, 1999).

Spain has the distinction of having the least impact from telework of the European Union nations. Interest among Spanish workers in telework is consistently low, although there appears to be interest among job seekers and among workers who would consider working in telecenters, but not in their homes, an interest shared by Italian workers (Guerrero, 2000). Spain has low access to communication technologies, with only 20 percent having Internet access as of 2000.

The true barriers to increased telework in France, Spain, and Italy have little to with access to technology, however. The barriers are higher and harder to scale, as they involve more challenging factors: culture and human relationships. Communication, management, and innovation differ greatly in these cultures from the other regions of Europe. Before deciding that telework cannot work in the warm regions, it pays to consider the cultural factors that have limited its acceptance to date.

CULTURAL IMPACTS

Culture can be defined as the collective patterns of behavior and expectations that we have learned through our associations and our upbringing. These collective patterns reflect the way people tend to act on the large, or national, scale rather than provide a template for action on the individual scale. Geert Hofstede refers to culture as the "software of the mind" (1997), a metaphor that is particularly apt in the context of this technological discussion. The cultural challenges posed by technologically mediated work is reminiscent of the story of the tower of Babel, a notorious instance of technology and communication mixing badly.

Hofstede suggests that cultures exists on a scale that begins at the national level and continues down a gradually narrowing path through regional/religious/linguistic groups to gender, generation, social class, and finally organizational groups. In addition, cultures vary on several dimensions: power distance, individualism, masculinity/femininity, and uncertainty avoidance.

Power Distance

Power distance describes how people react to the concept of equality and inequality in society. A high score on the power distance scale developed over 20 years of research suggests that workers are dependent on their bosses and unlikely to contradict them. A low score on this scale indicates comfort on the part of both workers and their bosses for a consultative, interdependent style of management. What this means in the workplace is that workers in a high power-distance environment tend to accept that their "place" is lower down than that of their boss, and they are comfortable with this. Workers in a low power distance environment believe that hierarchy exists for convenience but has no inherent meaning for them or their bosses. They expect to be consulted and that inequalities among them will be minimized. As a group, and in broadest brush strokes, the Scandinavian countries share low power distances; Germany, the United Kingdom, and the United States share moderate power distances, and the Latin countries (France, Spain, Italy) join together with South America and most of Asia to experience the highest power distances (Hofstede, 1997).

Individualism

In the same way as power distance, individualism reflects a significant distinction in the way people behave on the national level. This distinction is also reflected at the organizational level. Most cultures in the world are collectivist cultures—that is, people are more concerned with the power of the group than with the comfort or success of individuals. A collectivist desires good working conditions, skills training, and the opportunity to use skills on the job. Individualists want challenging work to do, freedom to do things their own way, and personal time to spend on their own activities. Individualism tends to correlate closely with low power distance and collectivism with high power distance, although this is not always the case. The highest scorers on the individualist scale included the United States, Great Britain. and Canada, all of which were low or moderate on power distance. The regions on the collectivist side of the scale, South America and most of Asia, scored high on the power distance scale. However, France, Germany, and Spain fell between the poles on individualism/collectivism, as did many of the Scandinavian countries, and Italy placed strongly on the individualist end of the scale (Hofstede, 1997). This system is not without anomalies.

Masculinity/Femininity

This scale measures the degree of assertiveness or modesty reflected in human behavior. Behaviors that reflect masculinity and femininity in today's society are quite closely tied to traditional patterns. For example, a focus on high earning, on recognition for contributions made, on advancement and on challenge for personal accomplishment are considered "masculine," whereas cooperation, good working relationships, living where one prefers, and security are considered "feminine." These traits or behaviors can be practiced by both men and women—they are not sex based. It is interesting to note that the decision to refer to these traits as masculine or feminine was based on the research results, which showed that the men and women who participated in the study (all employees of IBM worldwide) scored consistently on gender roles. The masculinity index is based on societies in which the gender roles are distinct—men are concerned with material success, and women are concerned with quality of life. Societies that are characterized as feminine are ones in which both sexes play the feminine roles. The most feminine countries in Hofstede's (1997) study were the Scandinavian countries and the Netherlands; the most masculine were Japan, Italy, and many Latin American countries. Firmly in the middle were the Anglo nations of the United States, the United Kingdom, Canada, and Ireland. As we progress through these dimensions of culture, it becomes more difficult to identify the cultures that will welcome technologically mediated relationships; cultural complexity becomes more apparent.

Uncertainty Avoidance

The fourth dimension of cultural comparison focuses on the ability of people to deal with ambiguity and uncertainty, and how much these things threaten their sense of security. The most anxious countries were the so-called warm countries, those where expressive behavior allows people to blow off steam. This includes the Latin and Mediterranean countries, as well as Japan. The least anxious countries were the Anglo countries and most of Scandinavia. A lower level of anxiety is correlated with weaker uncertainty avoidance and a higher level of anxiety with more uncertainty avoidance. Strong uncertainty avoidance creates a need to follow the rules, to go by the book, to play it safe. Weak uncertainty avoidance views change as a threat. People in strong uncertainty avoidance cultures like their jobs less than those in weak uncertainty avoidance situations where innovation, limited rules, and curiosity are tolerated (Hofstede, 1997).

The Chicken or the Egg?

When we consider the acceptance and prevalence of telework in relation to these four dimensions of culture, some of our assumptions need to be re-examined. Are the Scandinavian countries strong proponents of telework because of the early origins of telecommunications technology in these countries? Or because much of the population lives in remote areas? Or because the weather makes daily travel difficult and dangerous? Or is it because Scandinavian nations tend to be less concerned about power distance, have feminine structures in place, and experience little uncertainty avoidance and low anxiety about change?

Is encouraging telework likely to be a fruitless endeavor in the Romance language speaking nations because they do not prefer to work in isolation and make their own decisions, expecting their bosses to do that for them? Or because the home is the place for women, and men are supposed to be physically out in the workplace? Or because higher anxiety levels and a need to follow the rules and do things the way they have always been done blocks risk-taking and innovation?

In addition to the dimensions mentioned in this chapter, other dimensions play an important role in the patterns of acceptance of telework globally. These other dimensions include time, context, and proxemics and have been discussed in Chapters 4 and 5. In order to succeed, the introduction of these new workplace structures must respect the differences in each country in which they are being offered, with sensitivity to the varying cultural needs of the people who live and work there.

15

Going Home: A Longitudinal Case Study

In 1990, a small band of courageous innovators took their work home. Seven years later, a program had developed to serve 18 teleworkers who were processing transactions at home. By 2002, the band numbered 700 and included transaction processors, engineers, programmers, customer representatives, and managers. Something was going right.

BUILDING THE BUSINESS CASE

In 1937, George Putnam established a balanced fund with a flexible portfolio of stocks and bonds. George Putnam was the great-great grandson of Judge Samuel Putnam, developer of the Prudent Man Rule. This legal regulation directing the business of asset management required fiduciaries to limit their investments for others to those that a reasonably prudent individual would make. Putnam Investments has followed that watchword since its inception. In 1969, Putnam expanded into institutional management and was acquired the following year by Marsh & McLennan Companies, Inc. At that time, Putnam's seven mutual funds had assets under management of $1.5 billion. These assets grew to $43 billion by 1990 (www.putnaminvestments.com). In June of

Information is this chapter is drawn, in large part, from interviews and conversations held at Putnam Investments over a four-year research period. All quotations are accurate, all situations took place. I have changed the names of the individuals involved at all but the highest levels to protect their privacy and the confidential nature of our discussions. A description of the research methodology appears in the Appendix.

2000, George Putnam (son of the founder) stepped down as chairman and president of the firm's funds, leaving a legacy of conservative investment and assets under management of $370 billion (Kovaleski, 2000).

Innovation by Default

Putnam began its program of decentralization a decade earlier. Its first move involved shifting operations to Quincy, MA, from downtown Boston. Several high-performing employees tendered their resignations, unwilling to undertake the long commute south of Boston. The loss of these workers would have had a severe impact on the still-small company. Putnam's goal was to retain them and their valuable institutional memory. During the late 1980s, a sophisticated system that imaged all incoming mail had begun, and this technology opened the door to the idea of sending these valuable workers home, to perform transfer agency processes over the network full time in their own home offices. The first teleworkers ("go-homers" as opposed to the later "Work@Homers") operated almost as consultants, performing quality-control functions and the very limited processing permitted by the technology of the day. The program was an early success, retaining valuable workers on an ad hoc basis, and growing almost imperceptibly as individuals requested participation because of their special needs.

Incentives

Success stories do not occur without costs. Doing business was becoming ever more complex. The roller coaster stock market ride and the fund scandals of the 1980s and 1990s had thrown the investment world off balance and changed the way asset management firms operated. "Threatened by do-it-yourself investing and on-line stock trading" (Browning, 1999), Putnam had to find a way to adapt its proven model to the demands of the investment community. The cyclical turmoil of the stock market was replicated in the more conservative world of mutual funds. Never especially high-performing in the long term, mutual funds outperformed the Standard & Poor's 500 stock index less than half the time in their first 73 years of history (Zweig, 1999). The traditionally idolized fund manager was shown to have excellent reverse insights; that is, their forecasts were frequently off by 180 degrees, making advisors doubt the managers and investors doubt advisors.

Putnam Investments had never tended to the flash—the sexy, high-risk fund—and had a long-standing policy of team management of most funds (Carbonara, 2001). In the early 1990s, Putnam's investing strategy shifted from the fundamental research for which they had been known previously to mathematical modeling and computer analysis of companies' financials. Coupled with this shift and in the light of high turnover by individuals (Walmac, 1995), the remaining individual fund managers were replaced by management teams in an attempt to stabilize the funds. It was this staid image that bolstered the confidence of Putnam's customer—the mature, well-established investor who could afford to pay the higher than industry average fees that Putnam charged.

Labor force availability. As the meteoric rise of the market that extended over the second half of the 1990s showed no sign of slowing down, it became harder and harder to recruit workers. Asset management is a people-dependent business. Customers want to know what is happening with their investments, and advisors need service support from the fund management. The success of an asset management firm is nearly as dependent upon the ability to build relationships as upon the ability to actually manage assets. Answers to most questions are time-sensitive, and the whole process is driven by the hours the market is open. In a strong market, the phones do not stop ringing. The daily mail received by Putnam in their headquarters is measured by the pound—600 pounds is a heavy day, 300 pounds a light day. Twenty thousand to 30,000 individual transactions per day is normal. A great many people are required to handle the transactions in a timely way. To meet the need, in 1998, more than 500 telephone representatives worked Monday through Friday, 7:00 A.M. to 11:00 P.M. (and Saturday as well) in Putnam's Andover, MA, facility. Creativity helped to locate more of the needed representatives; an alliance had been made to provide jobs for students at a small, private college in Franklin, MA to alleviate some of the stress on the full-time workers. Eighty to 100 students worked part-time in a dedicated laboratory on the campus, learning about the industry while handling overflow processing tasks (Barney, 2000). Putnam also sought similar alliances at other educational institutions, but there simply were not enough skilled workers in the local area to fill all the available jobs.

A security blanket. It should come as no surprise to anyone that New England's winter weather is notoriously unpredictable. Sudden shifts in temperature, precipitation in varying quantities and forms of liquidity, and a population that seems to forget how to drive as soon as a snowflake appears create a logistical challenge for continuity and disaster planners. In light of the time-critical nature of the asset management business, representatives must be available regardless of what the weather brings. Putnam traditionally dealt with this problem by renting blocks of hotel rooms in Boston to house employees who could not get home or, once home, would not be able to return to cover the telephones in the morning. This was effective for the company's reputation for reliability, but it was expensive. And it was a poor solution for workers with responsibilities at home, young children, or personal needs of any kind.

Worker turnover rate. Order processing is boring work. It is repetitive. It is demanding. It is not creative. There is little fun to be found in this task. The telephone work is the glamour side of the business and, even at that, the glamour may be hard to find. The turnover rate for production employees—those answering telephones and processing transactions—was high, very high, on occasion spiking to over 30 percent. It is expensive to train new workers. The expense is so high, it seems out of line with the salaries that the workers earn. At the end of the 1990s, the cost to Putnam to recruit and train a single new production employee who was unlikely to meet productivity goals before six months of work was comparable to the annual salary for that entry level position, not counting benefits, which included a bonus plan, 401(k), and profit sharing.

Real estate and technology. Putnam Investments was founded in Boston, and it continues to use a Boston telephone exchange and main address. Despite the challenges of doing business in the financial district, there is a special aura about Boston for investment firms in Massachusetts. Overcrowding, high rents, and transportation disrupted by the Big Dig for a decade or more have generated movement from the central city to the outlying districts whenever more physical space is needed. As real estate prices escalated, the company sought office space further and further away from the Boston headquarters. Putnam began opening offices in the late 1980s in the areas surrounding Boston—first Quincy, then Franklin (1994) and Andover (1996), and finally Norwood (2001).

At the same time, Putnam, along with the rest of the world, fell in love with evolving technology. Encouraged by President Lawrence Lasser, they embraced as many technological solutions as they could find. While other firms were mailing marketing and financial planning materials in hard copy, Putnam was personalizing them and making them available on the Web. Their in-house technology group developed ways to integrate legacy systems with the newest advances, making possible specialized requests and up-to-the-minute customer advice (Clark, 1997). This technological skill would be the support for the vital teleworking and e-learning initiatives to follow. Also developed in-house, these initiatives helped move telework at Putnam from a program to an important aspect of their business-as-usual.

Restraints

There was little holding Putnam back from the revolutionary step of sending workers home. The general work environment was conducive to such a move: in 1997, telework (or telecommuting, as it was referred to then) was poised to take off. According to 1997 Department of Labor statistics, 21 million people were already teleworking, at least part of the time. The demand seemed to be high among workers, disgusted with commuting and having to juggle work with family demands.

There were technological constraints, of course. Costly upgrades and integration of legacy equipment had to be considered. Requirements for data security had to be addressed, along with the standard concerns about control and productivity. But these were insufficient to hold back the wider adoption of telework as a solution to the problems they were experiencing. The incentives far outweighed the potential drawbacks.

PHASING IT IN

Phase 1: The Intrepid Few (1990 to 1997)

Although stalwartly staid in their business operations, Putnam proved careful but clearly innovative in the use of technology. As early adopters of teleworking initiatives, they took creative steps to address the labor and real estate problems they faced. During the period from 1995 to 1998, Putnam tripled in assets under management, from $100 billion to $300 billion. During the same period, their personnel doubled. One third of the Putnam workforce was engaged in processing tasks, and demand for processors was increasing dramatically. But they were becoming harder and harder to come by. As Putnam continued to decentralize their operations, more workers were encountering commuting problems and were unwilling to relocate their jobs. By 1996, about 80 people (of the 1,000 processing agents) had resisted the job migration to new sites and were working at home, still on an ad hoc basis.

Phase 2: Earning the Right to Go Home (1997 to 2000)

Working in the office. A visit to Putnam's Andover installation in January 1999 caught us by surprise. Hidden in the woods of an industrial park, the installation was enormous. Seven attached single-story buildings, each the length of a football field, were named for local communities from Amesbury at one end to Gloucester at the other end. A small additional building of three stories was called The Tower, and housed a reception area, meeting rooms, the human resources department, and the training area. Each building was color coded, with furnishings that matched walls and carpets. The buildings had been purchased in poor condition and had been completely renovated before the staff moved in. Standard-sized windows were removed and replaced with large floor to ceiling panes, skylights were added, and a meandering central hallway meant to re-create the feeling of a New England town led from one building to another. A large atrium gave the impression of working nestled in a wild garden. Eighteen hundred parking spaces assured that everyone would be able to drive to work, a critical factor because there was no public transportation available nearby.

A tour of the structure began at the facility that housed IT support, generators, mainframes, power sources, and backup systems. Most of these ran without human assistance, the computers checking for problems and rectifying them before informing technicians that they had been corrected. Walking into this installation was like entering a science fiction movie—hushed footsteps on padded tile, wall-sized windows for observation of machinery and people, but not one speck of paper or dirt. This was a paperless environment; all receipts were scanned into computers and forwarded electronically. There was no reason to fear power fluctuations—900 rectifiers and matching automobile batteries served as UPS (uninterruptible power supply) for power failure and surge protection along with massive generators, robust enough to co-generate and sell electricity to the local power company, served as a backup system. These generators could easily supply power to the 1,400 homes in the local community.

The rest of the facility continued the illusion of a movie set. A conference room had walls that opened into enormous television screens for videoconferences with sites around the world. The conference table was wired for computer access, and the wall opposite the television screens contained a series of monitors behind sliding panels for presentations and multichannel observations. A touch screen on the conference table controlled the lighting.

The transfer area, where phone representatives and processors worked, was dominated by a raised platform (appropriately called The Bridge) where supervisors could observe the workers in their sawtooth-configured cubbies and, at the same time, monitor statistics regarding output, calls in, routing figures, and queues in real time. All these were displayed on ubiquitous screens whose readouts undulated, reflecting the dynamic data represented. Large LCD screens placed at strategic locations allowed all workers to keep updated on changes in the market, and oversized television screens provided continuous monitoring of CNBC for current world news. Workers sat in cubbies that provided an unexpected amount of privacy considering the sheer number of people and stations in the room. The management team also sat in an open area with cubbies in order to facilitate communication and create a more open feeling among workers.

Each town/building had centrally located meeting areas (town squares) for stand-up meetings. Those areas had skylights and permitted easy clustering for brief meetings, award presentations, and similar short get-togethers. A cafeteria with an extensive menu abutted a dry cleaner, a pharmacy, and an ATM. The whole place was surprisingly quiet.

The work. Beyond the management, sale, and trading of financial instruments, Putnam operates also as a transfer agency. Most of the workers process orders and perform customer service, interacting principally with brokers and dealers rather than directly with individual customers. These representatives are mostly college graduates, using this job as an entry-level position to the more prestigious and lucrative ranks of fund management. They receive five to six weeks of training, spend 12 to 18 months on the phones, and then often move to other areas of responsibility in the company.

Because of the mechanistic nature of the routine of answering the phones, the "agility model" was developed. This agility model allowed the representative to act as a single point of service for the client via the telephone, after which he or she could process the order. The vast majority of their phone work was inbound, and Putnam committed to having each call picked up within 20 seconds. Ninety-three percent of calls had to be answered in this time frame. As we were told, "It's all about the call."

The paperless environment had not yet taken over Putnam's operations, despite a staunch belief in the concept and in the vision that the shift had already occurred. Or, maybe it had, and the technology had outstripped the ability to keep up with language, resulting in an odd set of linguistic anachronisms. Discussing the processing operation, workers and managers alike consistently talked about getting "the paperwork" and filing "the paperwork." One worker described a process like this, "When I first work on an adjustment what I do is look through the paperwork to check and see if everything's in good order. . . . The next step would be to start processing the item . . . and then when I'm finished I just write down any work I've done. . . . We need to keep track of what we do, and then the next thing I do is send it off." When questioned about "looking through the paperwork," "processing," "writing it down," and "sending it off," the worker confirmed that "we image our system, so what that actually involves is waiting for our paperwork to come out." All that looking, sending off, and writing down related to purely electronic tasks despite the physical images it evoked—except among the night workers.

The second-shift workers had a different process for their problem transactions, although they used the same language. Here is where the paperless environment failed. One worker told me, "We have sheets where we take down a list, write down the number of the item we worked on. . . . This is keeping track of what we're doing. It's on paper. . . . I put it into a bin at the end of the night and somebody will pick them up . . . and put it into a database in the supervisor's office."

Work@Home. The Work@Home program grew in waves, tied to technology. As the OCR (optical character recognition) technology improved, all paper (mail, receipts, letters, trades, and other transactions) was scanned into Putnam's central system and routed to the appropriate queue for processing. The goal was to maintain a seamless and paperless operation, regardless of where the processing activity took place. Images were sent to queues organized by skill set so that the worker who received the task had the skills to handle it.

The Work@Home employees were treated the same as on-site employees in all respects, except for their specific work hours. By 1999, they were 150 strong, by which time the Work@Home program had been regularized from a special project to a full player in the business operation. With a proven format, now, remote workers could log on any time of day, from 2:00 A.M. to 11:00 P.M. On-site workers could do this as well, but they generally did not, tending to prefer more traditional work hours. As with on-site workers, every @Home transaction was handled twice—once by the processor, once by Quality Control—as part of Putnam's obsession with accuracy. Commitment to this level of accuracy required a significant amount of interaction among workers. When questions would arise about an account or a transaction, the home workers had several choices: They could call a manager, call a coworker on-site, call a coworker off-site, or check the online help screens for assistance. On-site workers had the benefit of walking over to a manager or coworker and simply interrupting whatever they were doing, whereas @Home workers had to hope that coworkers would interrupt their own work to help. This was not always the case, because the interruptions had a negative impact on productivity rates, which, in turn, could affect performance-based bonus compensation. The result was that @Home workers had a harder time performing the same tasks as on-site workers.

Challenges. One problem that arose was that physical separation and agility participation created a two-tiered employee system—the more elite on-site agility group and the unseen home worker. Under the agility model, when peaks in demand created slowdowns in transaction processing, processing was transferred to other workers in a lower job grade. The lower-grade workers were primarily @Home workers and were not college graduates. The distinction between the groups was exacerbated by the @Homers' inability to connect with coworkers on a personal level. One on-site worker said, "They [the @Home workers] have no interaction with different departments—you got [sic] to be able to walk over to different departments to ask questions."

Several of the problems that Putnam experienced in this wave of development were technological in nature. The telephone response task could not be done at home because the calls needed to be linked and switched at the site. All calls had to be recorded and the recordings archived for several years, but technical issues prevented calls from being recorded at remote locations. Because work was distributed based on skill set and calls routed to people who shared a particular skill set via an 800 number service, there was little point in including the @Home workers in the telephone queue. There were also problems with maintaining call answering times at remote locations. The 93 percent pickup requirement within 20 seconds could not be accomplished at a remote location, and the impact on service level would be significant if the phones were not answered promptly. In the words of Putnam workers, "It's all about the call."

Another technologically based problem had to do with monitoring employee work. The system described earlier where managers on the Bridge could monitor statistics on all worker activities on-site did not permit the managers to perform the same monitoring on @Home workers. They could only see what the remote workforce was doing by reading reports about what was done. Post hoc monitoring can easily result in a reactive rather than a proactive environment, creating tension and defensiveness among workers and their managers. A sense of superiority appeared among the on-site workers when talking about the Work@Homers: "They lose touch with us—they make so many mistakes." This claim had some basis in reality. The continuous flow of work in a home environment without disruptions or distractions lent itself to a trancelike state among processors. When confronted with unexpected items in their queue, Work@Homers complained, "You killed my zone." Although operating" in the zone" may be more pleasant than operating in the here-and-now, it does create absentmindedness in the performer that places speed above accuracy and personal record-setting games above precision.

A third technological limitation was really an operations environment issue. The cost for ISDN in New Hampshire was twice the cost of the same service in Massachusetts. The Andover office nearly straddled the border of the two states and attracted many workers from southern New Hampshire. Although willing to have employees work at home, Putnam did not want to undertake the expense of the setup, which could amount to as much as $6,000 per worker (beyond the cost of the router and associated charges). This meant that experienced employees who lived in nearby New Hampshire were unable to participate in the Work@Home program despite their qualifications.

Communication among the on-site and off-site workers became inconsistent. It was difficult for the remote workers to find a manager because, as one on-site worker explained, "their jobs don't always allow them to sit at their desks, you know; they're always on the phone with someone else so then they [the @Home workers] call me and see if they can get in touch with somebody." As workers interrupted one another, they often became agitated and reluctant to help out. We were told by one irritated processor, "If one person comes over, they ALL do." This person was particularly disturbed that she did not know the individual personally who was asking for help. She had gotten a reputation as a good source of reliable information because of a class she had taught the previous year, and people still went to her frequently for help. Her response? "It was only a one day class. I can't remember for the life of me who took it. It seems as if they all remember me, however!"

The personal communication networks of the on-site day workers were rich, but the @Home worker networks were less so. On-site workers were responsible for serving as support for teleworkers. They had to respond to questions; perform certain activities that were technologically impossible for remote workers; answer their telephones, emails, and faxes rapidly; and handle any physical paperwork promptly. They were frequently interrupted and, because the remote workers could not see what anyone was doing on-site, the interruptions often came at very inconvenient times. In order to be responsible and helpful, good team player traits encouraged in Putnam employees—the on-site workers had to sacrifice continuity in their own work processes, along with speed, accuracy, and the top performance ratings that would go along with these. Coupled with this problem was the reverse problem for @Home workers. When an on-site worker needed to reach someone at home, "Sometimes it's a little hard. . . . You call them, their phone's ringing and they're not answering and you don't know why and you know, you don't know if they're in the other room or they have a problem or . . . . a lot of the time they don't have access to printers up here so they want us to print stuff for them or do the stuff they can't do 'cause they're at home, stuff like that." Each group felt like it was expected to be on call all the time, or else have the worst assumed of them by others.

Training and socialization. In the late 1990s, the training was delivered in traditional modes for all workers. The basic training course for processors was five weeks of classroom learning, then on-the-job, feet-to-the-fire training occurred with real accounts and real customers. The average processor took about three months to attain 25 to 50 percent productivity, three to six months to attain 75 to 80 percent productivity, and six or seven months to reach organizational productivity goals. No one was trained in only one area; cross training and job enrichment was the standard. The college graduates who accepted these entry-level positions made a one-year commitment to the processing role, but had a career focus for their future. By the end of the probationary training period, workers had been thoroughly immersed in Putnam's structure and philosophy. Their personal networks included contacts in several departments, whom they could call upon for help. They had work friends with whom to eat lunch, share water cooler chat, and create a sense of personal affiliation. When asked what Work@Homers missed most about being out of the office, the answer often was the contact with these work friends: "The people contact, number one, definitely. Just even talking about how your day. . . . I still do that at home, but it's different when you're in there. You don't get to see the pictures, the babies that come in, and the everyday office chitchat. . . . It's very important to most people."

The intention of the training department was to make all work experiences opportunities for learning. For this reason, the main training manual was available online, along with a glossary, the Lipper Report for fund updates, and procedures pages. Dependence upon, or at least first reference to, these sources was encouraged before asking an individual for direct assistance.

Career paths for the college graduates in the office were clearly mapped. They were less clearly mapped for the non–college graduates. The Work@Homers had no path, at least in the beginning when the job had been designed for production work rather than as a career move. Though this frustrated some workers, most of those who volunteered to work at home did so for personal reasons unrelated to career development, and most of them intended to return to the office at some point in the future in order to advance.

Some of these issues resolved themselves naturally, with the evolution of the technology. The widespread introduction and lowered cost of cable and DSL made significant positive changes in Putnam's remote operations. As Putnam's training team partnered with the in-house technology group, new training models and delivery systems were developed. New methods were introduced to help remote workers get answers to urgent questions without interrupting on-site coworkers.

Phase 3: Recruiting to Go Home (2000 and beyond)

The Putnam Way is the conservative way, the well thought-out way, the carpenter's rule way (measure twice and cut once). By 1998, it

became apparent that Putnam was exhausting the available labor resources in northeast Massachusetts. Although there was a readily available worker pool in southern New Hampshire, Putnam had no desire
to invest further in real estate. It was logical to consider hiring this
nearby worker pool to work at home, but aforementioned constraints
kept this simple solution from happening. The local telephone company
was both expensive and uncooperative, and without ISDN, cable, or
DSL service, Work@Home could not occur in New Hampshire, even
with willing workers. Putnam's ability to recruit new workers was
further hamstrung by expensive advertising and job fairs that attracted
few qualified applicants. A nationwide search for available modern real
estate in an area with a concentration of skilled workers turned up
nothing—the country was in boom times, and as a result real estate costs
were comparable everywhere and locations with concentrations of
skilled workers had low local unemployment. Ken Daly, Director of
General Services, was challenged by the COO to "come up with a better
answer."

The better answer involved an updated replay of the first telework
initiative. The economic development groups in both Maine and Vermont got wind of Putnam's search for real estate and workers and were
eager to plug their own locations and residents. The governors of both
states got involved in the negotiations, and a creative and audacious
plan was hammered out: the states would advertise for workers whose
homes were ISDN compatible and would locate several colleges at
which Putnam could do training in much the same way as they had
done it in Franklin, Massachusetts. Then, the governors got the local
telephone companies moving and put together federal job-training
dollars to pay for the initiative. Putnam selected college partners in
Burlington, VT, and and Waterville and in Bangor, ME, as training sites,
creating technology centers that employed students in the evening and
trained workers to work at home without spending any time at Putnam
facilities in Massachusetts at all.

"Anything we do, anywhere, anytime." When Putnam began to consider
hiring workers in other states, they realized that they would have to
revise their existing training procedures. They could choose between
bringing new employees to Putnam for training, as they traditionally
had done, but the distance and expense were drawbacks. They could
provide training away from Putnam, in local small offices or strip mall
environments, but that did not quite suit the team culture of Putnam.
Or, they could train their new employees at colleges and then send them
home to work.

Their choice was a blended solution—to provide some of the training
at colleges, some electronically, and some in Putnam-like environments

created deliberately for the training process. They investigated the delivery of training off-site and electronically, and determined that their best bet was, once again, a blended solution. Instead of using an out-of-the-box e-learning system such as many of the local corporations were using or purchasing the services of an e-learning developer, they decided to use their in-house talent coupled with outside experts in training delivery. This blended approach fit the culture of cautious innovation very well.

Putnam's college partner in Vermont was selected through a purposeful search in Vermont and Maine for institutions that could provide the training services and the potential workers. This partner had both, along with 20 years of experience in delivering distance learning programs and adult education. The goal was to have the college train the new Putnam workers, and then have the workers go directly home rather than work in-house as previous groups had done—a revolutionary move that flew in the face of established wisdom about telework. The thought was to create a classroom with 30 terminals, train people for four weeks, send them home with their own terminals, and have college students use the training area to do processing when the Putnam training classes were not in session. The career path was to be formally established: Start in the call center at the College, and then move into other areas higher-level processing. Eventually a full career was to be offered, with promotions to supervisor and manager as natural in this environment as in the on-site offices.

The proposal met with wide acceptance and delight on the part of prospective employees. When the plan to hire 400 teleworkers (200 in each state) was announced, Putnam received 1,115 job inquires from Maine and 1,200 from Vermont in four days (Kovaleski, 2000). Ultimately, over 1,500 people applied for the first 50 jobs in Maine. Seven hundred applicants had to be turned down in Maine because of their obvious overqualification for the jobs. Clearly, the new pioneer was not the individual but the company. The employer could follow the labor force via technology, and instead of technology keeping people out, now it facilitated bringing people in.

Challenges. Once the decision was made to train new workers directly for the Work@Home program, issues of cost and quality arose. Some aspects of Putnam's programs did not migrate well. There seemed to be no way to deal with issues of culture, relationships, or the Putnam work environment with standard vendor packages. Vendor costs were outrageous, with estimates ranging from $12,000 to $40,000 per training delivery hour. The estimates for the total program ranged from $3.3 million to $10.8 million. This was not an insignificant undertaking.

Another concern was developing in the new employee a sense of respect for Putnam's culture of structure. Whereas some companies might want to encourage creativity in their employees, that was far from the mind of the Putnam development staff. They had no desire to develop creativity. According to training staff, "No one wants a creative transfer agent. We want to develop problem-solving capabilities and make people always aware of the second order consequences of their actions." In order to accomplish this goal, trainers had to be available at all times to monitor and guide the learning process—or so said conventional wisdom.

The ongoing concerns about post hoc monitoring of worker output had not yet been laid to rest. In an environment that employs production workers, control issues loom large. The demand for greater than 99 percent accuracy coupled with a continuous flow of work that suggested the importance of speed as well, measurement of key indicators became critical. The numbers can take on a life of their own, hypnotizing the casual observer into forgetting that the numbers represent people, their output, and their limitations. How could the numbers be monitored in real time, time enough to make necessary adjustments and corrections? How could telephone representatives, using the Agility model, access the backup they might need for accurate processing?

And, how was the new employee ever to learn the culture of Putnam? How could they develop the relationships so necessary for successful completion of tasks? How could the teleworker be integrated into the fabric of the organization if they were never to come into the office, never to report for training to Putnam's headquarters, never to meet their on-site coworkers in person? Who were the new employees who were willing to undertake this risk? Didn't this limitation set them up for failure?

Solutions. Putnam applied the same solution that had worked so many times in the past to this new set of challenges: They used their in-house talent to circumvent the need for expensive outside vendor packages. They developed their own 65-module training package, comprising 275 course hours and more than 10,000 instructional pages. The cost for the system came in at merely one-third of the lowest vendor estimate. An added bonus was a 35 percent reduction in overall training costs, with no loss of training personnel, who were reassigned to internal consulting and development duties. Best of all, according to company spokespeople, was the ability to replicate the Putnam work environment *exactly* in the training process.

The Putnam e-training program contains no training screens that "look like" the input screens; there are only screens that display actual processing tasks for the trainees. The result of a painstaking iterative development process that focused on the input of internal subject matter experts, the processing screens are meant to familiarize trainees with the live interaction and continuous workflow of the real work environment.

The live problem-solving was addressed by a series of pop-ups, dialog boxes, and instant messaging screens that allowed nearly immediate response to learner queries. Any technical issues were dealt with directly and instantly by the technical group in order to minimize technology-frustration on the part of those unused to working and learning online. Other, nontechnical questions were answered in a variety of ways. Moving a mouse over an unfamiliar term brought up a box with a definition. Self-tests after each new skill was learned allowed the trainees both to evaluate their learning performance and to gain an advanced piece of information that popped up when a question was answered correctly. A feature was developed in-house that allowed people to post anonymous questions. This relieved anyone of the embarrassment that might be associated with asking a dumb question—like "What is a mutual fund?"—and having one's name attached to it. This ability to ask anonymously encouraged people to investigate those areas they were unsure of, without shame or even their manager's knowledge. Plus, a series of JIT (just-in-time) training was developed. These brief (15 minute) training modules allowed everyone to keep skills up to speed, exactly when they were needed.

It became apparent that some of the assumptions that had guided programs at other companies were not appropriate when it came to the Putnam program. The initial launch of the Maine and Vermont training programs included sessions of traditional stand-up training to begin the acculturation process. In fact, Putnam personnel spent weeks on the college campuses as part of a socialization and relationship-building component of the training. The big question about culture building was about to be answered. When the first classes of 100 trainees went home to work, figures showed that this group performed as well after six months as the traditionally trained in-house workers—with only a .04 percent difference in productivity between the two groups, and a .06 percent difference in accuracy, with the higher measurement coming from the Work@Home agents. The decision was made to continue the blended style of training—part live, stand-up training and part e-learning.

Technological advances also eased some of the monitoring and control challenges. A system was developed that indicated the amount of time that was being spent on each item so that "you can tell when someone becomes active to an item and if there's [sic] big gaps between [transactions], you know there's something wrong, or if they are holding on to a certain item for a long period of time consistently you know that there is something wrong. So you do that in the office as well as out." The integrated management tools made monitoring production and troubleshooting simpler and more direct. Techniques initially developed for Work@Home staff migrated back to the office and were used for on-site workers as well.

Access to telecommunication devices permitted the new remote workers to take inbound 800 number calls similarly to the way they could be taken in the Andover location. If a manager pulled up the status of the call center on his computer, it would be transparent who was working in Maine and who was working within the four walls of the Andover center. Nearly 160 of the Work@Homers participated in taking calls at home in 2002, considerably easing the stress on in-house workers who previously had had to handle all telephone calls. In addition, the move to a web-based system allowed Putnam to deploy @Home workers to handle tasks that required letters of confirmation be sent to clients, which had been impossible in the past. As a result, fund accountants could now work at home and complete all the necessary tasks for their jobs.

The training programs were enhanced to begin their impact in connection with the hiring process. Flooded with a wealth of resumés and potential hires, Putnam developed a new screening model that reflected Putnam's experience in identifying attributes that successful teleworkers seemed to have in abundance, such as the ability to work independently, strong organizational skills and communication skills, and the way the person felt about the Web-based workplace. The goal was quality and the watchword, commitment, expressed by the maxim, "Hire quality people and they can do everything." They tried to identify people who were good risks to work at home rather than people like the manager who told us, "I know, for example, that I would probably make a rotten work at home person. I enjoy being with people every day. I also know myself well enough that I would be distracted by just throwing in that little laundry or do this or that while I was at home. . . . I know I'm not a good fit."

Blended learning gave way to blended staffs. The units began to maintain staffs that included both virtual workers and on-site workers, with all treated alike. Teaming became more of a way of life than ever. As new teleworkers were hired into the program, they were paired up with a buddy to give the new relationships a little boost. Worker after worker claimed "as a team we can all help each other out if we have questions," "we need to communicate to resolve any problems that come up or address any issues that come during the day so we work hand in hand in that the work that is done is checked by somebody else in the department," and "We're dependent on one another . . . my team works together in a group and I help out when needed." Deadlines were the same for all workers, whether in-house or @Home, and performance standards were met by all workers in both groups.

The long-standing problems with attrition and retention seemed resolved. As of December 2001, the attrition rate for a Work@Home production worker remained out one-half the rate of their in-office peers. Effective May 2002, the average tenure of an in-office production worker was 2.7 years; Work@Home tenure in similar positions was 6.5 years. The tenure of Work@Home and in-house telephone workers was identical at 2.0 years, but this was meaningful because the @Home telephone group was in existence for only two years. In addition, Work@Homers took 28.8 percent less sick time than their in-office counterparts.

The distance learning reduced the need to come on-site, and the colleges were used as a hub for periodic celebrations, holiday parties, and summer outings. Technology proved to be a community-building mechanism for the workers. Teleconferencing of major events created a sense of personal involvement in workers both on- and off-site. For example, when Putnam's Chief Economic Advisor conducted a presentation at the Andover location, more than 100 Work@Homers attended via teleconference and were part of the occasion in real time.

We were told by several workers that the first thing they did in the beginning of their shift was to "Say good morning on Mind Align (the company's chat room)." Early concerns about monitoring Mind Align chat content were put to rest by instituting the Larry Lasser Rule—appropriateness was determined by whether the writer would feel comfortable saying it to the company president. We were also told that some workers preferred a manager who works at home than a manager who works in the office, regardless of where the worker was located. Why? Because "The days she works at home it is actually easier to reach her and speak to her. She doesn't have the distractions of the office."

All around Putnam's training and hiring departments could be heard the sound of paradigms breaking. Training was being delivered nonsequentially. The focus had turned to hiring the correct people, regardless of the skill set they came in with. Learner-centric training took the place of traditional, front-of-the-room training for all employees. Self-designed and self-reinforced training became the new mode rather than the exception.

BULLISH ON TELEWORK

It only takes one anecdote to support Putnam's continued goal of expansion of its telework program. In February 2002, a tanker tractor-trailer ran a guardrail on the access road to the Andover business park that houses Putnam's operation. The exit from the expressway was blocked and all traffic detoured for miles. The accident occurred in the early morning hours, and workers from New Hampshire and Massachusetts could not get to the office in time for the 8:30 A.M. opening of the telephone center. Ordinarily, this would have spelled disaster for Putnam's emphasis on call completion. However, due to the extensive @Home program, they were able to contact 25 additional people at home who had not been scheduled for the telephones that morning. They logged on, and the phone center opened with no delay in service. That flexibility had been the initial goal of the Work@Home program, and it clearly had paid off.

A Look into the Future

- Putnam's past experience and present success help keep them attuned to future possibilities.
- Putnam's goals vis-à-vis e-training include expanding the program to all new hires, incorporating product and investment training as well as training for processors and telephone representatives.
- The selection and implementation of a formal knowledge management system is in the works and will permit a facilitated tracking process as well as clear identification of career trajectory for all employees, making it easier to hire the quality individual that Putnam seeks.
- Although no one had yet been promoted from working solely @Home by the time of this writing, the goal is to establish a formal career trajectory for the Work@Home employees, along similar lines to that of the more traditional workers.
- As of 2002, more than two thirds of the Putnam Transfer Agents were using ISDN lines. Although these digital access lines have broader bandwidth than the standard 3300 Hz available on analog lines and allow multiple activities on three channels concurrently (e.g. a 64 K voice communication channel, a 64 K communications link for data transmission, and a control/monitoring channel that, although slower, offers an additional communications link), they are not as fast or broad as DSL lines, which have very-high-speed upload and download capability. As telecommunications technology continues to develop, Putnam will be migrating its traditional ISDN lines for Work@Homers to cable and DSL service to enhance speed and access.
- A permanent commitment has been made to continue the Work@Home program. It's future growth will remain at 25 percent of the overall growth of the company. And, there is a pledge to

carry on the program growth in Maine and Vermont. As I was told, "We still owe those people who sent us thousands of resumés."

- The culture of Putnam Investments stems directly from its president, Lawrence Lasser. A perfectionist and proud of it, Lasser contends that good is not good enough, and the Putnam team ought not to be spending a lot of time patting itself on the back. Instead, they should be challenging themselves to be better, to do better, and to develop a stronger team.

Continuous improvement, constant re-evaluation and the setting of new goals, and teamwork rather than a star system has served Putnam well for a long time. That organizational model promises to endure, adding members to the team regardless of geography in the coming years.

Appendix—Methodology

Putnam Investments served as the pilot location for a multisite research study about communication and telework. The project began in the fall of 1998, with on-site research commencing in February 1999 and continuing through May 2002. The process that was followed encouraged the development of grounded theory, theory that arises from the data (rather than the collection of data that fits a preconceived theory). Grounded theory is particularly useful for managers—it is reality-based, and applications can be derived readily from it.

Research was conducted with significant assistance by student teams from Merrimack College, trained specifically to perform this research project. A list of these students appears at the end of this appendix. Each team was closely and carefully monitored through the course of the project, and they reported their findings each spring (both verbally and in written reports) to corporate representatives. The reports were well received and findings confirmed by the organizational representatives. In addition, as principal investigator, I personally conducted interviews at all levels of the organization and observed work processes over the entire course of the study. In all, approximately 250 hours were spent on-site in observation and interviews.

The research incorporated a series of ethnographic approaches designed to minimize researcher impact, while recognizing the unavoidable effect that the researcher has on culture. Theories of qualitative inquiry suggest that the presence of an outsider will always have an impact on natural interaction and emergent culture. Therefore in the course of the research, precautionary measures were taken as much as possible. Some of the qualitative methodologies that were used to compare the effectiveness and efficiency of electronic and traditional (nonelectronic) communication processes in the target agency and company included:

- Interpretation of mute evidence, as described by Clifford Geertz (1973): thick description and contextualization, not just "establishing rapport, selecting informants, transcribing texts, taking genealogies, mapping fields, keeping a diary, and so on" (6).
- Artifact analysis (printed memos, manuals, directives, bulletin board postings, and other documents) because "reading is an interactive process in which readers not only receive the text and its appeals to engage it and find it convincing, but also act on the text to create interpretations (Golden-Biddle & Locke, 1993).
- Content and context analysis: The interpretation of activities that comprise everyday life are the central items for analysis, not only as communication processes but as "situated content"—the location in which the interactions occur (Holstein & Gubrium, 1998).
- Observation of how well it appears that the communication systems work and the level of ease/difficulty in using the systems based on the "increasing recognition that the problem of understanding is not restricted to the study of past times and other societies—it applies to the study of one's own social surroundings too" (Atkinson & Hammersley, 1998).
- Symmetrical research: A process in which the participants are coresearchers and perform analysis concurrent with the researchers. The question addressed by the coresearchers was "What do employees at various levels in the organization say about the process of communication?" Validity was established through the coresearchers' review and acceptance, rejection, or reinterpretation of the researcher's initial interpretations (Janesick, 1998).

Distance worker dyads (research pairs) were identified the first year by the Work@Home liaison through a series of internal email memos at the vice presidential level. Thereafter a liaison for college relations undertook the responsibility to have managers identify worker dyads. Participation was voluntary, and all participants signed consent forms that made clear the purpose of the study. These workers, known in the language of grounded theory as coresearchers, were asked a series of questions about their work processes, method of communication, and style of interaction. Interviews and discussions with distance workers were accomplished both by telephone and in person. On-site workers were observed and extensive notes taken about their actual methods of work and communication, as well as about the general environment of their work groups. Interviews of supervisors and managers were also conducted to collect additional organizational data.

Initial network illustrative diagrams were created to describe the interactions among coworkers. These illustrations were presented to both sets of coresearchers (on-site and remote) for discussion and correction. After additional observation, these network diagrams were adjusted to reflect more closely the contact, methods, and frequency of contacts of the workers. Supervisors, team leaders, and managers were consulted about the processes and were asked a similar set of questions as those put to the worker dyads. Their responses were included in the network connection design, which often (but not always) corroborated the claims of the workers. Employees were interviewed both formally and informally over the entire study period. The final interviews focused on work satisfaction, feelings of affiliation, perceptions of self and others, and strength of connection with Putnam. The first and last interviews (formal) were taped and transcribed.

Researchers attended either formal feedback sessions of remote workers and of their managers, or the more casual team meetings of on-site workers. Initial findings were then triangulated with analysis of artifacts such as public web pages, intranet pages, the on-line reference manual, Work@Home participant and management manuals, handouts, internal publications, bulletin boards, and other artifacts. Extensive interviews were conducted at worker, supervisory, managerial, vice presidential, and executive levels throughout the study period, and transcripts were maintained. All quotes in the chapter are accurate, but confidentiality has been observed in their attribution.

Students Engaged in the Research

1999	Alyson King	2002	Stephen Basile
	Jeffrey Larcome		Brad Batchelder
2001	Mario Alvarez		Teresa DeLisi
	James Johnson		Patrick Egan
	Jessica Shea		Ed Johnson
	Elizabeth Ward		Alyce Koehler
			Chris Laird
			Kevin Mader
			Joseph Merry
			Rick Smith

References

21st century skills for 21st century jobs. (1999). Washington: U.S. Department of Commerce, U.S. Department of Labor, National Institute of Literacy, and the Small Business Administration.

Aeschylus. *Agememnon.* (1926). (H. Weir Smyth, trans.). Cambridge, MA: Harvard University Press.

Aiello, J. R., & Kolb, K. J. (1995). Electronic performance monitoring and social context: Impact on productivity and stress. *Journal of Applied Psychology, 80* (3), 339–353.

Alderman, E., & Kennedy, C. (1995/1997). *The right to privacy.* New York: Vintage Books.

Allenby, B. (2001). Vice President of AT&T, for Environment, Health, and Safety in a speech to a federal subcommittee on the topic of telework in America.

AMA 2001 survey on workplace testing. www.amanet.org

Argyris, C., & Schon, D. A. (1996). *Organizational learning II: Theory, methods, and practice.* Reading, MA: Addison-Wesley.

Argyris, C., & Schon, D. A. (1974). *Theory in practice.* San Francisco: Jossey-Bass.

Armour, S. (2001, June 25). Telecommuting gets stuck in the slow lane. www.USAToday.com

Atkinson, P., & Hammersley, M. (1998). Ethnography and participant observation. In N. K. Denzin & Y. S. Lincoln (eds.), *Strategies of qualitative inquiry* (110–136). Thousand Oaks, CA: Sage.

Augarten, S. (1984). *Bit by bit: An illustrated history of computers.* New York: Ticknor & Fields.

Avery, C., & Zabel, D. (2001). *The flexible workplace.* Westport, CT: Quorum Books.

Baker, W. E. (2000). *Achieving success through social capital: Tapping hidden resources in your personal and business networks.* New York: John Wiley & Sons.

Ball, W. L. (1994, December). *Commuting alternatives in the United States: Recent trends and a look to the future.* Washington: United States Department of Transportation.

Ballard, T. N. (2001, February 16). *OPM orders agencies to increase telecommuting.* www.govexec.com.

Barney, L. (2000, June 12). Putnam hires Maine residents at home. *Mutual Fund Market News,* p. 4.

Bartlett, C. A., & Ghoshal, S. (1992, September/October). What is a global manager? *Harvard Business Review, 70* (5), 124–133.

Baudouin, P. (1999). Conditions for the development of new ways of working and electronic commerce in France. *ECaTT National Report.* www.ecatt.com

Berlin, I. (1924). All alone. Irving Berlin Music Corporation.

Bloom, B. S., Mesia, B. B., & Krathwohl, D. R. (1964). *Taxonomy of educational objectives* (2 vols.). New York: David McKay.

Bluedorn, A. C. (1998, June). An interview with anthropologist Edward T. Hall. *Journal of Management Inquiry, 7* (2), 109–116.

Booz Allen Hamilton. (2002, April 5). Technology barriers to home-based telework. *The Status of Telework in the Federal Government.* www.gsa.gov

Brass, D. J., & LaBianca, G. (1999). Social capital, social liabilities, and management. In R. Leenders & S. Gabbay (eds.), *Corporate social capital and liability.* Boston: Kluwer Academic Publishers.

Brigham, M., & Corbett, J.M. (1997). E-mail, power and the constitution of organizational reality. *New Technology, Work and Employment, 12* (1), 25–35.

Brown, R. (1970). *Telecommunications: The booming technology.* New York: Doubleday.

Browning, L. (2000, January 14). Head of Putnam Investments says he'll step down in June. *The Boston Globe,* p. C3.

Browning, L. (1999, June 15). Putnam struggles to adapt. *The Boston Globe,* C1.

Bureau of Labor Statistics. *Employment projections.* www.stats.bls.gov

Burkhardt, M. E. (1994). Social interaction effects following a technological change: A longitudinal investigation. *Academy of Management Journal, 37* (4), 869–898.

Burkhauser, R., Daly, M., & Houtenville, A. (2000, January). *How working age people with disabilities fared over the 1990s business cycle.* New York: Rehabilitation Research and Training Center, Cornell University and the Lewin Group.

Burt, R. S. (1987). Social contagion and innovation: Cohesion versus structural equivalence. *American Journal of Sociology, 92,* 1287–1335.

Caldwell, B. S. (1997). Sociotechnical factors affecting communication and isolation in complex environments. In M. Mouloua & J. M. Koonce (eds.), *Human-Automation interaction: Research and practice* (298–304). Hillsdale, NJ: Lawrence Erlbaum Associates.

Carbonara, P. (2001, June). Putnam. *Money, 30* (6), 74.

Cascio, W. F. (1998). *Managing human resources.* New York: McGraw-Hill.

Casimir, G. (1999, August 31–September 3). Notions from the home: Changes in household activities due to telecommuting. *Proceedings of the Fourth International Workshop in Teleworking* (268–285). Tokyo.

Cauley, L. (2001, September 10). It's a jungle out there. *Wall Street Journal*, R6.

Chartrand, S. (1996, May 19). What your employer knows about you. *The New York Times*.

Clark, P. (1997, December 12). Putnam boosts adviser site with customization, planning materials. *Fund Marketing Alert, 2* (50), 1.

Clarkson, M. B. E. (1995). A stakeholder framework for analyzing and evaluating corporate social performance. *Academy of Management Review, 20* (1), 92–117.

Clinton, W. J. (1994, July 11). Memorandum for the Heads of Executive Departments and Agencies.

Cohen, A. (2001, Summer). Worker watchers. *Fortune/Cnet Technology Review*, 70–80.

Cooper, J. C., & Madigan, K. (2002, April 22). US: Don't mistake rising unemployment for a weakening economy. *BusinessWeek Online.*

Coulacos Prato, C. (2001, June 24). 'tis the season to skip out, slack off or take a slide. *The Boston Sunday Globe*, H21.

Coutu, D. L. (2002, March). The anxiety of learning. *Harvard Business Review*, 100–106.

Croci, T. (2002, April 29). Network World reports the first-ever decline in total network industry revenues. *NetworkWorld.* www.networkworld.com /press/2002_releases/pr042902.htm

Dalkey, N. (1969). *The Delphi method: An experimental study of group opinion*. Santa Monica, CA: Rand Corporation.

Deibel, M. (2001, August 5). Tax-hungry states go after telecommuters. *The Sunday Eagle-Tribune*, G2.

DeMarie, S. N. (2000, August). *Using virtual teams to manage complex projects.* Arlington, VA: PricewaterhouseCoopers Endowment for the Business of Government.

Deming, W. E. (1986). *Out of crisis*. Cambridge, MA: MIT Center for Advanced Engineering Study.

De Tocqueville, A. (1969). (G. Lawrence, Trans., J. P. Mayer, ed.). *Democracy in America*. New York: Harper Perennial.

Diekema, D.A. (1992). Aloneness and social form. *Symbolic Interaction, 15* (4), 481–500.

Donaldson, T., & Preston, L. E. (1995). The stakeholder theory of the corporation: Concepts, evidence, and implications. *Academy of Management Review, 20* (1), 65–91.

Donkin, R. (2001). *Blood, sweat & tears: The evolution of work*. New York: TEXERE.

Drucker, P. (1970). *Technology, management, and society*. New York: Harper & Row.

Drucker, P. (1954). *The practice of management*. New York: Harper & Row.

Edwards, R. (1979). *Contested terrain: The transformation of the workplace of the twentieth century*. New York: Basic Books.

Eoyang, G. H. (1997). *Coping with chaos*. Circle Pines, MN: Lagumo.

Erikson, K. (1986). On work and alienation. American Sociological Association, 1985 Presidential address. *American Sociological Review, 51,* 1–8.

ETO (European Telework Online). (2002, July 16). *European Council framework agreement on telework.* www.eto.org.uk

Fairfax, R. E. (1999, November 15). OSHA policies concerning employees working at home. www.osha.gov

Falling through the Net: Toward digital inclusion. (2001). Washington: National Telecommunications and Information Administration.

Farley, T. (2001). TelecomWriting.com's Telephone History Series http://www.privateline.com/TelephoneHistory/History1.htm

Farson, R., & Keyes, R. (2002, August). The Failure-Tolerant leader. *Harvard Business Review*, 64–71.

Festinger, L., & Carlsmith, J. M. (1959). Cognitive consequences of forced compliance. *Journal of Abnormal and Social Psychology, 48*, 78–92.

Fields, J., & Casper, L. M. (2001). America's families and living arrangements: March 2000. *Current Population Reports, P20-537.* Washington: U.S. Census Bureau.

Florida, R., Cushing, R., & Gates, G. (2002, August). When social capital stifles innovation. *Harvard Business Review*, 20.

Flutak, M. (2002, October 9). Teleworking booms in Europe. http://news.zdnet.co.uk

French, J. R. P., & Raven, B. (1960). The bases of social power. In D. Cartwright & A. F. Zander (eds.), *Group dynamics* (607–623). Evanston, IL: Row, Peterson.

Fromm, E. (1941). *Escape from freedom.* New York: Rinehart & Winston.

Fukuyama, F. (1995). *Trust: The social virtues and the creation of prosperity.* New York: Simon & Schuster.

Galinksy, E., & Kim, S. S. (2000). Navigating work and parenting by working at home: Perspectives of workers and children whose parents work at home. *Telework: The new workplace of the 21st century* (144-165). Washington: U.S. Department of Labor.

Geertz, C. (1973). *The interpretation of cultures.* New York: Basic Books.

Gleick, J. (1987). *Chaos: Making a new science.* New York: Penguin Books.

Goffman, E. (1961). *Asylums.* Garden City, NY: Anchor Books.

Golden-Biddle, K., & Locke, K. (1993, November). Appealing work: An investigation of how ethnographic texts convince. *Organization Science, 4* (4), 595–616.

Goold, M., & Campbell, A. (2002, March). Do you have a well-designed organization? *Harvard Business Review,* 117–124.

Gordon, G. (2000). www.gilgordon.com/telecommuting/adminfaq/admin01.htm

Granovetter, M. (1985, November). Economic action and social embeddedness: The problem of embeddedness. *American Journal of Sociology, 91* (3), 481–510.

Granovetter, M. S. (1974). *Getting a job: A study of contacts and careers.* Cambridge, MA: Harvard University Press.

Granovetter, M. S. (1973). The strength of weak ties. *American Journal of Sociology, 78* (6), 1360–1380.

Grantham, C. (2000). *The future of work.* New York: McGraw-Hill.

GSA Office of Governmentwide Policy, Office of Real Property. (2001, December). *Productivity in the Workplace.* Washington: U.S. General Services Administration.

GSA Office of Governmentwide Policy, Office of Real Property. (2000, December). *Real Property Performance Results.* Washington: U.S. General Services Administration.

Guerrero, M. (2000, March). Conditions for the development of new ways of working and electronic commerce in Spain. *ECaTT National Report*. www.ecatt.com

Hall, E. T. (1976). *Beyond culture*. New York: Doubleday.

Hall, E. T. (1966, 1982). *The hidden dimension*. New York: Doubleday.

Hall, E. T. (1959). *The silent language*. Greenwich, CT: Fawcett Publications.

Halpin, J. (2001). Productivity in the workplace. *Fortune Magazine Special Technology Issue*.

Hamilton, A. (1788). *Federalist Paper, 51*.

Hammer, M., & Champy, J. (1993). *Reengineering the corporation*. New York: HarperCollins.

Hamper, B. (1991). *Rivethead: Tales from the assembly line*. New York: Warner Books.

Harris, S. (2002) IP VPNs: An overview for network executives. *NetworkWorld*. http://nwfusion.com

Healy, B. (2001, July 19). Aiming to turn pain into gain. *The Boston Globe*, p. E1.

Heldrich, J. J. (1999, March 18). *Work trends: America's attitudes about work, employers, and government*. Center for Workforce Development at Rutgers University and the Center for Survey Research and Analysis at the University of Connecticut.

Helling, A. (2000). A framework for understanding telework. *Telework: The new workplace of the 21st century* (54–68). Washington: U.S. Department of Labor.

Herman, A. M. (2000, January 5). Statement on working at home. www.osha.gov /media/oshnews/jan00/statement-20000105.html

Hofstede, G. (1991, 1997). *Cultures and organizations: Software of the mind*. New York: McGraw-Hill.

Holstein, J. A., & Gubrium, J. F. (1998). Phenomenology, ethnomethodology, and interpretive practice. In N. Denzin & Y. Lincoln (eds.), *Strategies of qualitative inquiry* (pp. 137–157). Thousand Oaks, CA: Sage. 137-157.

Homans, G. C. (1950). *The human group*. New York: Harcourt, Brace, Jovanovich.

Hopkinson, P., James, P., & Maruyama, T. (2002, October 10). *Teleworking at BT: The economic, environmental, and social impacts of its workabout scheme*. www.sustel.org

Hopper, D. I. (2001, July 29). As authorities use more high-tech gadgets, legal battles await. *Sunday Eagle-Tribune*. http://www.Inventors.about.com /library/inventors/blradar.htm

Hymowitz, K. S. (2001, Winter). Ecstatic capitalism's brave new work ethic. *City Journal, 11* (1).

Jackson, M. (2002). *What's happening to home?* Notre Dame, IN: Sorin Books.

Janesick, V. J. (1998). The dance of qualitative research design: Metaphor, methodolatry, and meaning. In N. Denzin & Y. Lincoln (eds.), *Strategies of qualitative inquiry* (35–55). Thousand Oaks, CA: Sage.

Jefferson, T., to van der Kemp, M. (1902–1904). In A. Lipscomb & A. Bergh (eds.), *The writings of Thomas Jefferson, memorial edition*. Washington. 13:135.

Jesdanun, A. (2002, January 6). Using the office's Net system poses risks. *The Boston Sunday Globe*, G20.

Jesdanun, A. (2001, August 27). Net reaching growth limit as more devices, countries connect. *The Boston Globe*, C2.

Johnston, W. B., & Packer, A. H. (1987). *Workforce 2000*. Indianapolis: The Hudson Institute.

Joice, W. (2000). Federal telework topics. *Telework: The new workplace of the 21st century* (155–167). Washington: U.S. Department of Labor.

Joice, W. (1993). *The federal flexible workplace pilot project work-at-home component*. Washington: U.S. Office of Personnel Management Career Entry Group Office of Personnel Research and Development.

Kahn, R. E. (1995). The role of government in the evolution of the Internet. *Revolution in the U.S. information infrastructure.* Washington: The National Academy Press. www.nap.edu/readingroom/books/newpath/chap2.html

Kaplan, M. (1960). *Leisure in America: A social inquiry.* New York: John Wiley and Sons.

Kaplan, R., & Norton, D. (1996). *The balanced scorecard.* Boston: Harvard Business School Press.

Keenan, F., & Ante, S. E. (2002, February 18). The new teamwork. *BusinessWeek e.biz*, 12–16.

Kelinson, J. W., & Tate, P. (2000). The 1998–2008 job outlook in brief. *Occupational Outlook Quarterly.* www.bls.gov

Kistner, T. (2002, June 4). What's behind the telework slump? *NetworkWorld Fusion.* www.nwfusion.com

Kistner, T. (2002, May 7). What people are saying. *NetworkWorld Fusion.* www.nwfusion.com

Kistner, T. (2002, February 18). Telework industry comes full circle. *NetworkWorld Fusion.* www.nwfusion.com

Kistner, T. (2002, January 2). The death of telephone tag? *NetworkWorld Fusion.* www.nwfusion.com

Kistner, T. (2002, January 1). Gen X'ers want telework, study shows. *NetworkWorld Fusion.* www.nwfusion.com

Kistner, T. (2001, December 4). VAs leading the way. *NetworkWorld Fusion.* www.nwfusion.com

Kistner, T. (2001, November 27). Virtual assistant industry taking shape. *NetworkWorld Fusion.* www.nwfusion.com

Kistner, T. (2001, November 11). Telework gets strong backing form new consortium. *NetworkWorld Fusion.* www.nwfusion.com

Kistner, T. (2001, September 11). Can counting keystrokes be good for telework? *NetworkWorld Fusion.* www.nwfusion.com

Kistner, T. (2001, August 28). Coming to a city near you, perfect part-time jobs. *NetworkWorld Fusion.* www.nwfusion.com

Kistner, T. (2001, June 11). What (Virginia) businesses want. *NetworkWorld Fusion.* www.nwfusion.com

Kleinbard, D. (2000, November 9). The $1.7 trillion dot.com lesson. *CNN Money.*

Kobielus, J. (2001, June 25). P2P "fat clients" are wrong for Internet collaboration. *NetworkWorld Fusion.* www.nwfusion.com

Kolb, D. & Fry, R. (1975). Toward an applied theory of experiential learning. In Cooper, C. (Ed.), *Theories of group process.* London: John Wiley.

Korte, W. B. (1999). Conditions for the development of new ways of working and electronic commerce in Germany. *ECaTT National Report*. www.ecatt.com

Kovaleski, D. (2000, October 2). Putnam uses work-at-home option to lure staff. *Pensions & Investments, 28* (20), 71.

Kraut, R., Lundmark, V., Patterson, M., Kiesler, S., Mukopadhyay, T., & Scherlis, W. (1998, September). Internet paradox: A social technology that reduces social involvement and psychological well-being? *American Psychologist, 53* (9), 1017–1031.

Kruse, D. (2000). Comments on the economic and social impacts of telework. *Telework: The new workplace of the 21st century* (98–102). Washington: U.S. Department of Labor.

Kulish, N. (2001, August 6). Snapshot of America 2000. *The Wall Street Journal,* B1.

Kunkle, R. (2000, April). *Perspectives on successful telework initiatives*. Washington StateUniversity Cooperative Extension Energy Program. www.energy .wsu.edu

Kurzweil, R. (1999). *The age of spiritual machines*. New York: Penguin Books.

Lee, B. (2000). Putnam hires Maine residents at home. *Mutual Fund Market News, 8* (24), 4.

Levering, R., & Moskowitz, M. (2001, January 8). The 100 Best Companies to Work For. *Fortune,* 148–168.

Levine, J. M., & Moreland, R. L. (1990). Progress in small group research. In M. Rosenzweig & L. Porter (Eds.), *Annual review of psychology* (585–634). Palo Alto, CA: Annual Reviews.

Lindorff, M. (2000). Home-based telework and telecommuting in Australia: More myth than modern work form. *Asia Pacific Journal of Human Resources, 38* (3), 1–11.

Lipnack, J., & Stamps, J. (2000). *Virtual teams: People working across boundaries with technology, 2/e.* New York: Wiley & Sons.

Lipshitz, R. (2000, December). Chic, mystique, and misconception: Argyris and Schon and the rhetoric of organizational learning. *The Journal of Applied Behavioral Science, 36* (4), 456–473.

Lovelace, G. (2000). The nuts and bolts of telework. *Telework: The new workplace of the 21st century* (pp. 33–42). Washington: U.S. Department of Labor.

March, J. G., & Sutton, R. I. (1997, November/December). Organizational performance as a dependent variable. *Organization Science, 8* (6), 698–706.

McGill, M. E., & Slocum, J. W., Jr. (1992, Summer). Management practices in learning organizations. *Organizational Dynamics, 21* (1), 5–18.

McGregor, D. M. (1960). *The human side of enterprise*. New York: McGraw-Hill.

Mehra, A., Kilduff, M., & Brass, D. J. (1998). At the margins: A distinctiveness approach to the social identity and social networks of underrepresented groups. *Academy of Management Journal, 41* (4), 441–452.

Miller, J. (1975, June). Isolation in organizations: Alienation from authority, control, and expressive relations. *Administrative Science Quarterly, 20,* 260–271.

Mills, M. (1995). *The actor's studio—A look at Stanislavski's method.* www.moderntimes.com/palace/method.htm

Mintzberg, H. (1972). *The nature of managerial work.* New York: Harper & Row.

Mitchell, R. K., Agle, B. R., & Wood, D. J. (1997). Toward a theory of stakeholder identification and salience: Defining the principle of who and what really counts. *Academy of Management Review, 22* (4), 853–886.

Moss Kanter, R. (2001). *Evolve! Succeeding in the digital culture of tomorrow.* Boston: Harvard Business School Press.

Moss Kanter, R. (1989a, November/December). The new managerial work. *Harvard Business Review, 89* (6), 85–92.

Moss Kanter, R. (1989b). *When giants learn to dance.* New York: Simon and Schuster.

A nation online: How Americans are expanding their use of the Internet. (2002). Washington: National Telecommunications and Information Administration, Economics and Statistics Administration, U.S. Bureau of the Census.

Nationwide Personal Transportation Survey. (2000).

Nie, N. H., Hillygus, D. S., & Erbring, L. (2002). Internet use, interpersonal relations and sociability: Findings from a detailed time diary study. In B. Wellman & C. Haythornthwaite (eds.), *The Internet in everyday life.* Oxford, U.K.: Blackwell.

Nilles, J. M. (2000, October). Telework in the US. *Telework American Survey 2000.* International Telework Association & Council.

Nilles, J. M. (1998). *Managing telework: Strategies for managing the virtual workforce.* New York: Wiley.

Nupponen, T., & Vainio, M. (2000, June). Conditions for the development of new ways of working and electronic commerce in Finland. *ECaTT National Report.* www.ecatt.com

Nykodym, N., & Simonetti, J. L. (1987, June). Personal appearance: Is attractiveness a factor in organizational survival and success? *Journal of Employment Counseling, 24,* 69–78.

Orlikowski, W. J. (2000, July-August). Using technology and constituting structures: A practice lens for studying technology in organizations. *Organization Science, 11* (4), 404–428.

Osterman, M. D. (2002, January 15). The future of unified messaging. *Network World Newsletter.*

Osterman, M. D. (2001, March 29). Compress for success. *Network World Newsletter.*

Osterman, M. D. (2001, August 23). Downtime costs users. *NWFusion.* www.nwfusion.com

O'Toole, J. (1973). *Work in America.* Cambridge, MA: MIT Press.

Ouchi, W. G. (1980, March). Markets, bureaucracies, and clans. *Administrative Science Quarterly, 25,* 129–141.

Peters, T., & Austin, N. (1985). *A passion for excellence.* New York: Random House.

Peters, T. J., & Waterman, R. H., Jr. (1982). *In search of excellence.* New York: Harper & Row.

Pink, D. H. (2001). *Free agent nation: How America's new independent workers are transforming the way we live.* New York: Warner Books.

Pitkanen, K., and Thorslund E. (1999). Conditions for the development of new ways of working and electronic commerce in Sweden. *EcaTT National Report.* www.ecatt.com/country/sweden/nationalreport2.pdf

PMC (President's Management Council). (1996, January). *National Telecommuting Initiative Action Plan*. Washington.

Postman, N. (1993). *Technopoly: The surrender of culture to technology*. New York: Vintage (Random House).

Pratt, J. H. (1999). Cost/benefits of teleworking to manage work/life responsibilities. *1999 Telework America National Telework Survey* (a project of the International Telework Association & Council).

Pratt, J. H. (1997a). *Counting the Mobile Workforce, Bureau of Transportation Statistics*. Washington: U. S. Department of Transportation.

Pratt, J. H. (1997b). Teamwork, trust and technology. *Second International Workshop of Telework, Amsterdam 1997*. Work and Organization Research Centre Report 97.08.004.

Pratt, J. H. (1991). Trace behavior impacts of telecommuting following the San Francisco earthquake: A case study. *Transportation Research Record No. 1305*. Washington: Transportation Research Board.

Prusak, L., & Cohen, D. (2001, June). How to invest in social capital. *Harvard Business Review*, 86–93.

Public Law 106-346, Section 359. (2000, October 23).

Public Law 107-277, Section 630 (a). 1999.

Putnam, R. D. (2000). *Bowling alone: The collapse and revival of American community*. New York: Simon and Schuster.

Real Property Performance Results. (2000, December). Washington: U.S. GSA Office of Governmentwide Policy, Office of Real Property.

Reich, R. B. (2000). *The future of success*. New York: Alfred A. Knopf.

Review of Family-Friendly Workplace Arrangements. (1998, October 30). Washington: U.S. Office of Personnel Management.

Rook, K. S. (1985). Research on social support, loneliness, and social isolation. Toward an integration. *Review of Personality and Social Psychology, 5*, 239–264.

Rosen, E. (2002, February 11). No time for face time. *Network World*. www.nwfusion.com

Rosenbush, S. (2002, October 7). The telecom depression: When will it end? *Business Week*, 66–74.

Rosener, J. B. (1990, November/December). Ways women lead. *Harvard Business Review, 68* (6), 119–133.

Rosenwald, M. (2001, April 29). Long-distance teamwork. *The Boston Sunday Globe*, J1.

Rousseau, D. M. (1995). *Psychological contracts in organizations*. Thousand Oaks, CA: Sage.

Sakai, K. (1999). Telework in Japan: Where it is and where it is going. Presentation at ITAC International Conference.

Satcher, D., & Watkins, S. R. (1999, April 19). U.S. Surgeon General Satcher and Agriculture Undersecretary Watkins encourage participation in national TV turnoff week. http://lists.essential.org/commercial-alert/msg00008.html

Schonfeld, E. (1998, August 3). The network in your house. *Fortune Magazine*, 125–128.

Scully, M. (2002, May). Gender and "virtual work": How new technologies influence work practices and gender equity. *CGO Insights*. Boston: Simmons School of Management.

Senge, P. M. (1990). *The fifth discipline: The art and practice of the learning organization*. New York: Doubleday.

Sennett, R. (1998). *The corrosion of character: The personal consequences of work in the new capitalism*. New York: W.W. Norton.

Shah, P. P. (1998). Who are employees' social referents? Using a network perspective to determine referent others. *Academy of Management Journal, 4* (3), 249–268.

Smith, K. (2002, August 19). Western Isles set to benefit from the most extensive wireless broadband network in the U. K. *The Herald.*

Snizek, W. E. (1995, September). Virtual offices: Some neglected considerations. *Communications of the ACM, 38* (9), 15–17.

Sparrowe, R. T., Liden, R. C., Wayne, S. J., & Kraimer, M. L. (2001). Social networks and the performance of individuals and groups. *Academy of Management Journal, 44* (2), 316–325.

Sproull, L., & Kiesler, S. (1991). *Connections: New ways of working in the networked organization.* Cambridge, MA: The MIT Press.

The Status of Telework in the Federal Government. (2001). Washington: U.S. Office of Personnel Management.

Steiner, P. (n.d.). http:/cartoonbank.com

Stern, E., & Gwathmey, E. (1994). *Once upon a telephone: An illustrated social history.* New York: Harcourt, Brace & Company.

Stough, R., & Bragg, M. (2000, October 19). Fairfax Telework Conference Presentation Outline. (unpublished).

Sugarman, B. (2000, December). *A learning based approach to leading change.* Arlington, VA: PricewaterhouseCoopers Endowment for the Business of Government.

Sykes, C. J. (1999). *The end of privacy.* New York: St. Martin's Press.

Taha, L. H., & Caldwell, B. S. (1993). *Behavior and information technology, 12* (5), 276–283.

Taschek, J. (2002, January 14). 802.11a 5 times faster than 11b. *eWeek.* www .eweek.com/

Texas Comptroller of Public Accounts. (2000, December). Chapter 4: Human resource management. www.e-texas.org

Toffler, A. (1980). *The third wave.* New York: William Morrow.

Toffler, A. (1970). *Future shock.* New York: Bantam Books.

Tolly, K. (2001, February 5). The forgotten side of network security. *NetworkWorld Fusion.* www.nwfusion.com

Townsend, A. M., DeMarie, S. M., & Hendrickson, A. R. (1998). Virtual teams: Technology and the workplace of the future. *Academy of Management Executive, 12* (3), 17–29.

U. K. Labour Force Survey. (2002).

United States Census. (1997, 2000).

Vega, G. (2000). Building the case for telework. *Telework: The new workplace of the 21st century* (168–174). Washington: U.S. Department of Labor.

Vega, G., & Brennan, L. M. (2000a). Isolation and technology: The human disconnect. *Journal of Organizational Change Management, 13* (5), 468–481.

Vega, G., & Brennan, M. L. (2000b). *Managing telecommuting in the federal government: An interim report.* Arlington, VA: PricewaterhouseCoopers Endowment for the Business of Government.

Vega, G., & Hanlon, M. D. (in press). It's all about people. *The Virtual Organization*. Washington: U.S. General Services Administration, Office of Governmentwide Policy, Office of Real Property.

Vega, G., & Simpson, G. (2001). Please hold, I think my house is on fire. *People and the Workplace* (16–25). Washington: U.S. General Services Administration, Office of Governmentwide Policy, Office of Real Property.

Vroom, V. H., & Jago, A. G. (1988). *The new leadership: Managing participation in organizations*. Englewood Cliffs, NJ: Prentice-Hall.

Walmac, A. (1995, July). Why Putnam replaced its stars with a black box. *Money, 24, (7)*, 55.

Weinberg, N. (2002, August 27). Telework toolkit: For managing remote workers. *Network World Newsletter*. www.nwfusion.com

Weingroff, R. F. (1996). Federal-Aid Highway Act of 1956: Creating the interstate system. *Public roads on-line*.

Weisbord, M. R. (1987). *Productive workplaces*. San Francisco: Jossey-Bass.

Wellman, B., Salaff, J., Dimitova, D., Garton, L., Gulia, M., & Haythornthwaite, C. (1996). Computer networks as social networks: Collaborative work, telework, and virtual community. *Annual Review of Sociology, 22*, 213–238.

West, H. (2000). A practical approach to implementing teleworking programs. *Commuter Connections*. Washington: Metropolitan Washington Council of Governments.

Wetzel, K. (2002, March 13). Eating patterns in America revolve around idea of convenience. *Tribune-Review*. www.pittsburghlive.com/x/tribune-review/entertainment/s_60709.html

Wheatley, M. J. (1992). *Leadership and the new science*. San Francisco: Berrett Koehler.

Wilensky, H. L. (1963). The uneven distribution of leisure: The impact of economic growth on 'free time'. In E. O. Smigel (Ed.), *Work and leisure: A contemporary social problem* (pp. 107–145). New Haven, CT: College and University Press.

Woodward, J. (1965). *Industrial organization: Theory and practice*. London: Oxford University Press.

www.att.com/telework
www.census.gov/hhes/www/housing/census/historic/phone.html
www.tvdrawn.com
www.digitalcentury.com/encyclo/update/comp_hd.html
www.earlytelevision.com
www.fbi.gov
www.fcc.gov/mb
www.gsa.gov
www.inventors.about.com
www.irs.gov
www.islandnet.com
www.ivc.ca
www.japan-telework.or.jp
www.javaworld.com/javaworld/jw-10-1996/jw-10-connors_p.html
www.lindquist.com
www.ncpa.org

www.novia.net
www.pbs.org/internet/timeline/index
www.privacyrights.org
www.privateline.com/telehonehistory2a/ericsson.htm
www.putnaminvestments.com
www.sci.sdsu.edu
www.stats.bls.gov
www.technicalpress.com
www.telework.gov
www.teleworkarizona.com
www.workingfromanywhere.org
www.teleworkcollaborative.com
www.un.org
www.workandfamily@opm.gov

Zbar, J. (2002, September 12). Going totally VO. *Network World Net.Worker*. www.newfusion.com

Zbar, J. (2002, August 15). No more musical desks. *Network World Net.Worker*. www.newfusion.com

Zbar, J. (2002, July 11). Governor's support boosts telework. *Network World Net.Worker*. www.newfusion.com

Zbar, J. (2002, May 27). Avoiding the highway. *Network World Net.Worker*. www.newfusion.com

Zbar, J. (2002, March 18). Has Sept. 11 telework stuck? *Network World Net.Worker*. www.newfusion.com

Zbar, J. (2002, March 7). Look before you leap. *Network World Net.Worker*. www.newfusion.com

Zbar, J. (2002, February 7). Mapics learns a new way to work. *Network World Net.Worker*. www.newfusion.com

Zbar, J. (2001, October 25). Hiding in plain sight. *Network World Net.Worker*. www.newfusion.com

Zbar, J. (2001, September 13). Are you a typical teleworker? *Network World Net.Worker*. www.newfusion.com

Zbar, J. (2001, August 30). Employees drive Ford to adopt new workstyles. *Network World Net.Worker*. www.newfusion.com

Zbar, J. (2001, August 23). Does deducting your home office send a red flag to the IRS? *Network World Net.Worker*. www.newfusion.com

Zbar, J. (2001, July 27) Telework centers get mixed reviews. *Network World Net.Worker*. www.newfusion.com

Zbar, J. (2001, July 20). Another way to cut the commute. *Network World Net.Worker*. www.newfusion.com

Zbar, J. (2001, June 28). The manager in the mirror. *Network World Net.Worker*. www.newfusion.com

Zweig, J. (1999, April). Look back and learn. *Money, 28* (4), 94.

Index

ABOUT THE AUTHOR

GINA VEGA is Associate Professor of Management at the Francis E. Girard School of Business and International Commerce, Merrimack College, North Andover, Massachusetts.